Enjoy

Navigating a Life

Stephen Foster Briggs II

UNGAVA PRESS
BEECH ISLAND, SOUTH CAROLINA

Published by Ungava Press
Copyright © 2015 by Stephen F. Briggs II

ISBN: 978-0-578-16135-8
Library of Congress Control Number: 2015940299
Printed in the United States of America

Developmental Editor: Janet Martin Carmichael
Copy Editor and Proofreader: Lisa A. Allen
Photography: supplied by author
Book and Jacket Design: Linda Berry | Designer's Ink

For information and book orders, please visit the website
www.navigatingalife.com

To my family—past, present, and future—and to all those in this book who have touched my life, including my guardian angel, who I sometimes think of as my "lucky star" that saved me many times from foolish escapades and accidents. Those presences, sensed or real, allowed me to navigate life despite some rough waters along the way. To all of them I am grateful —including and especially Doris.

Acknowledgments

Over the past two decades I have written down many of the significant trials and tribulations of my life. I've always wanted to publish a book; however, I didn't have the foggiest idea where to begin. At the same time I knew I needed help sorting out what I thought was interesting but might not appeal to anyone else. I wanted the book to be for family, future generation, and a limited number of friends and acquaintances.

My good friend Pat Blewett from Aiken, South Carolina, came to my rescue, as he had just finished his book, *A Lucky Boy From Buffalo*, and highly recommended the team that had helped him. That was good enough for me.

I can't say enough about my editor, Janet Martin. She went beyond editing and became my partner in putting my stories, which were often too long and sometimes rather confusing, into readable form. In effect she was my co-author and more, as she not only kept me on track, but she also did some extensive rewrites of my clumsy prose. Her writing skills and intuitive ability to understand my goal were invaluable assets.

Next I wish to thanks Lisa Allen for providing my second edit and catching errors that had been missed.

Linda Berry, who did the book layout and cover design, provided the expertise to enhance the overall quality and appeal of the book through her creative talent. Her design of the cover provides the potential reader a reason to "peel back the onion" and look inside.

I must mention Doris, my wife of 30 years, who showed incredible patience when I was glued to the computer and she wanted to get online. She had to endure more than a year of this aggravation as the number of rewrites far exceeded my expectations.

Writing this book was a journey in itself. I traveled back in time to discover my family history within the global history of the past two centuries. I followed that history into the 21st century, taking particular notice of the ups and downs, the pitfalls, and the triumphs of my own life that have led me to where I am today. This memoir is part of my legacy, my gift, to the generations of tomorrow.

STEPHEN FOSTER BRIGGS II

Contents

The Ungava

SECTION I
𝒯he 𝒱iew 𝒫rom the 𝒮tern
(𝒫rologue)

Much of my life has been spent on a boat . . . actually, on all
kinds of boats . . . from skiffs to sailboats, from powerboats to
ocean liners.

For business and for pleasure, I've traveled all over the
world, met different kinds of people, and experienced varied
cultures. Within my life's boat I've navigated shoals and oceans,
reefs and rivers, waterways and beaches. There were times I got
stuck and times I bailed out. There were moments when my
boat leaked, and since a vessel can't skim water until the holes
are filled and the cracks are fixed, I learned my life would not
be smooth sailing until I corrected mistakes and repaired the
damage I'd done to others and myself.

Those familiar with marine terminology will recognize that
the front of the boat is called the *bow*. The middle is known as the
midship. The back of the boat is the *stern*. Running lights signal
direction: red lights on the left (or port) side of the boat facing
forward; green lights on the right (or starboard) side of the boat
facing forward; and rear (the stern) as indicated by a bright white
light. When at sea, you follow right-of-way rules: If you see red,
you stop. If you see green, you go. If you see white—the rear of a
boat going slower than yours—you give way to the other vessel.

It seems to me, at the beginning of life you sit at the bow, peering eagerly into the wind, with someone else driving as you skid across the water headlong in the green light of "go." Midlife, you're midship, throttling along capable and confidant, pretty much working with others while at the same time meeting difficulties, which signal red and necessitate a few "stops" here and there. At the end of life, well, you slow down and sit at the stern contemplatively, while steering and evaluating your journey in the white light of clarity as your eye is focused on the distant line of the horizon.

Here, you tell your story to others. And here, I'll begin. For the others in my life—my children, grandchildren, great-grandchildren to come, friends far, near, and dear—I'll say this: While motivated by goodness, I am no saint. Within these pages I tell you how and how not to live a life by describing how I lived mine. From the stern of my boat and presently in my seventh decade, I hope you'll say I've developed perspective.

SECTION II

Fore, Forward, "For'ard":

Toward the Bow of the Vessel

Playing on the beach at my grandparents' Briggs home in Naples, Florida

CHAPTER 1

Beginner's Luck (1936–1945)

I was born with beginner's luck. Of course, I didn't know how lucky I was on August 31, 1936, when I came forth as a howling infant at Columbia Hospital in Milwaukee, Wisconsin. Two years before, the stars had aligned themselves fortuitously over the beaches in Naples, Florida, stretching along the Gulf of Mexico. There my father, Stephen Albro Briggs [1], met my mother, Joan Taylor Nichols [2], in 1934.

For many years my father's and mother's families had vacationed in Naples, drawn by leisure water and hunting opportunities in that locale. Since the 1870s and 1880s, magazine and newspaper stories had described the area as abundant with fish and game, offering a temperate climate, and boasting a beautiful bay "surpassing that of Naples, Italy." Hence, the name *Naples* caught on.

My maternal grandfather and grandmother Nichols first went there in 1929, as my grandfather was an active fisherman. My paternal grandfather, Stephen Foster Briggs, had close friends who were well-known industrialists from Milwaukee, including Armin Slazanger, a private investor; Harry Bradley, of the Allen-Bradley Company, a maker of brand-name factory automation equipment, now owned by Rockwell Automation; Fritz McGinn, of Square D Company, now Schneider Electric; and Bill Uhelein, an owner of the Joseph Schlitz Brewing Company.

In the 1920s, there were only a handful of families who traveled to Naples in the winter, since the only way to get there was by boat from Fort Myers, which landed at the city pier. At the pier, a tram would meet you and take you to the Naples Beach Hotel. My guess would be that my parents met through social events, all of which were held at the old hotel. Around 1934, my dad's family, along with the Milwaukee group of friends mentioned previously, built homes close to each other on the water. The railroad reached Naples in 1927, and the Tamiami Trail from Naples to Miami was completed in 1928, but development did not begin in earnest until after the Great Depression and World War II.

Nevertheless, in its early days Naples was a promising place to visit, and it attracted people who made contributions to American business and industry that continue to this day. Growing up among my family and their friends during seasonal visits to Naples set my sights high and shaped the early years of my life.

Bea and Stephen Foster Briggs at their 40th anniversary celebration, 1950, in Naples, Florida

CHAPTER 2

Top Drawer (1934–1936)

I am a fan of sayings. They can be serious, frivolous, or fun. They can advise, cajole, or comment. One I particularly like is the expression *"top drawer"* as an indication of quality. The phrase is said to be Victorian, originating from a custom by the Victorian gentry who hid their most valuable items—jewelry, money, expensive clothing—in the top drawer of a chest in the bedroom. It was also an indication of social rank in society. Either you came from a "top drawer" family, or you did not. In my case, there was no question from which drawer my family came.

My parents' marriage in 1935 was a merger of sorts, the combining of two prominent families. My mother, Joan Nichols, was from Detroit, Michigan, and her father's family, the Nichols, originated in Scotland and came to America around 1700, settling in New Hampshire or Vermont, I believe, before moving to Crown Point, New York. From there they headed to Michigan, where John Nichols founded a company, Nichols-Shepard, in Battle Creek in 1848. Nichols-Shepard was one of the original manufacturers of motorized tractors and threshing machinery. The Nichols name was well known in Battle Creek, since the family was very supportive of the town.

My grandfather, J. T. Nichols (1868–1935), married Helene DeMorat [3] Nichols (1872–1955). Ultimately, she became my grandmother Nichols, whom I called "Duckie." She and

J.T. moved to Detroit, where he was a highly successful banker until the Crash of 1929 when he lost everything. Despite the loss, however, the family retained its high social standing, and consequently the match between my mother and father was considered a good one.

As I remember Mom, Joan Nichols Briggs (1912–1970), in her early years, she was 5'7" with dark black hair and green eyes. She was very kind and loving and extremely active in local charitable endeavors.

Dad, Stephen Albro Briggs (1911–1965), was about 5'8" with brown eyes and black hair. He was a very sensitive person and always the life of the party. He had a super personality and was well liked. He graduated from Dartmouth in 1934 and went to work for Briggs & Stratton, a company founded by his father and my grandfather, Stephen Foster Briggs.

My grandfather, Stephen Foster Briggs (1885–1976), was an inventive genius. He was born in Watertown, South Dakota, a descendant of Joseph Briggs, a blacksmith, who settled on Block Island just off the Atlantic coast around 1750. The island is part of Rhode Island, separated from the state's mainland by the Block Island Sound. The Briggs family migrated from Rhode Island to Connecticut, where my great-grandfather, Stephen Albro Briggs (1830–1907), was born in Stonington, Connecticut. From there they traveled west through Ohio and Minnesota before settling in Watertown, which in that day was the end of the railroad.

My grandfather Briggs (also referred to as SF) manifested an innate sense for innovation, which was evident to others even when he was still a youth. While attending South Dakota State College in Brookings in 1906, he designed and built a six-cylinder, two-cycle, air-cooled automobile engine. This was the first of many original inventions to come. In 1907, he graduated from South Dakota State with a Bachelor of Science degree in electrical engineering. During his senior year, the basketball coach, William Juneau, introduced him to Harry Stratton, who played for the

University of Wisconsin. The Stratton family had accumulated substantial wealth through the operation of grain elevators.

With financial backing from the Strattons, SF was able to start his business. He moved to Milwaukee, Wisconsin, and one year later in 1908 he built the "Superior" automobile, which was a full touring car. There were only three made, as SF could not obtain financing in Milwaukee. Even today, engineers still consider the "Superior" as one of the most innovative and advanced cars of that era. But the conservative bankers in Milwaukee in the early 1900s did not agree. They couldn't believe the automobile had a place in the 20th century. They were convinced that the horse was here to stay, but they weren't so sure about the car.

Nevertheless, SF and Harold Stratton formed a partnership in 1908 with the intent to produce automobiles. Eventually the company decided to manufacture automotive components and small gasoline engines, and later developed switches for controlling ignitions, lights, and starters on automobiles. The company manufactured door handles, window lifts, oil filters, carburetors, horns, and spring covers, as well as locks for switches, doors, and automobile compartments.

In 1910, SF married Beatrice Branch (1888–1979). My grandmother Branch's family [4] arrived in Massachusetts in 1638, having come from England where their roots can be traced back to the 1500s. They were reported to be descended from a Norman Knight. From Massachusetts they went to Norwich, Connecticut, and then to Tunbridge, Vermont. They ended up in the Yankton, Dakota Territories, where my grandmother was born. One of the family fables was that her father, John Elrie Branch, was an Indian agent to the Sioux Indians. I was very proud of this heritage, only to discover that actually he was a sales agent for Swift Packing selling to the Sioux.

My paternal grandparents' union was a lasting success, my grandmother later told me, because, "He makes me laugh."

I suspect more than laughter was afoot between them. Years later I came across a note my grandmother had written about meeting my grandfather in Chicago in 1919. She called the note, "Meeting 'S—'" and even now, long after both have died, I can still feel the romantic passion between them.

Here is what she wrote:

> A wireless. Two hours on a crawling limited. A choking gasp in a station. A yellow taxi. The hotel. Aimless hours on Michigan Avenue and in shops. There must have been dinner—night at last. A moon and its molten metal path across the lake. Another taxi. An obstinate guard to be won over. Hurrying, stumbling breathlessly down a long train shed. And at last your face, your hands, your voice.
>
> —B. B. B.

My grandmother Bea meeting my grandfather SF at the train in Chicago in 1919

Theirs was a fabulous life with a home at 1584 Lake Drive in Milwaukee and a second home known as "Pinewood" at Pine Lake in Waukesha County near the town of Chenequa, about 30 miles west of Milwaukee. They took regular trips to Naples, Florida, and subsequently owned a beachfront home there at 2700 Gordon Drive, built around 1936. Throughout their lives, wherever they lived or discovered a worthy cause, SF and Bea made it a point to be benefactors in terms of their outstanding community service, generous financial gifts, and college scholarships.

As the years moved forward, my grandfather, possessing an uncanny sense for business success, not only founded companies but also acquired them. In 1928, Briggs & Stratton [5] bought Evinrude Outboard Motors.

By the mid-1930s, during the years my own father began working at Briggs & Stratton, his father's genius for engineering was on full display. SF held 46 patents for invention. (At the time of his death in 1976, he was credited with more than 100 patents—many still in use in automobile and related industries.)

In 1936, SF made one of his many pivotal decisions: He turned his attention to the Outboard Marine Corporation (OMC) [6] to become president and director, leaving his old college friend and classmate Charles Coughlin to run Briggs & Stratton, while he remained as chairman. Based in Waukegan, Illinois, OMC made Evinrude and Johnson outboard motors.

The same year that SF made this strategic career move, I entered the picture. My mother and father responded by delightedly naming me after my brilliant grandfather. I became Stephen Foster Briggs II, newest member of a family favorably considered "top drawer."

Stephen Foster Briggs II (SFB II) with Grandmother Nichols, 1939, in
Grosse Pointe, Michigan

CHAPTER 3

Like a Chicken With Its Head Cut Off
(1936–1945)

Whenever I hear the expression about headless chickens, I'm reminded of my early years. My memories are fleeting—impressionistic even—and they have to do not only with events in my family's life but also those of the United States, since this country and the entire globe became involved in World War II.

In 1936, the year of my birth, several international events signaled forthcoming world change. George V (George Frederick Ernest Albert), king of the United Kingdom, the British Dominions, and Emperor of India, who reigned from 1910 to 1936, died. During his 26 years as king, he witnessed World War I; the expansion of the English empire; the rise of socialism, communism, fascism, and Irish republicanism; and the Indian independence movement—all of which radically altered the political landscape. Near the end of his life, he is said to have feared Adolf Hitler's rise to power in Germany within the Nazi Party. In 1933, he referred to Germany as a peril and predicted there would be war within 10 years.

His prediction proved correct. The king died on January 20, 1936. Seven months later, Hitler sent troops into the Rhineland on August 31, the day I was born. That same year, Italy's dictator Benito Mussolini made the cover of America's *Time* magazine—

the first among his eight cover editions. In November, U.S. President Franklin Delano Roosevelt won a stunning victory to serve a second term as president. Clearly, history was on the march.

In 1937, the year after I was born, my parents and I traveled to Europe aboard the *S.S. Deutschland* ocean liner. We lived in Zurich, Switzerland, in 1938, and there, my mother told me later, I spoke my first word, somewhat matter-of-factly from my timely perch on the potty. The word in Swiss German was *fartik*, meaning "finished."

That same year we moved to Antwerp, where we might have stayed had the war not begun in 1939. Mother and Dad returned to the States ahead of me, and—for reasons that remain unclear—I later followed them with my nanny on a separate ship. To the concern of everyone, German U-boats present in the English Channel delayed our ship for 10 days. My only memory of the experience was that of a traveling companion with the last name of Duffy who was in a barber chair getting a haircut. I was standing nearby waiting my turn when the rolling ship made him sick, and he "blew cookies" all over me. Despite an urgent washing of my clothes from this episode, and the menacing U-boats notwithstanding, we traveled safely to reunite with my parents in America.

For a time we lived in a rental house on Woodland Road in Lake Forest, Illinois. My father tried to enlist in the armed services to help with the war effort, but he was turned down because of poor eyesight. By now SF had formed OMC, and Dad worked in Waukegan, Illinois. The company subsequently assigned him the job of selling bombsights and other navigational equipment to Bendix Aviation located in Detroit. Since these products were produced in OMC's plant in Galesburg, Illinois, my family moved there, where my first childhood memories emerge and become clear, and the headless chickens made their lasting impression on my innocence.

Even then I had heard the expression "like a chicken with its head cut off." And while I thought it kind of silly, at the age of five or six I learned literally what it meant. My best friend was a school chum, Billy Simpson. Billy's parents were friends with my parents. They owned a farm near town, and we often visited on weekends for horse-drawn hayrides and cookouts. Occasionally, the Simpsons found it necessary to kill a chicken or two of the many that skirted all over the place, and when they did, Billy and I got to watch. It was not a complicated process. You held onto the squawking chicken, stretched its neck across a wooden stump, and WHACK! With an ax, you chopped off its head and let the body down to run. And it did! Watching those headless chickens take off, I learned the origin of the saying, because I witnessed chickens really running around with their heads cut off!

My school years began in the local Galesburg parochial school, St. Joseph, which I attended for two years. It was run by Catholic nuns, who were strict, and I remember being the object of discipline with a ruler smacked across my knuckles and a few chalky erasers aimed in my direction. Of course, such measures may have had something to do with misbehavior on my part.

We lived at 464 North Prairie Street in Galesburg. I remember my Aunt Helene reading to me *The Just So* stories by Rudyard Kipling. Tales like "How the Camel Got His Hump" and "How the Leopard Got His Spots" took my imagination far, far away.

Since this was wartime, our daily life was affected. Certain products were rationed, including sugar and meat. I learned to eat cornflakes without sugar, and to this day, that is the only way I will have them. I may use sugar on other cereals, but not on cornflakes! During World War II families came up with plans for enduring war's privations, and my mother was no exception. She had a small victory garden for vegetables. She baked bread and let it rise on the radiator. To keep me busy on rainy days, we pulled taffy.

Meat was rationed, so people we knew bought it "on the hoof," had it slaughtered, and stored it in rented freezer lockers from the local butcher. My father loved lamb chops—hard to come by back then—but he found a fine source in his friend Bernie Shimmel, who owned the Custer Hotel, and could procure lamb chops; that is, at least once in a while.

Some families had harder times than we did. I had two close school chums, Francais, who was Mexican, and another boy with the last name of Cronin. Francais's family lived in a less desirable part of town near the railroad tracks. We boys would walk along the side of the tracks to gather coal dropped by the locomotive so that his family could use it to heat their house.

When we heard from another classmate that his family was so large they were always short of dinner food, we found an empty barn with plenty of pigeons. We caught two and took them to his house. To our surprise, the family promptly let them go! Perhaps, we realized, our classmate was putting us on.

We played our share of tricks as youngsters. Cronin's family owned the local drugstore in Galesburg. Often we'd call the store and ask, "Do you have Prince Albert in a can?" When they replied, "Yes," we gleefully responded, "Well, you better let him out!"

One snowy winter day in second grade, Billy Simpson and I had a real scare. The previous evening we had built a snowman in the front yard of my house, and we had a snowball fight. The snowballs we didn't use sat out near the sidewalk all night and became frozen ice balls. Just for fun that afternoon after school, Billy and I heaved the balls at passing cars. After missing the first two, we scored a direct hit on the third car and broke the windshield. The glass injured the female passenger, and the driver chased us into the house. We were obliged to meet with the police, which was scary indeed. Fortunately, the woman needed only a few stitches, but Billy's and my punishment I considered severe. We were forbidden to play together for an entire month.

In my first two grade school years, I scored the typical bumps and bruises awarded to most young boys. One day some school bullies chased me, and I crashed into an electrical girder pole, receiving a cut so bad above my eye that it required a steel clamp. Fortunately, my father generally drove me to school, which he had done that morning. Seeing what happened, he took me to the hospital. Another time I was playing in the back seat of our car and managed to kneel on a light bulb, an injury requiring stitches in my knee.

A town tragedy occurred near the railroad tracks when two older students in seventh or eighth grade became stuck on the tracks and were killed by a train. The entire school attended the funeral, which was my first. The event made a lasting impression on me.

Overall, life in Galesburg in the 1940s was fairly simple: My father worked at the OMC plant in town; my mother and my Aunt Basie (Barbara Briggs McCulloch) joined the Red Cross. It was a thrill to watch the Red Cross motorcade run through the main street with my aunt driving one of the military vehicles.

I remember my father's favorite sport in the fall was going with his friends to the Illinois River to shoot ducks. When they returned, Dad, his friends, and I, alongside our cocker spaniel Rufus, would sit on the back steps plucking the birds (mallard and teal), which had been dipped in scalding water.

In the evening as twilight gathered around us, we listened to the radio. In fact, I suppose that's what most families did during those years. I recall one of our family visits with my maternal grandmother Nichols, "Duckie," at her home at 181 Lake Shore at the corner of Lake Shore and Moran in Grosse Pointe, a lakeside region in metro Detroit, Michigan. She lived in a wonderful old house with large front columns and a huge backyard with many trees for climbing. It became a ritual for us to join Duckie for cocktails (martinis we called "silver bullets") on her screened porch in the evening while we listened to commentators Gabriel Heatter or H. V. Kaltenborn report the news from the Allied front. Heatter invariably started his broadcast with a comforting catchphrase: "There's good news tonight."

Whether the war news was good or bad, I guess a child mostly remembers the good times close at hand, for I still can taste the shortbread cookies lovingly baked by my grandmother's Scottish cook, Sarah. On those occasions, I felt far, far away from the world war overseas. And, unlike the frenetic chickens running directionless across the Simpson farm, I felt safe and secure. I was content to nibble buttery cookies on grandmother Duckie's wide screened porch while the radio droned on.

SFB II (top row, far left) at Red Arrow Camp, 1946

CHAPTER 4

Wild as a March Hare (1945–1950)

The next few years of my life can be summed up in two favorite sayings: "Wild as a March hare" and "Happy as a clam at high tide."

Most people remember the hare from Lewis Carroll's *Alice in Wonderland,* madly offering tea to Alice, but not actually handing it over. The expression goes further back in time, however, even to the 1500s. It's noted in Chaucer, where "mad as a March hare" describes the mating season in spring and the foolish antics the male rabbits display to attract the attention of female rabbits.

While growing up it took me a while to be interested in the fairer sex. But right from the start, I was attracted to mischief, and that courtship would last my whole life long. Getting into scrapes with my friends invariably attracted the attention of adults who were determined to straighten out my zigzagging paths toward trouble.

We moved from Galesburg to Lake Forest, Illinois, in 1945 when I was nine years old. Our home was located at 921 Church Road, right behind the Winter Club, which dated back to 1900. In the winter the entire back area was flooded to create a hockey rink and a large area for recreational skating. Strange as it sounds, even though we lived very close to the club, I never learned to skate.

I attended the Bell School on Sheridan Road, owned and operated by Mr. Bell and his son Lex, who taught the eighth grade. The school was just north of the Presbyterian Church, a close bike ride or walk for me. It had no cafeteria, so I took peanut butter and jelly sandwiches for lunch. On Fridays the school offered a special treat: Campbell's tomato soup and grilled cheese sandwiches, all from a hot plate!

During these years my parents traveled extensively, so they hired Jane Demestre from Belgium to live with us, to cook, and to be my nanny. She had worked for my parents when we lived in Antwerp in 1938, and as things were very hard in Belgium after the war, she wanted to come to the States.

With Mom and Dad away, I was alone with Jane, and I learned a lot. She was tough! If I didn't eat my supper, it went back into the icebox and reappeared at the next meal. Further, I was not allowed to have milk with the meal—only after I finished. Thankfully, she did have a few endearing kitchen customs. She made the best boiled potatoes I've ever had, and she whipped up special pancakes with yarrow, dandelion, and ground ivy. Actually, quite good.

When Mom and Dad were home, I enjoyed formal dinners with them in the dining room. These were memorable—even elegant—occasions because Dad made the salad dressing in a silver dish that came on its own tray complete with olive oil, vinegar, dry mustard, salt, and pepper,

Dad had been to the Sorbonne in Paris during his junior year at Dartmouth. Naturally, he was a real Francophile, favoring the country's history, literature, language, and culture. He also loved Europe and went there at least twice a year on business. As a result, my family adopted the European tradition of having beer or wine with dinner. My parents' cocktail of choice was bourbon and water, which, as the years passed, became scotch and soda. I had my own little two-ounce beer mug so that I could drink with the adults.

In the evenings after I finished my homework, I was allowed my favorite treat—listening to the radio. We did not get a television until 1947 or 1948, and in the early days the reception was not very good, but we did have great radio programs. My favorites were "The Green Hornet," "Tom Mix," "The Shadow," and "Fibber McGee and Molly."

While during the evenings I enjoyed elegance (at least when my parents were home), during daytimes at school and afternoons at home or with chums I managed to get into my share of trouble. While I would like to say I was the first prankster in my family, I suspect that wacky behavior was securely implanted in my DNA.

One Saturday morning at home when I was in the fourth or fifth grade, I heard my mother complain to my father about a rabbit eating the flowers in her flower garden. It was located just below their bathroom window, and from the second floor she pointed out the ravenous rabbit to my dad, who happened to be shaving at the time. Seeing the rabbit below, he rushed down the stairs, grabbed his 12-gauge shotgun, and loaded it. But because he was in such a hurry he neglected to put on his eyeglasses. In his nearsighted frenzy, he ran back upstairs, shoved the gun through the closed window—which exploded in a shower of glass—and fired. The offending rabbit, having been duly warned by the loud confusion from the bathroom window above, merely hopped away. My mother was not pleased with this disaster. I thought it was terribly funny, but I had to wonder—was the "mad March hare" in this instance the rabbit or my father?

Meanwhile, I set about to carve out my own rabbit trail of misdeeds. Dunking girls' hair in inkwells in my school desk, shooting out gas lights with my Daisy air rifle on the block where we lived, smoking cigarettes with my school chum Wally Ross, setting off a small explosion with a chemistry set in his basement, and clandestinely sneaking him into the coal chute of the old McCormick Estate across from the Sacred Heart

School—all these pranks kept Wally and me busy. Some of them landed us before the police chief in Lake Forest, who showed us the jail cells in the police station while threatening us with incarceration and other terrifying consequences.

Although I was chastened by the threat of jail, of mischief I was not yet cured. In the spring of 1949, my family went to the Lake of the Ozarks for a fishing trip. It was June, and on the return trip home, we passed a bunch of fireworks outlets. Before the trip I had foreseen this opportunity and had in my pocket a large stash of funds to purchase cherry bombs, small rockets, and torpedoes. When my parents stopped for lunch, I made up an excuse to play outside. Secretly, I visited a fireworks store and surveyed the wonderful array of colorful explosives in bins and on countertops. These treasures were illegal in Illinois; you could not buy them there. With cash I had earned by working as a golf caddy at the Onwentsia Club, I successfully made my selections and hid my purchases in the trunk of the car.

Back in Lake Forest, I smuggled my loot up to my room without Mom or Dad knowing. I emptied my drawers in the clothes bureau and replaced them with all the exciting fireworks that I was going to sell at a huge profit. The next day at school I put the word out that I was having a special sale, and all kinds of kids—some I didn't even know—came in droves. The sale was going well until halfway through the second day. Somehow, my nemesis, the police chief, found out. He arrived on the scene, confiscated my remaining unsold items, and ordered me to his station for a stern lecture. He told me what I already knew: The sale of fireworks in Illinois was forbidden.

Ah, well. You'd think I would have learned something that time. My parents certainly did. In the summer of 1949, they sent me to Culver Military Camp near Lake Maxinkuckee, the second largest natural lake in the state of Indiana, near the town of Culver. There we campers were required to wear silly uniforms, and we spent our days marching most of the time. We lived in structures with wooden sides and tent tops. They were dreadfully hot; in the afternoons we sprayed them down with a hose to cool them off. The area where we went swimming was filthy. A band of gypsies was camped nearby, and when we swam we made sure our mouths were shut to avoid taking in one of the turds that floated by. Basically the camp was awful. I guess Mom and Dad felt I needed the discipline, and probably the fireworks sale did me in.

By contrast, prior to that summer, my camp experiences had been pleasant. I spent days at Camp Willowbank when I was around six or seven and boarded at Red Arrow Camp in Wisconsin during the summers of 1946 and 1947. That camp was located on Trout Lake in Woodruff, Wisconsin. We lived eight boys to a cabin. I had a friend from Milwaukee named Bob Buettner who was a wildlife enthusiast. With him we found snakes, frogs, salamanders—every living creature that crawled or hopped. We'd catch them and bring them back to the cabin for display. Water sports were big: canoe jousting, canoe races, and an event where you stood on the stern seat and jumped up and down to make the boat go forward.

In that ideal camp environment, I didn't play my cards right, or the devil got into me, or something. There were bunk beds in our cabin, and above me there was a boy from Palatine, Illinois, who was a chronic bed-wetter. Since I slept on the bunk below him, that created a problem. Eventually the counselors moved him, but not before the other boys—myself included— figured out that we could make him wet on demand. During naptimes while he slept, we took pleasure in putting his hand in a bowl of warm water. This only accelerated his bed-wetting problems. As usual, I didn't get away with my foolishness. Somehow the counselors found out, and we campers were forbidden to play sports for a couple of days.

While playing baseball at camp, I was chasing a fly ball in center field one day and fell and broke my wrist, necessitating a trip to the local hospital in Rhinelander. I particularly remember this incident, as Pat Harder, one of our counselors, and the fullback on the Chicago Cardinals' "Dream Backfield" [7] (the best in the league), had hit the ball. So my injury was, in effect, a badge of honor.

While growing up I was exposed to cultural events that I thoroughly enjoyed—among them, sports and music. Occasionally I went to Wrigley Field to watch the Cubs play. My hero was Andy Pafko. When I was about 12 or 13, Mom took me to the Chicago Symphony since she had season tickets. We went on Friday afternoons. The majesty of collected musical instruments and the beautiful melodies they created made a real impression on me. In fact, it was from those weekly excursions that I learned to enjoy classical music.

Between 1947 and 1948, Hans Snel, the son of Tilda and Hans Snel, Sr., came to live with us. The Snels owned the Briggs & Stratton distribution center for Holland along with Johnson and Evinrude Outboard franchises. Prior to World War II, when my parents were living in Europe, the Snels had become their good friends. They were special people. During the war, they hid about 15 Jewish children within their "extended family" from the Germans during the occupation of Holland. Hans's mother, Tilda, was German; consequently, the German military wanted her son to join their army. Hans's parents hid him in an underground tunnel in their backyard to keep him from being discovered. After the war, they felt it would be good for Hans Jr. to have a change of scenery, so he traveled to the United States and lived with another OMC family and with us for a year.

When he stayed with us, Hans was like a big brother to me, since I had no brothers and sisters of my own. I recall him being rather stubborn, and he frequently argued with my mom and dad.

While Hans was in Illinois, he went to Lake Forest High School. He brought the distance skates that he used in winter on the frozen canals of Holland. Those were the longest skates

I had ever seen, and Hans could cross the entire width of the
Winter Club ice in two strides. During warm weather he enjoyed
his other hobby as a long-distance bike rider, and together on
weekends we rode to Lake Zurich and back. Being as I was
only 12, this was a long trek for me. Irritated, Hans ordered me
around at times, and his belligerence bothered my mother. But,
even with that tension, I found it fun to be with him. After a
year it was time for Hans to return to Holland to finish high
school. His parents had wanted him to have a transition from his
ordeal living underground during the war, and his experiences in
America helped.

SFB II at Culver Military Camp, 1949

Mom and Dad (Joan Taylor Nichols Briggs and Stephen Albro Briggs) enjoying boating in 1948

CHAPTER 5

Happy as a Clam at High Tide
(1940s–1950s)

During the first half of my life, I was never more content than when I was playing on a Florida beach while listening to the ocean or operating a small outboard on a lake. In any locale where I could be around water and boats, I was happy . . . as happy as a clam.

If you have ever ordered clams in a restaurant, you may have noticed that when opened, clams appear to be smiling. Maybe the saying originated from that impression. Most people, however, think the expression, "Happy as a clam at high tide," was coined in the early 19th century in the northeastern United States, where clams are plentiful and readily enjoyed. There— as fishermen and clam diggers know—predators can't bother mollusks in deep water, because the mollusks can't be found! Safe and secure, they are blissfully embedded . . . as blissfully embedded as I was as a child growing up during the 1940s and 1950s in Pine Lake, Wisconsin.

My grandparents Briggs, SF and Bea (known as Tayto to the grandchildren) [8], had their summer house, "Pinewood," at Pine Lake. Located in the upper middle part of the state of Wisconsin, Pine Lake covers 703 acres and the water is clear and deep. During most of my childhood, my family enjoyed wonderful visits to Pinewood. My grandparents bought it some-time in the 1930s. They owned about 50 acres surrounding a large main house and a three-car garage with an apartment above with its own gas pump nearby. Behind the main house there were sleeping accommodations for servants. A fair distance away there was a cute cottage with a sleeping porch, and next door there was a large barn filled with equipment to manage the estate. A tennis court lay down the hill toward the water. At water's edge was our favorite retreat, "Snug Harbor," a two-bedroom cottage where it was fun to spend the night.

Located near the town of Chenequa, less than an hour's drive from Milwaukee, Pine Lake was the place where my extended family gathered happily for years. As a little guy of three or four, I visited there with my cousins Bobbie and Richie McCulloch. We scampered around having fun, especially building a fort out of the porch cushions, which were very large. My great-grandmother "Nanny" Branch, Bea's mother, would often visit on weekends.

As we got older, Richie and I thought up escapades, which often got us into trouble. When I was about six or seven, Richie and I sneaked up to the third floor, which was about half finished and included a large crawl space in the eaves. We were playing our fort game and became chilled, so we decided to build a fire with tissue paper. The paper ignited, smoke plumed, and fortunately my grandmother Briggs, who smelled the smoke, came running up the steps to put out the flames. Richie and I got into big trouble. Regrettably, it would not be the last time . . .

When we were eight or nine, Richie and I were allowed to take out the little boat without having parental supervision. The little boat was a pram, a lightweight almost flat-bottomed boat, about eight feet long with a small outboard motor around five horsepower, and naturally an Evinrude. One evening, however, alone, we rowed next door to play a trick on Brooks Ott, a neighbor a few years older, whom we did not like. Stealthily, we removed the outboard motor from his boat and hid it under the dinghy on their raft. The next day, the lost engine was reported as stolen. Chief Lutz and a group of neighbors conducted a search for the engine, only to find it (to their chagrin) located just a bit off shore on their raft. That escapade cost Richie and me another trip before Chief Lutz, and we both were grounded for a week.

Richie and I devised another ill-advised plan: He would row a boat while I swam across Pine Lake. Fortunately, Pops (SF) came along. After he lectured us about how foolish the idea was, he wound up becoming the rescue boat, as I gave up—gasping after swimming about 400 yards. Ah well. It seemed like a good adventure at the time.

As we grew older, our pranks became wilder. One afternoon Richie and I, equipped with our Daisy air rifles, decided to go on a big hunt. We ended up near Mrs. Vitz's barn. Mrs. Vitz was the grandmother of one of our good friends. For reasons I can't explain, Richie and I proceeded to shoot out most of the barn windows. *BANG! BANG!*

And you can guess what happened. Yep. The next thing we knew, we were at the police station, shaking in our boots before Chief Lutz. Things went from bad to worse. First, the chief scared us half to death. Second, our grandmother Briggs, Tayto, picked us up at the station and gave us a huge scolding. Third, and worst of all, we still had to face Pops. As one might expect, he not only gave us a very stern talk, but also he sent us to our rooms and banned us from playing together for several days.

Looking back, I can't remember how old Richie and I were when we were allowed to take out a regular-sized boat (a 12-foot car-top wooden Thompson) on our own. My guess is age 10 or 11, and the boat probably had a 10-horsepower motor. But, whatever! It was like having a driver's license. Now we were mobile.

Those were wonderful days. We hung out at the Swallow's home with their son Chip and his older sister Susie. We played with the four Ott children—Barbara, Shelley, and the twins,

Bobbie and Billy—and Tom Coleman, who lived next door. Mrs. Swallow was nice to us. The only time I remember her getting mad was when we kids had a fight in which the boys ganged up on the girls, peppering them with eggs, and prevented them from coming out from under the dock. But ultimately there was no harm done, only foolishness and fun. On rainy days our favorite game was Monopoly.

Not long after, I learned to sail a boat called a "cub" on Pine Lake. I was not very proficient; however, all the other families were big into sailing, and every weekend we enjoyed races for all different boat classes. Often there were scow races. A racing scow is a flat-bottom boat with a blunt bow and sideboards, which you climb out on to balance the boat in heavy wind. The largest is an "A" scow, which is 38 feet. These boats are extremely fast and are primarily found on lakes in the Midwest. Buddy Melges, from Lake Geneva, Wisconsin, made them famous when he helped defend the America's Cup in 1992. Up until then the East Coast sailing community looked down on those who raced on lakes.

Other competitions we enjoyed were normal races around a triangular course ending at a small island where there was a great deal of beer consumed by the adult racers. In addition, there were always frequent protests by various skippers who claimed they had been fouled.

Especially for kids, the full moon race was one in which the young people picked up greased watermelons floating on the water. Regattas were held in White Bear Lake, Minnesota; Lake Geneva, in Walworth County, Wisconsin; and Lake Winnebago, in Neenah, Wisconsin. Once Chip Swallow and I went to Neenah/Menasha to sail in the regional regatta on Lake Winnebago. At this event, Chip and I were almost last in our class, and in one race we managed to turn the boat turtle—we did a 180-degree flip and our mast wound up pointing down at the water! How embarrassing! It's not easy to get a boat mast unstuck in the shallow bottom of Lake Winnebago, so we were forced to drop out.

All in all, these water events were quite festive, and sometimes rowdy, but everybody—young people and adults—had an awfully good time. And throughout these good times, my "March hare" and my "happy clam" personas kept each other company.

One day when I was about 15, Richie and I conceived another hair-brained plan. We planned to take a group over to a party in Oconomowoc, in southeast Wisconsin about 10 miles away. We schemed to sneak into our barn at Pinewood at night to hot-wire the truck by taping a quarter to the back of the ignition. We figured we could go over to the party and be back before anyone missed us. With several friends in the truck bed, I pulled out of the barn. But I made a mistake, pulled the wrong knob on the dash, and activated the dumping feature to the back bed, which tipped my friends onto the ground in a torrent of screams and foul language. No one was hurt, but this mishap scared Richie and me bad enough that we eased the truck back in the barn and aborted our mission.

When I was 16 and had obtained my driver's license, I encountered a situation I did not know how to handle. An older friend, whom I won't name, asked me for a ride from Pine Lake to Milwaukee, where I was heading to a party at the home of Mr. and Mrs. Fitch. On the way over the boy—bigger and stronger than I was—asked me to stop the car to take a "whiz." I stopped, and I also got out to do the same thing. To my surprise, my riding companion approached me in a way that let me know he was trying to entice me to have sex. Well! I was so naïve; I had no sexual experience with the opposite sex, let alone a male. I was terrified! I climbed back in the car. He did, too. I drove at breakneck speed to town, dropped him off in Milwaukee, and steered my car toward the Fitch home, where the butler let me in. The home was a grand place overlooking Lake Michigan. When the butler took me to the dining room where Mr. and Mrs. Fitch were having dinner, I was mortified.

There was no party that I could see or hear. I must have made a mistake!

But then, another surprise for this day, the butler calmly opened a section of a paneled wall that revealed a stairway down into a huge elegant cellar, complete with a bar and more than 100 people. There were voices and loud music that I had not even heard upstairs. This party room had been constructed during Prohibition. Just like the movies! The parents of the young people below were dining elegantly in a formal dining room above while a party was roaring beneath their feet in rooms that looked like the interior of an ancient castle. I'll have to say, that last event was a sort of capstone for me, illustrating the surprises that prevailed during the years I grew up around Pine Lake.

There would be other unforgettable memories involving travel, car races, and deep-sea fishing. My parents, you see, did not let moss grow under their feet. Whether working or playing, they were always on the go. I've mentioned that my father loved everything French. Not surprisingly, one of his favorite French language expressions was *tout de suite*. Translation? "Right now," as in "immediately!"

1948 MG-TC, Mom and SFB II in Pine Lake, Wisconsin

CHAPTER 6

Toute de Suite, Right Now! (1947)

The fall of 1947 was a dismal time for Lake Forest, as the town became the victim of a major polio outbreak. The Bell School was closed down. Two of my friends, John Bent and Tony White [9], came down with the disease. I was with Tony the night before he went to the hospital, and it must have been a miracle that I never contracted polio, as it is highly contagious. Tony spent several weeks in an iron lung but finally recovered. We were advised to leave the Chicago area if possible.

As it happened, we stayed in Lake Forest for a while. During that time my mom didn't know what to do with me, so she got me started in stamp collecting. I would spend hours in the sunroom of our home organizing and looking up my stamps in the Scott Catalogue, a reference for stamps worldwide. Dad worked in the export division of OMC, so he brought home lots of stamps. As a result, I learned a great deal about geography through my collection since I looked up the countries on a world map. I thought the British Empire and the Belgian Congo had the most beautiful stamps!

After a while we did leave Lake Forest to visit Duckie's wonderful home on Lake Shore Drive in Grosse Pointe, Michigan. Grosse Pointe was (and still is) an affluent community in Wayne County that covers just over one square mile. Near Detroit, it borders the shores of Lake St. Clair and is known for fabulous estates, including the Edsel and Eleanor Ford House, at 1100 Lake Shore Drive. As mentioned earlier, my mother's family had moved to Grosse Pointe from Battle Creek. Duckie's home on Lake Shore was next door to St. Paul's Church, a French Gothic Revival style Catholic church with a wonderful view of Lake St. Clair. Duckie's husband J. T. worked for the family business, Nichols-Shepard. The company manufactured farm equipment and was the first to build a power thresher. I never knew that grandfather, although I understand that he was a successful banker in Detroit until he was wiped out by the Crash of 1929.

In the fall of 1947, we lived beside the lake and waited for the dreadful polio menace to pass. I worked on my stamp collection. Mom and my Aunt Helene, who was living there at the time, taught me all kinds of games, including gin rummy, backgammon, cribbage, canasta, and Russian bank, plus a little about bridge. Duckie used to play mahjong, which I never did understand.

At Grosse Pointe I spent countless hours in the backyard climbing trees as well as sitting on the front porch watching the ore boats pass by. Also known as lake freighters, ore boats are bulk carrier vessels that ply the Great Lakes. Classified as ships, but traditionally called boats, they carry materials, such as limestone, iron ore, grain, and salt, to populated industrial areas on the lakes. I determined their country of registration based on their flags, which I identified in my book on the flags of different nations, and logged this information into a notebook.

Following that spring and early summer in Grosse Pointe, we spent August and September at the Pine Lake cottage. My parents had become interested in car racing. They joined the Sports Car Club of America (SCCA), established only a few years earlier in 1944. The club, composed early on of mostly non-professional enthusiasts, began to support road racing, rallying, and autocross in the United States and developed programs for both amateur and professional racers.

SCCA emerged from the Automobile Racing Club of America, which had been discontinued in 1941 because of World War II. The sports club began to sanction road racing in 1948. SCCA's inaugural event was the Watkins Glen Grand Prix in 1949, and my mother was a timer for that race.

In 1947, Dad brought back an MG-TC from the UK. Through friends in Chicago he became interested in SCCA, and he and Mom were avid participants in the sport for many years. In the early days everyone drove his or her own car to each event, which also included a large amount of socializing. These events were held on private farms and included hill climbs, obstacle races, and even a few backward races. Road rallies were also very popular and were held on public roads. Each driver was given directions and a given time to the checkpoint. A driver was penalized for being over or under the allotted time. Not a speed race, the rally was judged on accuracy of navigation.

As time went on there were actual races held at diverse locations, such as the Studebaker Proving Grounds in South Bend, Indiana, and Elkhart Lake, Wisconsin, which still continue today. All events were built around picnic dinners and just plain fun.

Both Mom and Dad participated in as many races on weekends as they could, and after a couple of years they moved up to a MG-TD and finally a Jaguar XK-120. All participants were strictly amateur, and they used family cars for all events. This laid-back approach came to a screeching halt, however, when one member, Gentleman Jim Kimberly, showed up at Elkhart Lake with three red Ferraris in enclosed carriers and a team of mechanics!

My parents, you will remember, were drawn to excitement—travel, cars, hunting—and sports. I remember one time in 1948 when I was 12. Dad spontaneously decided that we would all go on a skiing vacation to Aspen. Dad had learned to ski when he was in college at Dartmouth.

For some reason, after considering ways to get there, he settled on the family Cadillac, and it must have taken us three days to cross the country. On the way out west, we stopped at a stream in Iowa for a picnic, where Dad spread out a blanket and we had his favorite lunch—freshly picked watercress sandwiches with a little French wine. We stayed at the Jerome Hotel, which was pretty much the only place in town. So far, so good.

But, on our first morning in Aspen, there were no lifts open at the base of the mountains. So Dad took off carrying his skis and climbed up a trail on Little Nell and maybe even higher. That afternoon he arrived at the bottom of the hill strapped in a toboggan, flat on his back. He had broken his leg. Just like that, our ski vacation was over after one day. The next day we left for home. *Toute de suite!*

My grandparents' Briggs home at 2700 Gordon Avenue, Naples, Florida

CHAPTER 7

Winter Term in Naples (1950)

Following the polio epidemic, we returned to Lake Forest and I went back to the Bell School. During the winter term of my eighth-grade year, however, my parents pulled me out of school since they had decided to travel to Europe. We spent Christmas in Naples, Florida, with my grandparents Briggs, and then I stayed there and was enrolled in the Hill School on the beach between Sixth and Seventh avenues south. There were only three other students besides myself. Going to the Hill School was a treat. Our lessons were on the porch overlooking the Gulf and beach, and Mr. Hill made sure we were through our lessons by noon!

Living with my grandparents while attending school was a wonderful experience. For entertainment, my friends and I had parties and went to movies held in the Quonset Building behind the Beach Store on Third Street. The Haynes family ran the Quonset Building and the soda fountain at the Beach Store, both of which became hangouts for young people in the town. We played tennis at our neighbor's sunken court, followed by lemonade in the courtyard, as Mrs. Uihlein (her husband William was vice president of Schlitz Brewery and established the Naples Water Works) would not allow us in the house.

While there were not many young people in Naples, every effort was made to find whoever was in town. We had great beach parties with bonfires that lasted quite late. Some parents worried about the lack of supervision for their daughters, so Peter Ordway (my closest friend and hiking buddy, whose parents were best friends of my grandparents) started the "Naples Social Services Club." This idea was designed to make parents feel at ease while their daughters were out at night, since Peter assured them that their daughters would have a good time in a safe and tranquil environment. When you consider that Peter was 17 or 18, about three years older than myself, this so-called "social services club" was a real joke!

My room at my grandparents Briggs' home at 2700 Gordon Drive was upstairs in the northwest corner—a long distance from Pops and Tayto's bedroom. Located near the back stairs off the kitchen, my room afforded the opportunity to sneak in and out at will, which on occasion I did. But my sneaking out did not mean that life with my grandparents was anything but a civilized experience—because it was.

They had a staff, Alma and Marshall, as well as Idela, who did the cooking. Marshall was in charge of the household as well as the serving. Alma was in charge of laundry and housekeeping. I spent a great deal of time in the kitchen and considered the staff friends.

One day Marshall and I took a bus to Fort Myers for the day, and I was surprised that I could not sit with him because segregation restrictions were still in place, and he was black. On Saturday nights he and I would visit "The Quarters" [10] to check on numbers from Havana, announced every Saturday evening on Radio Havana. There was no lottery in Florida then, but in the black community, playing the numbers was a forerunner of the state lottery today.

Gordon Drive leading to my grandparents' home was like most other roads in Naples—paved with shells. The area was undeveloped by and large. It was not unusual to see a distinctive blonde Florida panther occasionally crossing the road before it ducked into the lush enveloping growth of pinelands and mangrove swamp. There were only about 80 phone numbers in Naples and the population numbered 2,000. My grandparents' phone number was Naples #4.

Throughout the 1940s and 1950s, I spent my winter and spring vacations in Naples, where both my dad and mom's families spent the winters. In these days the town was basically a small fishing village compared to today's ranking as one of the top winter resorts in the United States. Back then the Quonset [11] Building, the movie theatre, doubled as a church where Catholic Mass was held on Sundays, as well as services for other denominations. If you got confused on the time to attend Mass, you could wind up at the Episcopal or Methodist service!

Before the widespread use of DDT, the mosquitoes in Naples would carry you away (DDT did not arrive until 1949). The horse flies were so large that my grandfather would try to shoot them with a BB pistol. Sometimes he would catch a horse fly and then stick a small piece of a broom up its tail end. The insect would fly straight up, a feat, in hindsight, I regard as a precursor to the first moon rocket launch!

Despite its remote environs, size, and worrisome insects, life in Naples was pleasant and busy. On Saturdays for amusement we watched a fellow named Chiz Rivers, the local water dowser, wrestle alligators at the Four Corners, bordering Fifth Avenue South and Ninth streets. Thursdays there was always dinner at the Naples Hotel, one block from the beach, where Duckie, my grandmother Nichols, spent her winters. Dinner was followed by bingo on the huge screened front porch complete with rocking chairs.

My grandparents Briggs built their home in Naples in 1936. The family vegetable and cutting garden was across the street on the east side of Gordon Drive in what is now part of Port Royal, considered today as a most lavish place to reside. During the 1950s, all the milk for the children of Collier County came from the Miami area. Because the milk was frequently spoiled, my grandmother urged my grandfather to start a dairy farm. The big mistake was that he hired a manager from Wisconsin to run the operation, because Wisconsin was the leading dairy state. Unfortunately, Theron Ridge had no knowledge of what type of dairy cows would survive and produce milk in southwest Florida. After about two years, the dairy venture failed.

Pops had a photography studio, which at one time employed 12 to 15 people and made and distributed films for OMC. Pops also developed and printed his own bird photographs and produced films, including *Gooney Birds, Toy Story,* and *Inagua Flamingoes,* among others.

In 1952, SF was rated one of the "very finest bird photographers in the world." That same year, his photographs were displayed at the Kodak Information Center in Grand Central Station in New York. Over his lifetime, he photographed 40 different species of water birds. For his work he designed and built a special 16-millimeter twin reflex camera with matching six-inch cine ektar lenses—one for the picture and the other attached to a ground glass lens for focus and composition. The lenses were interlocked for accurate focusing. Disney and Warner Brothers purchased footage he shot of flamingoes in their habitat. Any money he received from the sale of footage was donated to the National Audubon Society. Toward the end of his life, he donated his photography equipment and many pictures to his alma mater, South Dakota State College in Brookings.

As distinguished as he was, with all his business, civic, and amateur accomplishments a matter of public record, he simply was "Pops" to me, and I loved spending time with him. One favorite activity was to go down the Shark River on his boat, the *Ungava,* to fish for snook. These drab colored fish have a distinguishing lateral black line on their sides, stretching almost head to tail. They live in the tropical waters of the Western Atlantic Ocean and the Gulf of Mexico, and they are the finest eating fish I have ever enjoyed. It seemed like every trip we would catch at least one or two 30-pounders. What a thrill!

Every day before lunch at 11 a.m., Pops and Tayto would take their daily walk to the Naples Pier and back. Other family members who might be in town and I would join them. Dinner was promptly at 7 p.m., with the cocktail hour beginning at 6 p.m. Sunday lunches were a formal affair. Pops fixed his famous "rum dums," a drink made up of two ounces of light rum, usually Santa Cruz, which he brought back from Cuba on his boat, plus grapefruit juice from his grapefruit grove nearby, and a one-ounce portion of Myers's dark rum, with fresh ground nutmeg floating on top. All in all, it was a civilized existence, indeed.

After my winter visit of several months in Naples, I moved back to Lake Forest following my parents' return from Europe, but I went back to Naples in June following my eighth-grade year. In honor of my successful graduation from the Bell School, my parents gave me a week of tarpon fishing at Boca Grande, which in a word was FANTASTIC!

SFB II in 1950, tarpon fishing in Boca Grande

Chapter 8

Tarpon Fishing (Spring 1950)

Boca Grande is Spanish for "big mouth" and recalls the shape of its port. It's a small residential community on Gasparilla Island in southwest Florida, known for its charming downtown, deep blue water, beautiful beaches, and fabulous fishing. My family and I stayed in the Gasparilla Inn, originally opened in 1913. The inn is named for a 17th-century Spanish traitor-turned-pirate who buried his riches on the island, although they were never found. It is an exquisite resort, built to attract first-class travelers, and known as a top place to capture one of the world's best sporting fish, the tarpon. Back then the inn maintained its Old Florida air, when everyone seemed to know you and the names of arriving guests were posted on the bulletin board.

The morning after arriving, Mom, Dad, and I got up early, and by sunrise we were cruising through the Boca Grande Pass. We were not alone. There were wall-to-wall boats on the sparkling Atlantic and the tarpon were rolling in the waters all around us. But, oddly enough, they weren't striking. Suddenly without warning, everyone's luck changed. At once, fish were jumping and being hooked everywhere. My mother's line, as well as my own, were screaming out, carried by the vigorous fish. In the chaos, sometimes two tarpon were on a line at the same time! More than once a tarpon hooked by another boat jumped into our boat over the transom. What a sight!

Tarpon are large fish native to the Atlantic and the Indo-Pacific oceans. They are the largest species of herring, and both species may be found in saltwater and freshwater habitats. These fish grow to between four and eight feet long. They can weigh as much as 280 pounds. Their backs are a bluish green and they have silvery scales covering their bodies, but not their heads. Their eyes are large, their mouths are wide, and their lower jaw juts out as if the fish wants to insult you for marauding his territory! When you hook him, a tarpon will jump out of the water and put up a fearsome fight, and that makes him a challenge to catch. All in all, tarpon are among the great saltwater game fish. Their leaps are spectacular, and their fight to be free, heroic. Unfortunately, their meat is bony and not good to eat, so most tarpon are released after being caught. Tournaments are held year-round, however, since catching tarpon makes for a wonderful sport.

That day, after both my mother and I hooked a fish, our ship's captain headed for shallower water to get away from the other boats. In response, the fish jumped even more. I remember that my tarpon weighed about 100 pounds. He must have jumped 20 times in two hours! What a thrill! It was surely the best tarpon fishing available anywhere—and a fantastic graduation present for this delighted 13-year-old boy.

The Canterbury School logo

CHAPTER 9

Canterbury (1950–1954)

After my halcyon days as a youngster spent in Naples, Florida, and Pine Lake, Wisconsin, why, after graduation from the eighth grade, did I land in a Catholic prep school several hundred miles from home in a place I had never seen?

Why? My parents never explained. As a youth, I found it a mystery. But as an adult, I've gleaned a few clues . . .

Quite often my parents left me with my grandparents Briggs for extended periods while they traveled. And, yes, I managed to get into some juvenile mishaps, which may have aged Pops and Tayto a little bit. After all, I was 13, visiting with them, and enjoying my spring term at the Hill School on the beach. But I must say I thought my mischievous episodes were minor . . . like the day I brought home a large snake from the garden and let it go on the patio. That terrified my grandmother. Then there was the time I missed the brakes on the Cushman scooter and crashed it through the door of the boathouse. My grandfather didn't like that too much. And there was the occasion that I took the small outboard boat down to Marco Island without telling my grandparents—even though all I did was have lunch with a friend of my Dad's. That was definitely worrisome to everybody. And, oh yes, there was the Culver Military Camp summer experience—not the normal fun and games, if you remember— with its strict counselors and disciplined regimens. My parents clearly felt I needed that discipline. So, those clues were apparent. And finally there was the clincher: I remember a conversation in late summer between Mom and a friend of hers . . .

Mom was out in her garden. She saw one of her neighbors, and they began talking. Mom must have said something like she thought I might be more than a handful if I spent my teenage years at the local high school. What, she asked, did the neighbor think? Brightly, the neighbor responded that her son had gone to a nice Catholic school named Canterbury in New Milford, Connecticut. The next thing I knew, I was on the train, headed for New York City en route to Canterbury. Imagine that!

On the journey, I was seated in the coach section, which was stuffy and you had to sit up, so I walked back to the club car, which was last in the train lineup. It had a wonderful sitting area; the entire back was solid glass. The next morning when I arrived at Grand Central Station, I was met by a school representative and transferred to the New Haven Railroad for a trip to New Milford, a place I had never even visited.

Canterbury School was (and is) a Catholic college preparatory school, offering grades 9–12. It was founded in 1915 by two men: Henry O. Havemeyer, descendant of a wealthy family in the sugar refining business, and Nelson Hume, a Catholic schoolmaster. They wished to establish a Roman Catholic school for boys, who would be guided by religion and prepared to attend Ivy League universities. Some remarkable people have graduated from Canterbury. The school's website lists, among others, author and mythologist Joseph Campbell; actor and producer/director Mel Ferrer; television personality Dominick Dunne; venture capitalist and trustee of Hearst Trust William Randolph Hearst III; Peace Corps organizer Sargent Shriver; and former President John F. Kennedy.

In the 1950s, Canterbury was an all-boys boarding school (girls were admitted in 1973) that was taught by lay instructors,

who were regular teachers not in the priesthood, with Father
Quinn as chaplain. Total enrollment was around 135 students,
so our classes were small. In my freshman year Mass was
compulsory every morning. Later on that practice changed and
each house had its day on a rotation system. In addition to Mass
in the mornings, chapel was required every evening at 5 p.m. I
had difficulty making both Mass and chapel on time. On many
occasions I ran up the hill, tying my tie (we always wore a coat
and tie), with Phil Brodie, my favorite teacher, yelling, "Briggs
we are about to start! You're going to be late! Hurry up!" I can
tell you it was a real pain to run up the hill early in the mornings,
especially during the winter months.

As a freshman I lived in North House, so named for
its position on the north end of the campus. Our corridor
housemaster was "Wild" Bill Dalton. I don't think he was much
older than we boys were. My roommate was John Kliegl, with
whom I shared numerous adventures. We had an excellent
collection of movie star photographs that we had cut out of
Parade magazine and pasted on our walls. The school frowned
on this, but we didn't take them down. Generally, John found
dorm life confining, and frequently he would climb out the
window and crawl along the roof to visit a classmate while
we were supposed to be studying. When our housemaster
"Wild" Bill was not around, our favorite activity was "corridor
hockey," for which we used a rolled up pair of socks as the puck.
As you can imagine, it was a rough sport with lots of body
checking into the walls and doors. Sometimes we got so loud,
the headmaster, who lived under us at the end of the corridor,
named Walter Sheehan and also called "Twit," came charging
up in a highly agitated state to reprimand us. On another
occasion we dismantled the fire hose and used the nozzle as a
trumpet. These and other rule infractions led to a meeting with
the headmaster, who warned us that if things didn't calm down,
some of us might be expelled.

Among the faculty, which was excellent, I should mention that Phil Brodie was everyone's favorite teacher. He was probably in his late 60s at the time, a real "Mr. Chips." He had a wonderful Arkansas accent; he was stern, but always fair. He taught Latin and Greek as well as coached the swimming and track teams—overall a real institution at Canterbury. One impressive detail was that Mr. Brodie was a Rhodes scholar. Another significant detail was that if you couldn't finish the *New York Times* crossword puzzle and you gave it to Mr. Brodie at lights out, he would complete it and put it back under your door to be discovered the next morning.

In the 1950s, Canterbury paid its faculty the amount it cost to send a boy there for a year. Even to this day I am amazed that the school was able to attract such talented teachers at those prices. One explanation was that we were all basically family. Also, the discipline and high moral standards, as well as quality students, appealed to many "top drawer" teachers who were mainly staunch Catholics.

Everyone was required to attend all meals, and we were assigned different tables each week. The tables had a master and a mix of different forms or grade levels. Each week we anxiously checked the list posted outside the dining room to find out whose table we had for the forthcoming week. We hoped to be at our favorite master's table, as some were a lot more fun than others.

The food at Canterbury was definitely not mom's home cooking. To me the worst dish was tapioca pudding, which we called "fish eyes," because of the large tapioca bubbles that stared back at us from the little bowls. The mashed potatoes were a close second—cold and lumpy. Also, I drew a pass on the hot cereal, which seemed disgusting to me.

The kitchen crew was Asian, and the waiters were students. On one occasion my roommate John picked up some pebbles from the chemistry lab that gave off smoke when dropped in water. The next day at lunch, the student waiters dropped a handful of pebbles in the washing tubs as they passed by. What a great idea! Wrong! Regrettably, our knowledge of chemistry wasn't what it should have been, and the pebbles turned all the silverware black. As a result, we students spent most of the next day cleaning it.

Rules were strict. We were not allowed to leave the campus except for Sunday afternoon walks and only for one weekend per semester. Family could come and take us out for the day or a dinner, but we had to be back in the dorm by 8 p.m. In the fall, our walks would lead through the woods to an apple cider mill nearby. Utilizing (there again) our expert knowledge of Chemistry 101, we brought the cider back to the dorm with a plan to make it hard cider. Most of the time it exploded under our beds, which frequently required a visit with the headmaster. More adventurous students would sneak into town, which was off limits as they often got into fights with the local townies.

In the spring our walks led to an abandoned stone quarry that was an excellent swimming hole. It had a sheer drop of 30 feet to the water, except in one place where you could climb down and dive in from about 10 feet. This, too, was off limits, but for us it was a welcome change from the confines of the school.

On the one weekend per term that we were allowed to leave campus, most students went home if they were from New England. Those of us who lived far away visited classmates or traveled to New York City. The state of New York had a drinking age of 18, so we prepared ourselves with fake driver's licenses for when we were carded. Upperclassmen provided these for a price. Our favorite meeting place was beneath the clock at the Biltmore Hotel across from Grand Central Station. We'd hang out in the lounge hoping to meet a visiting young lady or two from some of the girls' boarding schools. On occasion we got student rates at the Biltmore, then jammed in five or six kids by dividing the mattresses and box springs and putting both on the floor.

My first experience in New York City was Thanksgiving 1950 during my freshman year. My Aunt Basie McCullough rented a suite at the Pierre, a luxury hotel originally built in 1930 on the Upper East Side, across the street from Central Park and steps away from fabulous shopping. She invited my cousin Bob, who was at Choate, a private college-preparatory boarding school in Wallingford, Connecticut, his roommate, and me. This was my first time in the Big Apple, and all expenses were paid. WOW! What an introduction to the city at a level I would not see again for many years! One night she took us to our first Broadway play, *Finian's Rainbow*, followed by dinner at Sardi's where the actors often arrived. Another night, after an elegant dinner, we went to the Bowery district to the Bowery Follies, a successful bar that attracted down-and-out bums as well as tourists, politicians, and actors. Ex-Vaudeville entertainers sang and danced for the patrons over sawdust-sprinkled floors, and we had our picture taken with them. During the visit we also took a Hansen cab ride through Central Park. We had breakfast at Rumpelmayer's, a popular tea and pastry rendezvous for New York children, located at the corner of Central Park South and Sixth Avenue. We enjoyed a trip to the top of the Empire State Building, then the tallest building in the world. We also took in the view from atop the Chrysler Building, we visited Rockefeller Center, and we saw the Rockettes at Radio City Music Hall. My favorite experience was the boat ride around Manhattan.

As for restaurants and bars, we went to Jimmy Ryan's, where Sidney and Wilbur de Paris played Dixieland music (in my opinion New York's answer to the Preservation Hall Band in New Orleans). We saw ageless ballet dancers at the Club Del Rio; we attended the Big O, or Orpheum, featuring Sallie and Tessie Coal, and danced with middle-aged women in risqué 1920s ball gowns. On Sunday before boarding the train back to Canterbury, we hit a jam session at the Child's Paramount.

All in all, it was an enjoyable overdose of entertainment and a magical trip for us all.

Back at Canterbury, entertainment was a bit more mundane. On Friday and Saturday nights, we sat on the floor in the lounge of South House and watched black and white Westerns, which were the highlight of the week.

Everyone at the school was expected to participate in sports, and most freshmen played on the midgets' football team. Back then, I weighed 150 pounds, so I ended up on the JV team, but despite my promising size, I failed athletically to live up to expectations. In the winter I made the swim team, which required us to swim 100 laps per practice; but even though I was selected to swim the 440, I didn't excel.

Sophomore year was terrific, as Mr. Brodie was our corridor master along with his wife Pooh. They were kind to us but stern when enforcing the rules. That year the Detroit Tigers were in the World Series. Our school was small, and we supported family teams. Micky Briggs's [12] family owned the Detroit Tigers, so we had great interest in the games. It was against the rules to listen to radios in our rooms, but many of us had small portable ones that we hid under our pillows. Mr. Brodie, ever alert, caught us, but he didn't take away the radios for long.

That year I joined the camera club. For some reason the darkroom seemed to me to be a perfect place to try to smoke cigarettes. Wrong! I was caught and almost asked to leave school. That made an impression on me, and I never smoked again.

On the rare holidays or weekends off campus, we enjoyed our freedom—home-cooked meals, plenty of sleep, and the absence of homework. One weekend I went to my roommate John's home on Long Island. We ventured into New York City for excitement, and we found it! At a random club we went into the back room to dance with some damsels. But John got in an argument with one of them, and the next thing I knew, he'd pulled out his switchblade. At once, two plainclothes federal agents showed up, escorted us out, and explained that we'd made a big mistake trying to dance with the lesbian ladies who frequented the club. Lesson learned.

That year the student body experienced a significant letdown in the generally moral atmosphere of the school. A senior stole the math final and, perhaps, the English final as well. The exams were locked in the bedroom closet within the home of Ed Lindman and his wife. We had heard, but couldn't verify, that the senior and his friends got into the house, removed the closet door, retrieved the exams, and then reinstalled the door without waking the Lindmans, who were asleep in the bedroom. Unlikely story, but whatever caprice took place, the culprit(s) got caught indirectly through their own misguided efforts.

The thieves were smart enough not to perform spectacularly on the exams; rather, they turned in tests that were about equal to the average of the grades they had achieved during the year. However, their entrepreneurial instincts outwitted them. For $5 to $10 each, they sold the purloined copies of the exam to some less stellar students, those you might say who were not the sharpest tools in the shed. These bright lads, who had never performed well academically, were suddenly able to turn in perfectly flawless tests! As a result, Professor Lindman became suspicious and the entire student body had to take the exams again.

During the summer of 1953 between my junior and senior terms at Canterbury, I convinced my mother to let me borrow her 1952 MG-TD for a cross-country excursion. I was 17, likely bored, and I wanted to head west. In late July my friend Dave Allen and I set out from Lake Forest, Illinois, for California. We were loaded down with peanut butter, cornflakes, nabs, and other miscellaneous supplies, as well as two sleeping bags, a little cash, and my mother's gasoline credit card.

We found the drive across Iowa and Nebraska boring, but soon we came upon a great location just outside of Reno, Nevada, by the Truckee River. We took on the town and found it a real treat with bright lights, gambling, and beautiful women, most of who were a bit older than we were. One night we were able to sneak into a girlie show without an ID.

After Reno, we headed to Los Angeles, where we stayed several days with my Aunt Basie and Uncle Robert McCulloch [13]. Then we traveled to the North Rim of the Grand Canyon and had a breakfast of pancakes, which we cooked on a grill we manufactured with a church key and a wastebasket. Before leaving, we drove a golf ball into the canyon.

We were supposed to head home after the canyon, but we were a few days ahead of schedule so we judged that New Orleans was a cultural must for two 17-year-old lads on their first cross-country getaway. On the way we passed through Arkansas where we were halted by a construction site. We met a man nearby who was working on his lawn. We began to chat with him, and he invited us in for coffee and biscuits. He said his wife was out, and why didn't we spend the night? We thought a bed was better than the sleeping bags on the ground, so we said yes. One night turned into two, and he showed us his town. It was hot in Arkansas; there was not much air conditioning in those days, but he had a huge attic exhaust fan that worked wonders after dark.

Once we reached New Orleans we found cheap accommodations at the YMCA, which proved to be a great location. We worried we would not be served liquor, but Bourbon Street opened our eyes; in fact, we did not miss even one bar or one girlie show. The transvestites fooled us, but Bourbon Street was a paradise for two kids slightly underage. After three days we were broke and exhausted. Dave was past his due date for arrival home, so we headed to Lake Forest, intending to drive straight through the night.

All went well until we reached Missouri around 4 a.m. Dave was driving; I was sleeping. All of a sudden, I awoke to the car bumping and the sight of wooden fence posts flying in all directions! We had plowed along a farmer's fence line and landed almost on his front porch! To our horror, the farmer stood on the porch with a loaded shotgun. We exchanged unpleasant words, and he threatened to shoot.

"Let's get out of here!" I shouted at Dave, who drove the MG out to the highway as quick as he could. On that surface we traveled about 500 yards with the right front wheel bent awry before we came to a stop. We made it over the hill and out of the farmer's yard, thank heavens, and I hitchhiked into town to arrange for a tow truck. The garage mechanic in town had never seen an MG, and he assured me that no one in the area could repair it. My only choice was to call my dad and ask him to solve the problem. Dave and I headed back to Lake Forest on the bus.

My senior year I lived in a single room in Middle House. My prized possession was a Columbia 360 record player with two speakers, which played 33-1/3 rpm records. That year I became editor of the school newspaper—a real mystery since English was not my strong suit. I also enjoyed the debate team.

Although improved, I still had not outgrown my "March hare" streak, and I had difficulty concentrating in study hall without cutting up and disturbing the entire room. For punishment, I was given the task of picking dandelion heads until I filled a wastebasket.

We had an unusual custom at Canterbury of three-day silent retreats. These were exercises in discipline and self-control, I suppose, but the students appreciated them—not because of the spiritual emphasis so much as the retreat meant no classes for three days. Even our meals were silent—not offering the customary banter we enjoyed. Our one outlet came in the afternoons before chapel. Then we were able to take walks and talk, which was a real treat!

In the spring of my senior year, following a break spent in Florida, I convinced my parents that it would be okay to drive Mom's MG-TD back to school. Two classmates squeezed in, and we headed north from Naples toward Connecticut.

Now, I knew that cars were not allowed at Canterbury, so I made sure we arrived right at 10 p.m. on Sunday night, which was the deadline to return. The next day I met with the headmaster, who requested that I remove my car since they were not allowed on campus. I told him it would take me three days to drive back to Lake Forest; so, after much discussion, he allowed me to store it in the barn. Since I'd always had a good relationship with my housemaster, I convinced him that if the car were not driven on weekends, it would require extensive repairs. Once again, after much discussion, I prevailed and he let me take it out every other weekend for a couple of hours.

Despite its strict atmosphere and the regimentation, Canterbury was a wonderful experience and it taught me valuable life lessons. There I learned the importance of high moral principles. In addition, the instruction in Christian doctrines laid a foundation for success among many of my classmates. The academics were excellent, and the vast majority of our class was headed to an Ivy League college. The faculty was caring and dedicated. To this day, not only can I recite all their names, but also I can recall much of what I learned every year. Upon entering Canterbury, I was scared and in shock. Plus, I ranked near the bottom of my class. By the time I graduated, I had gained confidence and focus, and I ranked fourth, near the top of my class. Part of my success I attribute to the fact that Canterbury offered few outside distractions.

College, on the other hand, with distractions galore, would offer me a real roller coaster ride.

Bell Tower, Cornell University

CHAPTER 10

How Can You Be Lost When You Don't Know Where You Are? Cornell (1955)

After a successful programmed existence at Canterbury, I launched into the next few years with misguided abandon. In some respects I was immature, I grant you. But in others, I was advanced. You see, my years at Canterbury were interspersed with family vacations and travel both within and outside the United States. Those experiences and the people we knew offered me educational opportunities far beyond textbooks.

In 1951, for example, I attended a boat show in New York City on Ralph Evinrude's boat, *Chanticleer*, a luxurious 110-foot yacht, one of only two ever built. Mr. Evinrude was the president of OMC, and on the return trip I was flying back to Milwaukee on a DC-3 owned by the company. The two of us became involved in a game of gin rummy, and by the time we reached Milwaukee, I was pretty far ahead. Now, Mr. Evinrude hated to lose, so he ordered the pilots to circle the field for about an hour (at who knows what expense in fuel) until his luck changed!

That same year I stayed at the elegant Drake Hotel, built in 1920, on Chicago's Gold Coast. My mother, father, and I made two trips to Havana, Cuba, in March 1952 and 1953. With my dad I enjoyed a trip to Southampton, New York, in May 1954 for a major sports car race. With my mom in August that year, I was invited by Jim Pigott, a good friend from school, to visit Seattle where he lived and to go on a camping and fishing expedition to Pincher Creek, Alaska, a stream not far from Anchorage.

These trips were spaced between events that I mentioned earlier with SCCA races, which were held in Janesville and Elkhart Lake, Wisconsin. There, road races were hosted on public county roads during the 1950s.

Such adventures contributed to my varied geographical background, and they were unusual, I'd say, for a boy heading off to college. The only problem was, with all that exposure to exotic places and relative open-mindedness, my mind was closed. Or perhaps I should say "fastened" to one singular ideal: I wanted to be an engineer like Pops—Stephen Foster Briggs—whose name I'd inherited and whose talent and experience I hoped to repeat.

Big mistake! But I can't say I wasn't warned at the time. My college advisor at Canterbury told me flatly that I was crazy to go to engineering school. But I was determined, and so off I went to Cornell.

Cornell University is an Ivy League research university located in Ithaca, New York. It was founded in 1865 as a land grant institution by Senator Ezra Cornell, who offered his farm in Ithaca as a site and $500,000 of his personal fortune as the initial endowment. Senator Cornell was a broadminded fellow. He is quoted as saying, "I would found an institution where any person can find instruction in any study." By that he meant opportunities of all kinds. And his prediction came true. Cornell boasts Marshall Scholars, Rhodes Scholars, and Nobel laureates affiliated with the university. The institution also was recognized as technologically innovative.

If you'll recall, my grandfather Briggs held more than 100 patents to his name during his lifetime. He was my inspiration, and Cornell, his alma mater, seemed to be the place to realize my own aspirations and dreams.

But when I landed on the Cornell campus, I lived in temporary dorms left over from World War II. The classes were tough, and I hated the labs. Even though I'd graduated fourth in my class at Canterbury, I was terrible at college mechanical drawing, which no one ever fails, and my performance in physics and chemistry sadly loomed not far behind. In short, the courses were killing me. And make no mistake: That fact was obvious to others.

Across the hall in my dormitory there lived a short, rather obnoxious student from Brooklyn. He was exuberant in his expectation of my failure, and he insisted on betting me that I would fail the chemistry final. So, I took the bet—$5—and lost. I failed chemistry, but I didn't fail to pay him back. Much to his chagrin, I decided to pay my debt by giving him 1/4-cent stamps (legal tender). And much to my enjoyment, I learned that for several months afterward, he cussed me out every time he sent a letter home, since it took 28 stamps, which represented seven cents!

The main difference between Canterbury and Cornell (in addition to heightened difficulty) was the number of distractions; that is, the freedom to do what I wanted. And I did! I enjoyed fraternity rush, all the parties, and visits to the different campus houses. At the time Cornell had 56 fraternities and sororities. About half the student population joined them. I joined Kappa Alpha (KA) fraternity, only to find out that my grandfather Nichols, also a graduate of Cornell (and whose grandfather was an inventor who started the Nichols-Shepard Company in Battle Creek, Michigan, in 1848), had been a member of KA. That coincidence fueled my hopes to succeed at Cornell. The Nichols family had started a company that became an important supplier of the farming industry, producing the steam engine tractor in 1854 and the first "vibrator thresher" in 1859.

Naturally, I might have concluded that college success lay in the genes. If so, my failure lay in the distractions. Not only did

I enjoy all the social events, I succumbed to late-night games of cards, notably bridge.

The truth was, while I disliked the academics, I enjoyed the school. The area around Ithaca was great and the campus itself was fabulous. The location on the hill above Cayuga Lake was spectacular, and the buildings throughout the campus had an Old World feeling to them. I remember winters when we borrowed dining trays from Willard D. Straight Dining Hall to slide down to our freshman dormitories.

After the spring term of my freshman year, due to my abysmal performance, I was asked to leave Cornell, and I went home to Lake Forest. But I didn't stay there long. My father got busy and arranged for me to go to Mexico City to live with a good friend of his on the conditions that I work hard and go to school. Without blinking, I promised to do both.

I said to myself, *Even though I was a lost student at Cornell, I am a fairly accomplished traveler for a kid my age. So, how hard can Mexico be?*

Mexico City College campus, postcard circa 1955

Chapter 11

Mexico City (April 1955)

My bravado faded quickly. Leaving the United States I became nervous and even scared about going to a foreign country with a language I did not speak. After a brief stop in Austin, Texas, to visit a young damsel I had met in Naples several years before, I was off to Monterey in my Nash Rambler, which had reclining seats that went almost flat and on which I spent several solitary nights.

The road was terrible—a dirt track in the middle of desert country. Breaking down was not an option, and fortunately my car held up. By using sign language I somehow found the home of the family in Monterey with whom I was to stay before proceeding to Mexico City. The Hintons were friends of my dad, and they turned out to be very nice. Jim Hinton knew a lot about plants and the environment. I learned that his father had been the famous botanist in British Columbia who had discovered that rubber trees were bisexual.

During my stay Jim enthusiastically insisted that I go hiking, climbing, and walking in the local hills near his home with him as well as camping at his "Pulki" ranch, which was about an hour and a half away. It was a delightful visit—so much so that in having a good time, I neglected to call home. My parents, meanwhile, had made repeated calls to Mexico City. They thought I had come to some terrible fate at the hands of bandits in Mexico. Thankfully, not true. But, on the other hand, before I left Monterey for Mexico City, Jim assured me that the roads were "loaded with banditos," and I must be extra careful. Funny thing, driving to Monterey I must have been too young and innocent to be afraid while driving through desert land and sleeping in my car at night.

Once I reached Mexico City, I had first-class accommodations, since I had my own little "casita" away from the main house. Just up the road lay Mexico City College, where I took a couple of classes in the mornings. In the afternoons I worked in the parts department of Commercial Euzkadi, the Johnson Motor distributor.

In those years Mexico City was relatively clean and safe, so I spent my evenings exploring the city and its various places of amusement. One evening a group of us from the college hit virtually all the nightspots, and then at about 4 a.m. we headed down to the market. This was where all the "crazy gringos" wound up. When the sun emerged over the horizon, I was aghast to discover that none of us had any pesos to pay for transportation home. But—not to worry. I conceived the brilliant idea that we should convince the local shoeshine boys that we would do the shining for them—for 50 percent of their profit—so that we could earn some pesos. With our limited Spanish, this sales job became amusing, and eventually we convinced them that we would all have fun. The result was that for the next hour or so we Americans cheerfully operated the local shoeshine service.

Later after coffee and snacks, I wandered off to find one of the Paseo de la Reforma cabs that ran up and down the road. These cabs were like modern-day mini buses that picked up people and dropped them off along the Paseo de la Reforma for one peso. Since I was staying in a home on this road, they let me off right outside the gates.

Another evening I attended a party hosted by two of my college friends who lived in a location that was actually a series of straw rooms on top of an apartment building. The place was cheap and kind of funky and fun when it didn't rain. This event was my first exposure to marijuana, which seemed to be the levity of choice except for those of us who still preferred Carta Blanca or Dos Equis. A highlight of this evening was to watch limos and other fancy cars come and go on the street below us. It seems that this particular straw rooftop palace was right above the best whorehouse in Mexico City. I guess you could say acquiring such knowledge was part of my Mexican education.

Late that summer, Mother called me to say that Dad had had a serious heart attack. When he was out of the hospital, she told me, they were going to Cape Cod for four weeks. Would I join them?

Right away, I quit school, packed up my things, and left for the Cape. I was grateful for my few months in Mexico. The experience had given me an understanding of foreign culture and a smattering of Spanish—both of which would become useful later in life.

SFB II, front row, KA Fraternity, Cornell University, 1956

CHAPTER 12

Loose Ends (1955–1956)

In the fall of 1955, I returned to Cornell for another try. I was required to retake all the classes that I had failed—chemistry, physics, and mechanical drawing. All were still a problem. By the end of the semester, I was given one more chance; I was placed in the Division of Unclassified Students. This classification provided me the opportunity to take courses at any of the schools at Cornell. My student advisor suggested I try some easy liberal arts courses, such as Song Bags 101 (part of a series on the history of American music), so that I could raise my grade-point average before re-entry into the Mechanical Engineering School. Once again, I didn't listen. I flunked my final for mechanical drawing, thereby setting a school record. I'm pretty sure that I am the only person who failed the course not once, but twice! Everybody always said nobody at Cornell ever fails mechanical drawing! *Hmmm*. It seems I had a problem drawing a straight line with a ruler. Of course, there were other problems, too—those same old distractions—the fraternity house and the game of bridge.

By Christmas it was time to head home. My good friend Fredi Sewera from Graz, Austria, and I were supposed to drive to Lake Forest with Bill North and John Fell Stevenson, whose dad, Adlai Stevenson, ran for president. They were to pick us up on their way from Harvard en route to Lake Forest. But for some reason, Fredi and I canceled that plan and headed out on our own. When we reached the Indiana turnpike, we encountered a terrific blizzard. Cars were stalled all over the road, and some had slid off the road. Visibility was only a few feet, and I remember seeing what must have been a circus truck of animals—giraffes and elephants, among others—wandering loose. We got to Lake Forest around 3:30 a.m. When my mother came into our room about 6 a.m., she was surprised to see us. There had been a terrible crash on the Indiana Turnpike, she said, and tragically Bill North, our friend, had been killed. She thought we were in the crash with him, and, while she despaired of his loss, seeing us brought her thankful relief.

After my second try at Cornell as a freshman, I spent the spring of 1956 working at Johnson Motors in Waukegan. Dad had arranged the job for me, as he felt it would keep me out of trouble. I worked with the experimental engineering department in the factory. Punching the clock at 7:30 a.m. was difficult, so sometimes I had one of my co-workers punch me in.

The summer of 1956 was approaching. I was asked to be an usher in my cousin Bob McCulloch's wedding in June in Bel Air, California, which is an upscale residential area near Beverly Hills. Following his wedding, Bob had planned to spend the summer traveling in Europe, so that left his room open. I convinced my parents that I could live in his room and earn credits from the University of California, Los Angeles, during the summer. What a great idea! And what a great summer! Classes were five minutes away and scheduled in the mornings; in the afternoons, Santa Monica Beach was 15 minutes away, where I could rest and recuperate at the Beach Club. During those months I even got to see Harry Belafonte perform live at the Hollywood Bowl.

I should mention that while I was taking in the rays of sunny California, I applied to several schools, including

UCLA, Pomona, Occidental, the University of Arizona, and the University of California, Berkeley. Much to my surprise, none of these institutions of higher learning felt I was up to their standards. Imagine that!

Fall was looming, and I had no place to go. I was at loose ends. At this point, my father stepped in to define my future.

Entrance to Babson College

CHAPTER 13

Babson Institute (1956–1959)

I had been home about 10 days from my laid-back summer in Los Angeles when my father called me aside to speak to me about something important. I listened politely, and then with disbelief. He gave me two options: I could find a school that would accept me that fall, or I had the privilege of becoming a U.S. Marine. Surely he was kidding! No, he was not. And to complicate matters, I had a timing problem. It was one week after Labor Day, and all the schools were well under way. Things were *not* looking good.

Sometimes I think there is an angel in heaven that looks after bad boys. Well, not bad, really. I'll say unfocused, indifferent, lackadaisical, fun loving, or maybe just immature. Whatever. I had all the symptoms. Coincidently, my angel appeared as a friend of my father's who was visiting with my family for a few days. His name was Bill Less. We were at dinner one night and the topic of discussion drifted to my problem with getting an education. I mentioned Dad's proposed options and told Mr. Less that I was not too excited about becoming a Marine at the moment. He took that in with a slight smile and asked if I had ever considered the Babson Institute.

"Never heard of it," I quipped. "But I'm sure I would love it!"

Right away, things began to look up, for he said that he was a good friend of Roger Babson, the sole financial support for the school. Also, he said, "I'm a trustee and can probably help to get you in on short notice." Wow!

With absolutely no hesitation I told him, "Please proceed with all haste!"

And he did. After dinner, he picked up the phone and talked to Roger Babson, and the very next morning I was on my way to Wellesley Hills for an interview. Eureka! The interview went well; I started school the next day. I called my mother and urged her to please send me some clothes!

The Babson Institute (renamed Babson College in 1969) was founded in 1919 by Roger Babson, an entrepreneur, businessman, and economic theorist who believed that experience was the best teacher. He had graduated from the Massachusetts Institute of Technology. At Babson, he constructed a curriculum consisting of both class work and business training. He hired businessmen as faculty over academics and stressed the importance of practical experience.

Babson was a welcome change from Cornell, where I hated my classes and most of the professors. In 1956, Babson was popular because it was a three-year business school offering a regular four-year degree. The Korean War (1950–1953) had ended and the Vietnam War (1959–1975) had not yet begun. The average age of the entering freshman was 21, and most of us had either attended another college or were coming from the U.S. Armed Forces. Babson Institute had only recently become accredited; the rumor was that long-term Mayor James Michael Curley in Boston owed Roger Babson a favor, and the school's accreditation was the result. Babson's theories about stock investing had far-reaching implications. He predicted an economic crash in 1929, just before the Wall Street calamity that resulted in the Great Depression. Fortunately, he had believed his own prophecy and converted his investments to cash.

Roger Babson was the single driving force behind the school. He was the Prohibition Party's candidate for president in

1940, so he allowed absolutely no drinking on campus. If caught, violators were immediately dismissed. Women were not allowed in the dormitories. These strict rules encouraged us older students who had cars to leave campus on the weekends. We were fortunate that the great city of Boston was nearby with plenty of girls' schools in the area.

Babson's location offered access to the northeast; it was close to the best colleges in the nation, providing the institute with distinct academic advantages. Babson shared professors with Harvard, Northeastern University, Massachusetts Institute of Technology, Boston University, and Boston College. This practice benefited Babson, because its recent accreditation meant that people no longer considered it a second-class school. I found it excellent. The Babson experience was unique. In most courses the school followed the Harvard "case study" approach to learning. Unlike Cornell, many professors at Babson were business entrepreneurs—active in the fields they taught. This made the courses come alive compared to the static feeling I'd experienced at Cornell. This aspect I truly enjoyed. Meanwhile, I began to think that at Cornell I had chosen the wrong major in the first place.

At Babson, the business law professor was a practicing lawyer. My economics professor, Dr. Wertheimer, who taught money and banking, had been an advisor to the Republican Party and still spent one day each week in Washington. His experience provided us with a real feeling for economics as seen through the lens of the nation's capital.

I chose economics as my major with a minor in the stock market. Since we were on a three-year curriculum schedule to earn a four-year degree, we carried 20 to 22 hours of classes per week, compared to the general load of 15 hours at other schools. During our senior year we spent an entire semester writing our industrial analysis, which was like a mini graduate thesis. Naturally, with my family background, I chose the outboard marine industry. Under this system of education I thrived, and unlike my debacle at Cornell, I did very well. Babson's case system meant that you could take your chances studying selected cases and hope that one was used. Or—an even better scenario—the professor didn't call on you!

I benefited from Babson in many ways. The emphasis on entrepreneurship enhanced my confidence and prepared me for business opportunities I would embark on soon, as well as entrepreneurial exploits I would attempt later in life. But also I benefited from Cornell. Even though I didn't succeed scholastically, I did learn something valuable, and it is this: Every child is born with DNA from his ancestors. He inherits generational talents, leanings, and longings, and those often guide his choices. But, in the final analysis, he must recognize what he enjoys. I chose Cornell because I thought I wanted to be an engineer. Why? Because my grandfather had been an engineer. But I was not cut out for it. I didn't like it. Bumping aimlessly from one school to another, I found ultimately what I enjoyed—the thrill of being in business. With help from caring people, I navigated choppy waters and discovered my strengths.

So, having learned that lesson, I feel confident in saying that no life ever repeats another. Each life is unique. And for that reason—if for no other—you must believe in yourself.

CHAPTER 14

Babson Off Campus (1956–1959)

While Babson offered terrific learning exposure during the week, on the weekends it was a wasteland. With no alcohol and no girls on campus, we male students had to use a certain amount of ingenuity to round out our exposure to the fairer sex. Babson scholastically was known to encourage entrepreneurial endeavors. So, we thought up a few.

My freshman year, the fall of 1956, we Babson men looked around and realized we had a problem: Our dates that semester came primarily from Pine Manor in Wellesley or from Wellesley College. Since no girls were allowed on campus, it became imperative to find a place to take our dates. And to complicate matters, almost all of our friends had two-seater cars. We managed to locate a friend with a station wagon, however, and in that we set out to locate the closest place to take our dates for the cheapest price. We found a one-room apartment in Wellesley Hills located above a hair styling establishment. Since we were in a business school, we felt it appropriate to give our new endeavor a name. We chose to call it the "Jiffy Eraser Company." Since it was only two minutes from campus, five minutes from Pine Manor, and only 10 miles to Wellesley College, the Jiffy Eraser Company became a popular place. But soon the location developed a problem: Because it was used almost daily, the apartment was consumed with the odors of stale beer and cigarettes, making it almost unbearable. Before long, we realized that our growing business had outgrown our facility. The Jiffy Eraser Company was bursting at the seams. It was time to find another location . . .

After logging many miles, we located a terrific cabin in Westwood on a lake. The cabin had three bedrooms, a huge fireplace in the living room, and a decent kitchen. We called this newest entrepreneurial business the "Westview Athletic Lodge." Financially, it represented a major expansion, as we had been paying about $125 for the Jiffy apartment, and the Westwood cabin rent was $600. We realized we needed more paying members, which we had no difficulty recruiting. Our lease stipulated that (of course) the cabin would be used primarily for studying in a quiet atmosphere. Even though it was a good 25-minute drive from school, and therefore somewhat inconvenient, the business boomed. We shut down our membership at 12, since demand was high due to the three bedrooms for R&R.

During winter break, we made the business decision to save working capital by turning off the cabin heat. Big mistake. The pipes froze, and the repairs forced us into bankruptcy. In addition to that, several of our guests from Pine Manor and Wellesley were signing out for the Westview Athletic Lodge, and many were signing out for overnights to the lodge, which was supposed to have its own chaperone. Both the cabin landlady and Wellesley College called the Director of Student Affairs at Babson, wanting to know about Westview. Quickly, the cabin was traced to the "Gang of 12." Needless to say, we were requested to shut down immediately.

With Westview closed we desperately needed a new location for R&R. I found the answer in my good friend Charlie

Bonanno, whose family had a fabulous summer camp on Little Squam Lake about two hours from school. It was a bit of a trek, so we mostly went on weekends. In the winter the place attracted only the most adventurous souls, since the location required hiking through snowdrifts to reach it. We received permission to use the camp only if we assured Charlie's parents (who were extremely strict) that the sole purpose was to study! This meant after visits everyone had to wait outside while Charlie and I crawled through the entire cabin, room by room on our hands and knees, to remove any stray bobby pins or long hair that might refute the study story.

I'd like to say that my entrepreneurial failures to date attractive girls were uncharacteristic of my success in romantic pursuits, but I can't. To tell the truth, the opposite is true. My life with girls was sketchy from the start. Maybe it's because I was an only child and didn't have a sister to play with, or fight with, or whatever siblings do. I don't know. But the girls came and went so fast, it was difficult to even catch their names. Let me see . . .

When we lived in Lake Forest and I was in seventh grade, I had a crush on Merrill, who everyone considered sort of a townie. But I remember being very excited when I sat next to her on the hayride at her house in West Lake Forest, considered real country.

Sometimes I had a babysitter named Sally who worked at the Winter Club. This was a treat, as I had a real crush on her. She was probably around 20 and I was all of 11 or 12. I liked it when she read to me in bed or invited me to sit on her bed while she read. Wow, the imagination one could conjure up even at a young age!

In seventh grade we all went to dancing school at the Winter Club, and our teacher was Mrs. Emma, the wife of Mr. Emma, who owned the Deerpath movie theatre. Dancing school was embarrassing, and I remember having to go ask the young ladies to dance and then writing their names in our dance card. Those were formal occasions, and the girls were all decked out in elegant dresses and white gloves and the boys wore coats and ties.

That same year there was a Friday night when I went to the movies with Lisa Woods, and we sat up in the balcony at the Deerpath. Mr. Emma patrolled the theatre and did his best to stop all necking; however, the balcony was the last place he patrolled. Lisa, as I remember, had just gotten eyeglasses, and my big ploy was to try and share her glasses. I told her I could see better with them.

By eighth grade I was trying to learn more about the opposite sex. I was successful in finding an excellent teacher. She lived about four blocks away and was a real tomboy. Betty Ann was considered a townie, and she was one or two years older than I was. I recall that we played all the games, and I received a quick course in the various sexual parts of the female and male anatomy. Seeing them didn't teach me how all this knowledge was to be used, but it was a fun learning experience.

Later on, I had a crush on Marina Galitzine. She lived just across the street, so I would sit at my window with binoculars trying to watch her get ready for bed. Naturally she always pulled the curtains, and I thought she never knew I was spying. Some years later I learned that she was spying back on me!

My parents were good friends of Ki and Sonny Chappell. Their daughter Susie was in my class, and I really admired her but never got anywhere, even though I tried my best through prep school and even in my early days of college. Her brother George was a good friend, though he was a year older than I was. One time George and I biked down to the lake, and while we were up on the bluff we noticed that two young ladies were on the beach sunbathing without any tops. We decided that we could ride our bikes down the bank through the woods and get a closer look. My problem was that I was so busy looking, I didn't see the city sewer drying system, and I rode headlong into our city septic pool! I was covered from my head to my toes with gross, smelly filth. When we arrived home, my mother made me take my clothes off outside. They went directly into the incinerator.

Perhaps that last incident is a good metaphor for my early love life. My adventures all seemed to end the same: crash and burn.

Older and in college, I still failed to encounter romantic success. To get dates I even tried flipping burgers at the Wellesley College Well, which was the snack bar for the college, located in a basement. No luck.

I seemed to do better on vacation. At least I had a few adventures . . . like those in the summer of 1957 when I traveled through Europe with my good friend Fredi and later when I visited my parents in Nassau.

In Europe I stayed first with Fredi's family in Graz, Austria, and spent most of the day with his mother and grandmother while Fredi was at work. They spoke no English, and I spoke no German. The family was very proud of their shower, the first one in Graz! Fredi insisted on the shower after his first term at Cornell. While in Graz I attended my first opera, which was spectacular, even though I didn't understand a single word.

From Graz, Fredi and I traveled all over Europe, including far-flung places like Positano, on the Amalfi Coast in Italy, and Oslo in Norway. In Sweden we visited an OMC distributor and his wife, who was in her early 30s. One afternoon, she and her husband invited Fredi and me to join them in their sauna near the water. When we arrived they were wandering around with no clothes on. This was our first experience with Scandinavian nudity, and it was a real eye opener in more ways than one.

After Fredi and I returned mid-summer from Europe in August 1957, I was provided with another cultural opportunity to meet damsels in a foreign country.

Mother and Dad had moved to Nassau, as Dad was CEO for OMC International. The company had moved its office from Waukegan to Nassau for tax advantages. At that time, if you reinvested your overseas profits outside of the United States, you did not have to pay U.S. taxes until you brought the money back.

Not long after their move, Mom asked if a friend of mine, B. J. O'Connor, and I would drive their two dogs and other valuables from Lake Forest, Illinois, to Nassau. So we loaded up the family station wagon and took off, arriving safely with everything intact. My parents were grateful for this delivery, and as a "thank you" gift they bought us two tickets to Havana and gave B. J. and me a small amount of spending money.

Fidel Castro had not yet come to power in Havana, so it was still a wide-open playground for the American tourist. Once B. J. and I arrived, we had no idea where we should begin our fabulous adventure, so we asked the cab driver to take us to the Hotel National, reportedly the best in Cuba. We decided this would act as our headquarters. Our first stop was the men's room, where we stashed our ditty bags of travel items and clothes in a locker. We were not sure where we would wind up that evening, or even if we'd stay together, so we agreed to meet up the following day between noon and 1 p.m. After that, we jumped in a taxi and commanded the driver to, "Take us where the action is!"

Big mistake. He did. By the wee hours of the morning we must have gone to every sleazy bar, including Sans Sousi, the famous exotic casino and bar. As you can imagine, we were well oiled on Cuba libres (rum and Coke) that cost about 25 cents each. Somehow in all this partying, I lost B. J.

Alone, sitting in a bar, wondering where I would spend the night, I struck up a conversation with a young woman who also was seated at the bar. She listened to my bedtime predicament, assumed I must be U.S. military, felt sorry for me, and said she could arrange for me to stay in her hotel. Lucky me!

The next morning, I told her about B. J., my friend, and she said, "Go get him. You both can be guests of the hotel." What a happy surprise! For the next four or five days, we explored every nook and cranny of Havana. We'd all gather in the mornings with our cafe Cubana—wonderful Cuban espresso—and our female friends discussed their previous night's adventures. Much of this was in Spanish, so I understood only enough to catch a drift of what had gone on.

Then, on the last day of our stay, our lady friends told us to hide up on the hotel roof. It seemed the owner was looking for two gringos who were staying and not paying. B. J. became alarmed. He said we should "haul ass and get back to the States PDQ (pretty damn quick) before we got in real trouble." I agreed.

We gathered our ditty bags and took off on foot. We'd gone about two blocks before we realized that we were being followed. We feared someone was going to hit us up for our free room and board, so we ducked into a nearby church, stayed hidden for about 30 minutes, and escaped by a side entrance. We hailed a cab and told the driver, "Take us to the airport the most direct way—no stops!" Amazingly, we caught the next Pan American flight to Miami.

As interesting as these excursions with women were, they were only drive-by encounters—not romance, not love. At the time, as the song lyrics go, I was "looking for love in all the wrong places."

I began to wonder if I'd ever find it . . .

Lorna

CHAPTER 15

Meeting Lorna Elwood Sargeant
(Spring 1958)

I n the spring of 1958, my luck with romance began to change. A roommate of mine arranged a blind date with a young woman named Lorna Sargeant. A complete stranger to me, she was attending Bradford Junior College in Haverhill, Massachusetts; she was from Denver, Colorado; and she was the good friend of a girl my roommate was dating. You never know what you will get on a blind date, so I was pleasantly surprised to see a pretty brunette with expressive eyes who was not only thin and athletic but also had a wonderful personality that attracted me immediately. Here was a young woman with class! Not only was she well educated, but also she was adventurous as well. Also—and this was significant—she met my family's standards of the kind of girl I should bring home to dinner. Others I had dated did not rise to the benchmark; that is, they were not quite top drawer. Lorna was different.

On our first date, we went to a drive-in theatre. Young people nowadays may not remember these places, but they were fun. You bought your tickets in a booth outside an enormous parking lot wrapped around a huge constructed screen 30 or more feet tall. When you drove past the ticket booth, you were directed along rows across the parking lot, which actually had poles with metal speakers hanging from either side. You pulled beside a pole, rolled down the window on the driver's side, unhinged a square box speaker, hitched the speaker with its own metal hook to your window, and rolled the driver's side window back up halfway. Then you settled back to listen to the speaker's static music and its crackling lines voiced by your favorite actors projected on the giant screen. Despite the challenges of scratchy audio, the experience was enjoyable for families, children, and lovers. Sometimes little children lounged on the hood of the family car in their pajamas, propping their heads up on fluffy pillows. Parents in the front seat could see over their heads and simultaneously enjoy a reprieve from entertaining their little ones. Lovers on dates stayed inside the cars, naturally, because that was the point of a drive-in theatre: You could snuggle and kiss in your own private world, while before you in Hollywood brilliance beamed Rock Hudson or John Wayne, Doris Day or Marilyn Monroe from the open-air screen.

I was a little nervous on this double date, and I remember that we all shared a pizza. I can't remember the drive-in movie feature that night. My attention was focused on Lorna. Sometime during the evening, on the ruse that I was an experienced stamp collector (remember that I had collected stamps as a boy), I peeked at a letter Lorna had tucked in her pocketbook. It was an innocent pretense to make sure of her name, because I wanted to see her again!

When I asked Lorna for a second date, she accepted. We arranged to meet at the Copley Plaza Hotel in Copley Square in Boston at the Merry Go Round Bar, a festive scene, and one of my favorite places. I was nervous about seeing her again, so much so that I hardly could attend class that morning at Babson. By that afternoon, my stomach was all butterflies. Anticipating our meeting at 4 p.m., I put on my best brown Brooks Brothers suit over a white button-down shirt and a red tie. I arrived at the Merry Go Round Bar ahead of schedule—unusual for someone who generally runs late. The bartender knew me from previous visits, and since it was happy hour, he was serving two drinks for the price of one. I ordered a Manhattan, which was really two drinks. I sat at the bar to wait as it revolved (it actually was a merry go round). When Lorna arrived, she was all dressed up, and I didn't recognize her. But then I realized who she was, greeted her, moved to a small table next to the bar, and gave her order to the waiter who was serving us. He asked what I wanted to drink, and like an idiot, I ordered another Manhattan. As I sipped my drink, I felt a large bubble in my stomach that became a burp, and then culminated in my "tossing cookies." Unexpectedly, I vomited all across the table and all over my best suit!

Quickly, I rushed off the men's room to clean myself up. Dabbing soap and water on the front of my shirt and suit, I stayed a rather long time, and eventually Lorna entered the men's room to see if I was all right. I was terribly embarrassed. Obviously, I was in bad shape, yet Lorna quietly and simply helped me clean up. I appreciated her kindness, knowing all the while that this was not a good way to begin a relationship. Then, the night got worse. We left the bar, and while looking for a place in Cambridge to eat dinner, we became lost. I only barely got her back to Bradford on time—and that was without dinner! Believe it or not, despite this clumsy beginning, we continued to see each other whenever possible. Then June came, bringing summer break, and Lorna went home to Denver.

During 1958, Lorna spent her junior year at school in Paris. Christmas was coming, and I wanted to see her. I called her father, who was less than enthusiastic about the idea. "She's in Paris to be educated," he told me. "She shouldn't come home until the school year is complete."

I made a counteroffer: "Then why don't I travel to Europe to see her?"

Again, he was not receptive. He made me promise that first I would talk to my parents about the idea. My mother was disappointed that I would not be home for Christmas, but she gave her blessing, so I had secured parental approval. That accomplished, I faced the next problem: how to finance my travels.

You will remember that I was pursuing a major in economics and a minor in the stock market while at Babson. Well, the previous summer of 1958, I had worked at OMC selling Cushman three-wheelers. I figured out the cost to ship these vehicles from Lincoln, Nebraska, and then by ocean freight to Havana. My co-worker at OMC and I had sold about six or seven carloads to Cuba when my boss called me into his office. It seems that we had made an error in our calculations, since we neglected to add in the ocean freight and we had priced them delivered to Havana. That meant we were giving away $50 with every vehicle. My boss said gruffly, "The more you sell, the more we lose." Aha. That debacle became another lesson in economics for me.

Nevertheless, I had invested my savings of $600 from summer earnings at OMC in Haloid Xerography (later known as Xerox), a newly listed company. As it happened, I was able to sell my holdings for $3,200, thus making the profit that would finance my European adventure.

It was great to see Lorna again. We rented a small Renault and drove through France and Spain. Our destination was the Island of Majorca. (I might add that Lorna's parents thought we were going skiing with a group from her school, an impression we did not disavow.) On our trip, we discussed marriage but realized that because her parents were very conservative and staunch Episcopalians, we had a problem. I was Catholic. Overall, however, our time together was meaningful, and we made plans for her to meet my parents in Nassau, and for me to

meet hers in Denver. We would try to see each other whenever
we could.

Upon returning to Paris, I bought a little extra time to
return to Babson after Christmas by locating a doctor who
agreed to send a telegram to the college. In it he stated that I had
a serious ear infection, and I could not travel for a week. When I
finally reported to Babson, not surprisingly, the school nurse was
very skeptical.

I was facing my last semester at Babson, and I was
extremely busy with my studies and writing an industrial analysis,
a major thesis on an industry. You had to get a passing grade on
this project to graduate. As mentioned earlier, I chose the marine
industry, and I came up with a solid A to graduate in April 1959.

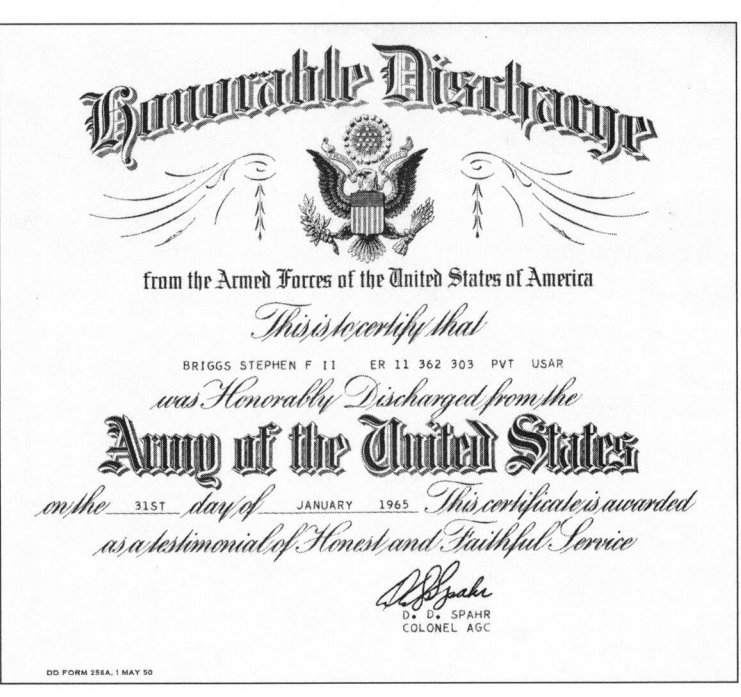

United States Army discharge papers

CHAPTER 16

Port Dix, New Jersey (April 1959)

The year 1959 was somewhat pivotal in terms of U.S. international relations. The seeds of the Vietnam War (never declared) were sewn earlier. The Korean War had ended in 1953. Then, in 1954, Vietnam was divided by the Geneva Accords into two countries: North Vietnam, with a communist government under Ho Chi Minh; and South Vietnam, with a democratic government under Ngo Dinh Diem.

In 1959, Ho launched a guerilla campaign in South Vietnam, led by Viet Cong units, in an effort to unite the country under communist rule. The United States, fearing the spread of communism, trained the Army of the Republic of Vietnam (ARVN) and provided military advisors to help fight the guerillas.

America became actively involved in 1964 when North Vietnamese torpedo boats attacked a U.S. warship in the Gulf of Tonkin. Congress passed the Southeast Asia Resolution giving President Lyndon B. Johnson authorization, without a formal declaration of war by Congress, for the use of "conventional" military force in Southeast Asia. American ground forces were deployed in 1965 and stayed until the fall of Saigon in 1973.

As a senior at Babson in 1959, I knew, along with everyone else, that you had to serve in the military unless granted an educational deferment. This meant that as soon as you graduated, you were drafted. My friend Charlie Bonanno and I decided we did not like the idea of two years of military duty, so we researched the best way to meet our requirements.

In the 1950s, you could enter any branch of the service for six months and then spend the next six years in the reserves. This duty entailed monthly meetings and training for two weeks every summer. The idea appealed to us, since we thought we could figure a way out of the six-year obligation at a later time. The Air Force seemed to be the best deal, and we applied for that and the regular U.S. Army Reserves. Some of our friends liked the National Guard, thinking they would be the last to go overseas in combat. But Charlie and I thought the Guard marched in too many parades, and we didn't want to tie up more weekends than absolutely necessary. More seriously, we knew that the National Guard had been called up by the governor of Tennessee in 1956 and by the governor of Arkansas in 1957 to deal with integration unrest. It seemed like dangerous duty to us, and we didn't relish the idea of waving bayonets at our fellow citizens to help quell the racial discontent.

Since we did not hear from the Air Force Reserves, we thought we had better sign up with the Army Reserves or we would be drafted for two years after graduation in April. So we sent the Army our applications in January 1959. As luck would have it, once we signed up with the Army Reserves, we were accepted by the Air Force Reserves! But it was too late.

The way it turned out, the Army was a breeze for me, and sheer hell for Charlie. During basic training he questioned every action and tried to make sense of what we were required to do. When we reported for duty, we encountered nothing but lines to process us through everything from haircuts to acquiring equipment. This slow inefficiency seemed a total waste of time to Charlie. Other things bothered him, too. We were issued brown boots but told they were supposed to be black. Charlie insisted on the right color and size. That was a joke, because they didn't care. The color was our problem to solve with extra elbow grease and boot polish. He questioned why he had to be up at 4 a.m. only to stand in line for two hours before breakfast. He learned the answer: Do it the Army way.

Back then our drill sergeants were generally black or Korean vets (or both), and they both disliked white college graduates. Many of them had endured bad experiences in Korea with ROTC officers who were college graduates but not respectable leaders. Being a white college graduate, I thought I'd better find someone who knew the ropes and could keep me out of trouble. By the second day I located a fellow barracks mate named Brooks, who had been in the Marines for six months but refused to go to his reserve meetings. As a result they gave him a choice: spend two years with the U.S. Marines or two years in the Army Reserves. He found this option made his life easier. He made his choice, and he knew what to expect. He felt that six months in the Army with meetings and summer camp for six years was far superior to going back into the Marines, which almost killed him.

One night on an overnight camping maneuver, Brooks was my pup tent mate. The entire operation was conducted in the cold, pouring April rain. When erecting our tent, I didn't pay much attention to protocol, but rather followed Brooks's suggestions. When we returned—cold and wet—after training, we found our tent soaked inside as we had neglected to dig the proper trench around it to drain the rainwater. The rest of the evening we spent cleaning our weapons in a dark, cold, wet environment.

While Charlie spent hours trying to understand Army training, I spent hours figuring out how to get through it with the least amount of energy and aggravation. On one of our night maneuvers, we were made to crawl under barbed wire fences with our rifles. Live machine gun fire rattled above our heads. Land mines exploded all around us. It was a cold, rainy night, and our sergeants urged us to hurry up and complete the course so we could do it again. On my second run through I came to the conclusion that we were out there for a set number of hours no matter how many times we crawled through the course. Why hurry? My solution was to lie still in the middle of the course and rest until the all-clear sign. When the sergeant kept poking me, I moved on a few yards. At the end of the exercise, most of the others had gone through the course five or six times; during the same amount of time, I made one and one-half trips. Compared to me, they were much muddier, much wetter, and way more exhausted.

After spending eight weeks in the Army, I had developed techniques to beat the system, so I signed up for on-the-job training (OJT). OJT as a clerk typist was a breeze; however, I learned to type only 15 words per minute. Life was better in other respects, too. From a large mess hall, we were assigned to a small company unit where the food was excellent. Also, in OJT we had more free time.

We still had our onerous duties: kitchen patrol (KP) and guard duty. Guard duty meant a lot of walking and staying up nights, plus it was boring. KP, while most people hated it, could be fun if you got the right job. It helped to arrive early to wait in line since you could select your job based on the time you got there. Even so, I learned not to move too quickly because the job was measured in time, not performance. Whether peeling potatoes or mopping the floor, it was best to proceed at a slow pace, since you never finished anyway, and you saved your energy.

From clerk typist training I was moved to another company to serve out the last two months. With only eight weeks to go, I figured I could slack off a bit. The first rule was to lay low and not become obvious. When I arrived at the new company and checked in to get my room assignment, I was told that there was no place at the moment. "Check back in four or five hours. We'll find you a place," the admissions officer directed. Right away I realized this was the opportunity to find my own place. I scouted the area and soon discovered an empty barracks just outside the company perimeter. I planted myself in the orderly room, which was nicer and more hidden than the regular dormitory area. For the next 7 to 10 days, I was never found as I did not report for roll call in the morning and I was not on the company roster.

Finally, my luck ran out. In the company there was another Briggs who was well over six feet tall and black. One day when I was returning from the PX, having my customary tea while reading the *Wall Street Journal*, I was stopped by the other Briggs. He wanted to move in with me, as he claimed he was taking the heat because I was lost. I let him share the room, and two days later we were both caught. I was obliged to explain to the duty sergeant that I had taken the empty room because I knew there was no room left in the company barracks. I'm not sure he was convinced.

The main goal of our company commanding officer (CO) was to work our asses off every day and give us the least amount of sleep allowed. He was determined to build the streets around our company's barracks with bricks. Thus, we would rise an extra hour early in the morning and work an extra two hours in the evening (supposedly our free time) to build those streets. During the project, loud speakers blasted patriotic military music loud enough to make us deaf. One of his favorite pastimes was to volunteer our company for every conceivable parade. Personally, I was not excited about marching on hot days. After one parade I discovered that there was a shortage of rifles, so I volunteered to work in the supply room on parade days. Because I passed out rifles, the supply ran out before I got one. This worked for about five parades before I was caught and required to participate. Actually when I heard the CO was coming, I escaped to the bathroom where I thought I was safe. Wrong! Pounding on the door, the CO hollered, "Briggs, how many parades have you marched in?"

Oh, well! Thank goodness I was a short timer. In mid-October I was discharged.

As for my reserve duty—monthly meetings and two weeks of training every summer for six years—I missed those fun activities. When I enlisted, I knew I was going to Belgium where there was no active Army reserve. The Army considered having me attend my two-week summer reserve training in Germany, which was the nearest place to Belgium, but then it determined that the distance from Belgium was too great. Thus, the Army declared me exempt from reserve duty. When I returned to the States two and a half years later, I knew that if I sent the Army papers with a United States postal location, the military would send me off to reserve training stateside, since I originally owed them six years. I asked a friend of mine, Jao Tito from work in Belgium, to forward me the location papers every year, which I signed and returned to him to send from Belgium to Germany. No reserve duty for me!

Charlie's fate took a different twist. We were on the buddy system and were supposed to stay together after basic training. However—poor guy!—he ended up at Fort Sill, Oklahoma, driving tanks in 100-degree weather. To this day he claims an old girlfriend of mine had a connection in the Command Company and arranged for me to stay at Dix while he went off to Fort Sill. Not true! He survived Oklahoma (barely), and when he went back to Boston he took over Bonanno Linen Service, a family business in bad financial condition. This situation allowed him to get out of his reserve obligation. Based on his Babson education, he modernized the plant and initiated a highly successful marketing program. Eventually, he sold out to Cintas for several million dollars. So, he didn't do half bad!

CHAPTER 17

Marriage to Lorna (November 1959)

During the time I was in basic training at Fort Dix, I had written to Lorna's father, asking if I could marry his daughter, who was still at school in Paris. In June, on her way home from Paris, Lorna came to Fort Dix. As was proper in those days, she stayed with my friends Emmy and Jim Kearney, who lived just outside the base. Jim was stationed at Fort Dix. He was from Princeton, New Jersey, and had been a classmate of mine both at Canterbury and at Cornell. He and his wife were good friends, and, in addition to the time when Lorna visited, I spent several fun weekends with his family.

A few years prior, in 1957, Mom and Dad had rented a house on Cable Beach in Nassau, capital of the Bahamas, and during that time they decided to build a home at Lyford Cay (the very first house built there), on a prime beachfront lot. It was a mammoth undertaking. Work progressed extremely slowly, and during construction something always had to be ripped out and done over. Disgusted, Dad went to check on the job and found most of the workers sitting around playing checkers. He asked, "What are you men doing?" To which they replied, "We working for you, boss."

Dad tried to engage some other workers in a dialogue, only to discover they spoke no English. Next he learned they were illegal Haitians, hired by the Bahamian workers, for two shillings per hour. Furthermore, he found out that if the Haitians would not work for the low wages, the Bahamians would turn them into the immigration department and they would be deported. This duplicitous scheme meant that Dad was paying the Bahamians four to five shillings per hour so they could stay home, work another job, or simply hang out at a local bar.

Despite the setbacks, assorted delays, and reconstructions, the home turned out to be spectacular, and it was featured in *Florida Architecture* magazine. My room in this fabulous house was on the opposite side from my parents, on the other side of the swimming pool. Also, it was beside the entrance and part of the guest suite. I had my own living room, complete with kitchen facilities and a bar. These were important features for a college student visiting at vacation times. Naturally, I took advantage of this wonderful set up.

My parents were free spirits, always into one caprice or another, and living with them was sometimes hilarious. They were both given to a certain amount of whimsy, particularly Dad, who enjoyed doing anything out of the ordinary. Because he was head of OMC International, Dad had an affinity for those things that originated from his distributors' countries. Somehow, when my parents first arrived in Cable Beach, they acquired an ocelot, whose name I can't recall, and a pet bird named George. The ocelot, also known as a dwarf leopard, is a wild cat that comes typically from South America. George, a colorful Macaw parrot, probably came from the same neighborhood, as the birds are native to tropical Mexico and South America. Mother claimed that George was a mean bird and she didn't trust him. (Macaws are exuberant and given to screeching at times; plus, they like to bite.) But the ocelot was the first to go. Within six months he died a mysterious death. Dad was distressed and claimed that

Mom had poisoned the cat. Ah me, a charge with no proof! George the parrot stayed around longer, but sadly, I can't recall what fate he ultimately faced.

I had started working at OMC International in Nassau during the summer of 1958, and then went back after being discharged from the Army. There I was a sales trainee learning the ropes of international trade, customs regulations, and collection and payment options, such as letters of credit, open accounts, and sight drafts, which were drafts to pay drawn on a local bank that had to be paid prior to goods being released from customs. I lived with my parents in their fabulous house at Lyford Cay on the beach. It was a good place to be, even without Lorna, and I was content to know that she was in Denver, planning our wedding.

I was thrilled to be marrying a special person whom I loved and was acceptable to my family. I looked forward to a fun-filled life with someone who shared many of my interests and who promised a calm, organized life. With these expectations, in early November 1959 I went to Denver for the wedding and some elaborate festivities. The parties, given by friends and family, were fun and seemingly endless.

My bachelor party was held at the motel, Riders Manor, where most of the out-of-town guests, including my parents, were staying. The bachelor party started off relatively calmly until sometime after dinner when, fueled by many toasts, the evening turned rowdy. In college, one of my favorite expressions was to call people I was dubious about "turkeys." Now, it was late November, around Thanksgiving, and my best man, Charlie Bonanno, my friend from Army and college days, remembered my fondness for turkeys. So, when he introduced his speech to "roast me" before the guests, he miraculously produced a live,

25-pound turkey! Mayhem erupted as all of us decided to play
with the turkey, which was loose and scared to death. Someone
even suggested that I should kiss the turkey! In the uproarious
confusion and ensuing damage, the turkey suddenly escaped and
headed down the corridor at a fast clip, shitting as it went. To
make matters worse, my parents, aunts, and uncles were partying
in one of the rooms near ours, and the frantic turkey joined their
party, tried to fly, and racked up more damage. Oh boy! In the
end the cleaning and damage bill amounted to several hundred
dollars. Late that night Charlie went to the motel kitchen to try
to resell his turkey. Ultimately, he had to beg someone to take it
for free.

　　November 29,1959, was a glorious day for a wedding. Of
course, as the groom, I experienced the usual nervousness. Also
I had some anxiety that my best man Charlie might not get me
to the wedding on time. I needn't have worried. The wedding
was beautiful. It was followed by a lovely reception at the Denver
Country Club. After the reception Charlie drove us to a local
motel to spend the night before we left on our honeymoon. He
had a bottle of champagne and insisted on coming into the room
to consume it. Lorna thought he would never leave, because he
spent a rather long time reviewing our many adventures together
and crying over our parting.

　　Our honeymoon lasted almost a month. It began with a
visit to my Aunt Jane and Uncle Dr. Jack Briggs [14] in Bel Air,
an affluent neighborhood in Westside Los Angeles, California,
where we stayed in their guesthouse next to the swimming
pool. From there we visited my Aunt Basie and Uncle Robert
McCulloch [15] at Thunderbird Country Club in Palm Springs.
His house was written up in *Life* magazine, as he designed many
novel features, unheard of at the time. Among the features I
remember, there was a sunken tennis court where the lights came
out of the ground at night to light the court. Around the pool
there was a lazy Susan chaise lounge that rotated with the sun

for an even tan. At the outside bar he designed bottle holders that held six bottles in each well. When one bottle was finished, another would pop up! Another unique feature—the beds in the house were electrically operated like hospital beds so the maids did not have to lean over to make them. Finally, as Uncle Robert enjoyed chess, he also had a full chess set at the pool that was made up of nearly full-sized characters, each about four feet tall.

From Palm Springs, Lorna and I went to Mexico City, where we rented a car and visited places like Cuernavaca, San Miguel de Allende, Pátzcuaro, Ixtapan, and finally Acapulco. There we had luxury accommodations at Las Brisas.

After these honeymoon travels, it was time to begin life as a married couple. We thought it a good omen that on our flight back to the States there sat the actor Jimmy Stewart—right in front of us—loaded down with three or four huge sombrero hats.

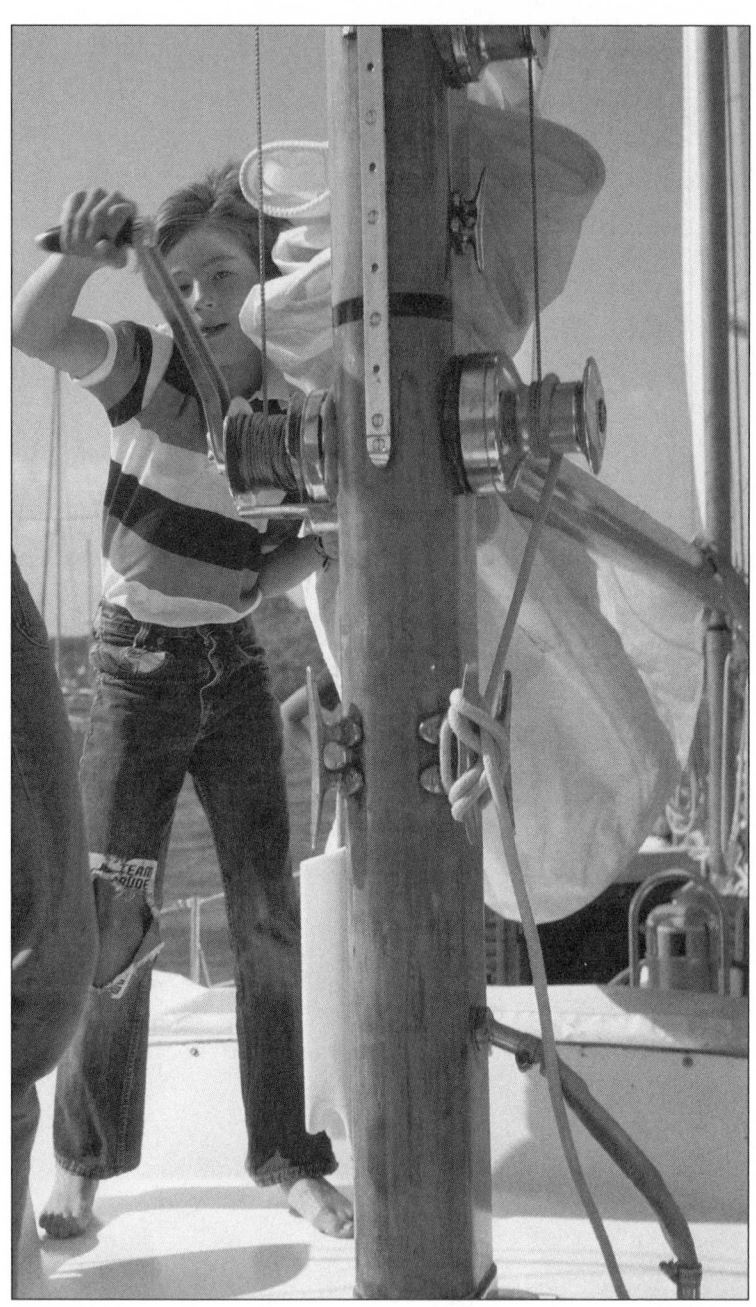

SFB II's son, Stephen, sailing

SECTION III
Midship

Lorna and SFB II's apartment on the sea in Knokke, Belgium, second balcony

CHAPTER 18

Arriving in Belgium (January 1960)

After our honeymoon and first Christmas as a couple, Lorna and I began to prepare for our move to Belgium in January, since I was to become the Northern European Sales Representative for OMC. My starting salary was $5,500.

Although World War II ended in 1945, Europe in 1960 had still not fully recovered from the bombing devastation it experienced nor the damage to its economy that the fighting had inflicted. Bruges, a medieval city, fortunately had escaped the bombs, and its beautiful architecture (some buildings date from the ninth century) is bordered by cobblestone streets and crisscrossed by canals. In fact, the name *Bruges* likely derives from an Old Dutch term for "bridge."

The city is small, oval shaped, and located in the province of West Flanders in the Flemish Region of Belgium. It borders the North Sea. Sometimes referred to as the "Venice of the North," Bruges shares the designation with other canal-accessible northern cities like Amsterdam.

Its port named Zeebrugge (Bruges-on-Sea) is the second largest in Belgium and important to all of Europe. Today, Bruges has significant economic strength due to tourism, silks, tapestries, art, and chocolates. Artisans and craftsmen abound. But in 1960, the town had not recovered from the war; it was still largely agrarian and its mood was not the magical fantasy that you will find these days.

Furthermore, if you look at modern postcards of Bruges, you will notice that they are taken in bright sunlight or at night, when the lighted medieval buildings rise picturesquely above dark ribbons of canals. There is a reason for these selective kinds of shots—sunlight is rare in Bruges! Even Belgians are skeptical about the weather, which is cold and damp. In July and August, the temperature climbs only to 70 degrees, and rainfall averages eight inches per month. By October, chill is in the air.

When Lorna and I arrived toward the end of January from New York, it was a dark, overcast day with lots of wind. My boss Alfred Wend met us and drove us to the apartment he had rented for us overlooking the North Sea. It was spacious and the furniture was early Victorian style, but it was dark, dingy, and drab. That first night we sat in our new living room having a drink while the curtains blew toward us at a 45-degree angle from the wind off the sea. We were tired; I didn't feel well. We both stared at one another dismally sharing our first dreary impressions of Belgium.

Afterward, we walked to a small restaurant where we were the only guests. Because my stomach was upset, I chose to order something plain like a hamburger. I noticed the term *filet American* on the menu, which seemed to be just what I wanted. While we were having some wine after ordering, I noticed that a young boy went out the door and jumped on his bicycle. I learned later that he was on his way to buy the food for our dinner. It certainly was fresh; however, when my burger arrived uncooked with a raw egg on the top, I learned that in Belgium steak tartare and filet American are the same dish.

At dinner, Lorna and I decided that we would search for another apartment. Within a few days we found one at 201 Digue de Mer in Knokke. It was small, but brand new and nicely furnished with comfortable chairs and a living room couch. Our bedroom was just large enough for a double bed. It had another interior bedroom the size of a small closet. The kitchen was tiny;

however, the appliances were new and included a mini Hoover washer/dryer combo all in one. Best of all, the cozy living and dining area overlooked the sea, since we were on the second floor. Our rent was an affordable $250 per month including furniture. In the winter the restaurants would deliver four-course meals to your door at no extra charge. A boy on a bicycle brought each course in its own set of warming dishes, stacked and hung, amazingly, from the handle bars. He left the warmers and then returned the following morning to pick them up.

There was only one drawback to our location: It was above one of the most popular discos in Knokke. While in winter, despite the cold wind, it was pleasant to sit and have coffee under the heaters and watch the world go by without a crowd, in summer the people flocked to this area, and the noisy nightlife created a totally different atmosphere!

Somewhere during those early days of marriage, travel, and relocation between November and January, Lorna muttered the French phrase, "Je suis plein." It didn't strike home exactly, because we generally ate well, so "I am full," was an appropriate statement to make. But, when she repeated the phrase, I caught on.

"Je suis plein" can also mean "I'm pregnant!"

Spring in Keukenhof, Holland

CHAPTER 19

Outdoor Flowers and Offshore Deals, Belgium (1960)

The Knokke/Le Zoute area where we lived was a wealthy resort community and a neat place to be. But as I mentioned earlier, Bruges still had not recovered from the war, the city was dingy, and the majority of the population rode bicycles. The people seemed drab and listless, and the town lacked vibrancy.

Living in this foreign land so soon after we married was hard on Lorna. For one thing, I held a time-consuming, responsible position, being in charge of sales for OMC for the northern part of Europe. The factory and office were in Bruges, which was about a 25-minute drive from home. Also, my job involved foreign travel, sometimes for weeks at a time, and because I spent most of my time either at the office or traveling, Lorna had many lonely hours in Belgium with no family or friends. This hardship was made worse by the winter weather— more miserable than one can imagine—with cold winds off the North Sea. Then, too, she was pregnant for the first time. Fortunately, she spoke French, which softened the experience of waiting for a baby to be born far from her home in the United States. Although I knew she found her predicament difficult, Lorna never complained or told me she was unhappy. She was a real trooper.

When her delivery time drew close, Lorna's doctor told her to call him any time, day or night. He even gave her the phone number of his girlfriend, who lived near to us! One night about midnight Lorna called him and he came right over. He decided she should go to the clinic "toute de suite!" (right away!), so off they went in his VW Beetle!

The next morning Lorna was having severe labor pains, but the nuns were not available since they were at Mass. Actually, it was the cleaning woman who called the doctor and helped Lorna walk to the delivery room. After Mass, the nuns arrived to help with the birth. Our daughter, Alexandra Sargeant Briggs, "Sandy," was born September 2, 1960.

Lorna's room in the clinic was large and overlooked a pasture. In fact, when the window was open you thought the cows might come right in. You could hear their mooing just outside, and since there was no screen, they would frequently poke their heads inside the room! The nuns required that Lorna drink plenty of hot milk, which she did not like, so I bought some cocoa to add to it. During her stay at the clinic, the nuns were amazed that she spoke three languages—French, English, and American. They also were fascinated by her nightgowns, which were much fancier than they had ever seen.

Lorna and Sandy stayed at the clinic for 10 days, all paid for by the government, and we received a bonus of $100 from the government for having a baby. When they came home, the government sent around a registered nurse every couple of weeks for the next three months to make sure the child was being well cared for by the family. Interestingly, at that time in Belgium every child was sent an $8 per month milk allowance until the age of 18. We held Sandy's christening at the small church in Le Zoute, which had a beautiful outside area where Mass was held in nice weather.

As a new couple with a new baby, our favorite activity on weekends was to take Sandy in her stroller and wander around town looking at the great old mansions or traveling to The Zwin, a park in the north section of town.

Our travels led us to other quaint, inviting places. On Fridays, we frequently found ourselves in an intimate restaurant in Zeebrugge, where the specialty was moules and pommes frites (mussels and French fries). We could eat all we wanted for just 50 francs, the equivalent of a U.S. dollar. At Le Siphon in Damme, chefs cooked steaks on an open wood fire, and we ate family-style alongside other guests on large tables with checkered tablecloths.

We saw the huge flower show held every five years in Ghent. This extravaganza attracts several hundred exhibitors from more than a dozen countries and regions. The flower-covered architectural shapes and the sheer volume of beautiful indoor blooms were staggering. We also visited the Kukenhof gardens in Lisse, Holland, open every year since 1949. It is a 70-acre parkland that claims to be the world's largest flower garden. There we found meandering canals, tranquil swans, and glorious color—red, gold, orange, and purple—among the seven million tulip, jonquil, and hyacinth bulbs planted by hand.

In Knokke, we had cocktails at a wonderful hotel, La Reserve. We went to the casino next door, where we saw Harry Belafonte and also the French singer Dalida.

Lorna's best friend at the time was an English lady named Moya Hueis. Moya was married to a Belgian who was head of the local brewery in Bruges. It was through Moya that we found Sandy's first nanny, a lady named Mire Morel, affectionately called "Zu Zu."

While these early months with Lorna and Sandy were peaceful and pleasant, my job in sales for OMC, by contrast, presented international challenges that were complicated and occasionally fraught with peril.

Lorna and I had bought an Opel Record when we first arrived in Belgium. That had been fine for the two of us. After

Sandy was born, however, we needed another car. I ordered a gray Fiat 1500 convertible, which I planned to pick up at the factory headquarters in Turin, Italy. Meanwhile, Dad called from Nassau with the request that I investigate an investment deal in Libya.

"All right, I can do that," I answered, figuring I could visit Tripoli, take care of Dad's request, and pick up the car in Italy on the way home.

Tripoli, often called "The Western Tripoli," is the capital city of Libya. It is located in northwestern Libya along the Mediterranean coast, and it is the country's largest city and chief seaport. My father explained that there was an Australian living in Libya who had valuable knowledge that he wanted to sell to the oil companies and this Australian fellow needed offshore partners to make it work. My job was to determine whether the Australian was legitimate and whether we should become involved with him and his friends.

When I arrived in Tripoli, the Aussie met me at the plane and took me to the only hotel in the center of town. We went out for dinner at the yacht club, and he explained the scheme. At this time only one or two companies had the oil concession for all of Libya. The government was getting ready to pull those concessions and auction off more than 80 percent of them to other oil companies. The companies holding concessions were allowed to keep only 10 to 15 percent, and the balance would go back into the pool for auction. I believe Caltex was one of the two.

Because the companies were returning concessions on which a lot of oil was known to exist, their geology reports became extremely valuable and worth stealing. The Aussie claimed to have the contacts to get him the information about where oil was located on the concessions being returned to the government. What he needed was to be able to compensate his sources through offshore banks. The Aussie wanted the payments from the prospects to remain offshore, because there were severe currency restrictions in Libya. Also, he stressed, it would be unsafe if the scheme were discovered. This all sounded a little wild to me.

This Aussie was a real trip, and after dinner we went to his home where he showed a home movie of his escape from Egypt with his Arab wife. The film was shot from the back of a moving jeep speeding across the desert with bullets flying all around. He spoke two dialects of Arabic, and he assured me his plan would work. He already had the informants lined up, he said, and once we had the data it would be an easy sell worth millions.

That first evening was an eye-opener, and he made plans to show me around the next day. When I returned to my hotel room at around 10 p.m., my room had been taken completely apart. Clothes were strewn about, and everything had been stripped and gone through with a fine-toothed comb. When I reported this incident to the hotel, the attendants only shrugged their shoulders, so I cleaned up my room and tried to get some sleep, which was extremely difficult.

The next morning the Aussie picked me up, and I told him about my room being ransacked. His response was that he should have warned me that the only visitors in Tripoli then were CIA or oil spies looking for information. The fact that I was an OMC salesman made no difference because no one believed it, so my room was searched. The Aussie felt it was no big deal. We spent the day visiting the marine locations and an oil refinery.

That night we enjoyed a delightful dinner al fresco. We had acquired another overseas visitor for dinner. After we finished, the Aussie asked us if we wanted to go to the casino. When I explained that I didn't gamble, and it was not covered by my expense account, our host said, "No problem." He said that the evening was his treat, and we each would receive 1,000 Libyan pounds to use at the casino. When I objected, he told me the money was useless to him. The currency exchange controls were so tight he couldn't take Libyan money out of the country, and he had rented all the safe deposit boxes that the hotel would allow him. Then he revealed that this was money he had acquired through the sale of his valuable data. Dubious as I was, at this point all I could do was think, *Hmmm.*

As soon as I landed in Milan, Italy, however, I called Dad and told him I thought the whole deal was a little dicey and he should decline. Then I picked up the Fiat in Turin and returned home to Bruges.

Map of the Middle East

CHAPTER 20

Middle East Adventure (1960)

Following my trip to Libya in the spring of 1960, I was approached about a new position by my OMC boss in Nassau, whose name was Wally Britt. He wanted someone to explore the possibility of selling our outboard motors and to locate distributors in the Middle East. Was I interested? While other salespeople could have gone in my place, the situation was complicated. Tensions were high in that area of the world, particularly between Israel and its neighbors. In those days you could not travel to an Arab country if you had a stamped visa in your passport for Israel. As I did not have one, I was selected to go.

By way of background, briefly, I can tell you that the nations of Turkey, Syria, Lebanon, Jordan, Iraq, and Saudi Arabia were once part of the Ottoman Empire, a vast holding that was broken up into these nations after World War I (1914–1918). Following World War II (1939–1945), Israel, in 1948, declared itself an independent Jewish nation, but not without bitter fighting, which continued between Arabs and Jews.

In subsequent decades two persistent issues dominated and troubled the Middle East: oil and Arab–Israeli hostility. Both issues are still in evidence today. Oil brought economic progress and dazzling modernity to several countries, especially in the Arabian Peninsula. Arab–Israeli hostility directly involved the surrounding countries of Syria, Lebanon, Jordan, and Egypt, and indirectly all the countries of the region. Hostility provoked two full-scale wars in 1967 and 1973, plus several bloody disturbances on—and within—Israel's borders.

In 1960, the oil industry had not yet transformed the region with its glittering wealth. But Arab–Israeli hostility generated suspicion and unrest. For this reason, the fact that I had not traveled to Israel made my proposed exploratory trip to the Middle East on behalf of OMC less likely to be viewed with skepticism.

And make no mistake: The idea to explore possible market development in foreign countries was right in line with the OMC company goal of dominating the outboard industry overseas. During the late 1950s, OMC's main objective was expansion of business in Europe as well as the rest of the world. The plant in Belgium was built to improve access to these markets, which were now opening up after World War II.

Travel to the Middle East was a lengthy preparatory process. I had to request a visa from every country on the trip: Yugoslavia, Lebanon, Iran, Iraq, Kuwait, Aden, Somalia, Eritrea, Sudan, and Egypt. In a few cases, obtaining a visa required a personal interview with the consulate in Brussels to make sure I had no Jewish ties. One of the major stumbling blocks was that we had an outside attorney on the OMC board who was Jewish. However, we worked through that, and soon I was on my way to the Middle East.

YUGOSLAVIA

Known as the Socialist Federal Republic of Yugoslavia, the Yugoslav state was formed in the aftermath of World War II, and then dissolved in 1992 during the Yugoslav Wars. It was a socialist state and a federation made up of six socialist republics: Serbia, Croatia, Bosnia and Herzegovina, Montenegro, Macedonia, and Slovenia. Serbia included two autonomous provinces: Kosovo and Vojvodina. Translated, the word *Yugoslavia* means "Land of the South Slavs."

When I traveled there in 1960, the trip represented my first visit to a communist country. My interpreter and guide—a government official—met me at the airport. She was in her mid-30s, very attractive, bright, and pleasant. She delivered me to my hotel and met me for breakfast early the next morning. Actually, except for sleeping, she was assigned to me from the time I arrived until I left. At our meeting with the various government officials, I was offered coffee, and at that time I really preferred tea. However, realizing that refusing coffee might be considered impolite, I asked for coffee, as any good American should early in the morning. The first taste was terrible—so strong I decided to get it over with quickly by drinking it all at once. Big mistake! This was my introduction to Turkish coffee. Aaagh! I found my mouth full of coffee grinds and proceeded to chew and then swallow. Thus I learned my first travel lesson in what became my new "culinary experience."

The trip did not prove successful in terms of acquiring business. As I remember, the Yugoslavian government asked for a bid on some motors; however, the red tape and lack of hard currency made the order quite unlikely.

BEIRUT, LEBANON

I will never forget the beauty of this city at that time. It was truly a little Paris with snow skiing only an hour away. I stayed at the St. George, which was a famous hotel on the water. I could watch the water skiers from my window with the snow-covered mountains in the distance. Lebanon was a good market for its size, and I had a great contact, or prospect, to become a new distributor. He was an Arab who had been educated in the States and was truly fond of Americans. At dinner one evening he spent two hours trying to prepare me for the rest of my journey by explaining how I should act and what I might expect in the various Arab countries. Although his advice was helpful, I must say the trip proved more traumatic than I could have imagined.

While he discussed my prospective travels, I had my second lesson in "culinary experience." As a first course, we had sheep eyes—a real delicacy. Now my problem was, not only did I *not* want too eat them, but also they sat alone on the plate, so there was nothing to hide them under! No lettuce, no parsley, nothing! So I followed my first rule of travel, which was to always have a cold bottle of beer handy to wash down any surprises. That saved the day, or evening, shall we say.

My next destination was supposed to be Baghdad, but I wound up going to Tehran instead.

TEHRAN, IRAN

The flight on Iranian Airlines was dramatic. We had a slight delay leaving Beirut because one engine was barely functioning. After we were in the air, the passenger next to me asked what I did for a living and why was I flying Iranian Airlines. "I am an Outboard Motor salesman," I replied, an answer he did not believe. He informed me that the only Americans traveling in the Middle East were government employees, CIA spies, or officials of the Ford Foundation. He went on to explain that the U.S. government had issued a directive that no government employee was allowed to travel on Iranian Airlines because of its poor maintenance record.

Hmmm, I thought. *Not much I can do at this point.* I landed in Tehran and checked into my hotel only to learn that it was a national holiday, so no businesses were open for two days. Rather than sit around the hotel and be bored, I stood around out in the lobby for a while and found a group of Americans who were boarding a tour bus. I didn't realize until later that it was a private tour for Aramco [16] employees who were on holiday. It was a great way to see the city and they felt sorry for me being alone, so a group of them took me out to dinner. The next day I met with our distributors and explored the city, which was fascinating.

BAGHDAD, IRAQ

The following morning I was up at 5 a.m. to catch the early flight to Baghdad. As I went through immigration, the man in charge looked at me and said, "Where is your exit visa?" I replied that I had checked with his consulate in Belgium, and a visa was not required. Obviously, this made no difference to him, so I asked how I might obtain same, and he informed me that once I applied it would only be 10 to 14 days! Fortunately for me one of our distributors happened to be in line and came to my rescue. Off he went with my passport, and 10 British pounds later, I had my exit visa.

BAGHDAD JAIL

Landing in Baghdad around 8 a.m., I proceeded to immigration only to receive a shock. The officer looked at my passport and my yellow international vaccination document, and then two armed police confronted me and escorted me to a small room that had about five or six other travelers—all Arabs. There was no English spoken, and after about 20 minutes, we were all loaded on a bus and off we went for about a one-and-a-half–hour ride. We made a turn into an area containing a rather imposing prison structure, and suddenly I realized I was in big trouble!

One of my major barriers was language, so when I was taken inside to the head warden's office I immediately started jumping up and down, screaming, "Embassy!" After a while they got the point and I was handed the phone, which did me no good as all the numbers were in Arabic. Grudgingly, the warden dialed the phone, and I was connected to the British Embassy. Obviously they had few dealings with Americans, so I suppose they couldn't differentiate between American and British.

After about 15 minutes, which seemed like hours, I did get the chance to speak with the American consulate. He advised me that I had a big problem, as I was already in jail and it would be difficult to spring me in less than 10 days.

"What is the problem?" I wanted to know. And then I found out. The entire problem had arisen because I did not have a cholera vaccination, so I was to be quarantined for 10 days. The consulate explained that this situation arose because I had arrived from Tehran and not Beirut as originally planned. Coming from Beirut, no vaccination was required.

Oh, great, I thought. *Ten days in a Baghdad prison.*

The embassy went on to instruct me not to accept or eat any food, because I would surely become ill. Also in the prison they would try to give me a shot, an injection. I was to resist it at all cost, since the needles were less than sterile. As a parting token of hope, the embassy said it would send a driver to pick up my passport and deliver my food rations. They also promised to do everything they could to spring me in less than 10 days. After hanging up, I slipped into a funk as they took me to my little room with a cot and a sink in the corner.

The toilet was eastern style (a big hole) and located down the corridor. It was used by a large population with bad aim, and the fermentation odor was not to be believed.

As predicted, shortly after I was in the room, a nurse, who neither spoke nor understood English, arrived with orders to jab me. I raised such a ruckus that immediately out of nowhere appeared two armed guards who were to camp outside my room for my entire stay. Next my captors brought in prison food, which I could not identify, so I quickly pushed it back out the door.

After two or three hours, my care package from the American Embassy was delivered. My diet for the next three days was canned cocktail sausage, bananas, and Coke.

The prison authorities requested my passport and I gave it to them. In turn, they gave it to the chap from the American Embassy. A few minutes later I heard someone yelling at me in English from outside. The prison room had a small balcony, which overlooked the boundary wall, and this chap was yelling up from over the wall. He emphasized how much better off I would have been if they had been able to intervene at the airport, but they would do their best, and he would be back the next afternoon.

Wonderful. So I now had 24 hours to sleep, read, and look out the window. As luck would have it, the only book I had was *Lolita,* not too great under the circumstances. The real challenges were first preparing myself to use the toilet and then trying to sleep. By causing a scene when I arrived, I now had two guards who didn't bother me, except they had a radio and played loud Arabic music all night long. I can usually sleep anywhere, but that was a real challenge even for me.

The next day I couldn't wait for my American visitor, who arrived as planned in the afternoon. His news was somewhat disturbing. First, they tried to get me on a plane to Kuwait, but there was a big problem. Kuwait was my next scheduled stop; however, when I left Belgium, I did not have a visa for Kuwait because I was supposed to pick it up in Tehran. I had forgotten to take care of that task. *Dumb me.* I didn't think this would be a problem, but the Kuwait Embassy had no visa for me. Secondly, the Americans had tried to book me back to Beirut, but the only space available was on TWA, an American airline, and a non-Arab was not allowed to fly between Arab countries except on an Arab carrier. Another thought they had was to book me through to Greece; I would get off in Beirut and thus continue my trip. By now, however—disgusted and worried—I was ready to abort the mission and return to Belgium. Ultimately, TWA had no space after all, so I sent my embassy friend away with instructions to get me out of Baghdad the quickest way possible. He promised to return the next day with a plan. So, I faced another 24 hours of the same worrisome ordeal. Upon his return we did the same bit of yelling back and forth over the wall. This time the news was good. The American ambassador had run into a friend from the Kuwait Embassy and had procured my visa. I was also extraordinarily lucky. The Iraqi plane only flew three times per week and was always overbooked; however, it was going early the next morning and they had gotten me on board. All this made me very happy! I was told that a car with a driver would pick me up at around 5 a.m. the next morning.

Anticipating departure, I was up at 3:30 a.m., waiting to be taken to the car. But to my dismay, 5 a.m. came and went with no car showing up. By 5:20, I panicked and tried to sneak past my guards, who were sleeping with the very loud Arabic music blaring. I guess I made it about 30 yards before they were after me and I was back in their control. Again, I caused a scene screaming, "Embassy!" and acting out charades for a telephone. After several minutes they got the point and delivered me to the warden who was asleep. It took several more minutes, which seemed like an hour, to convey my request. He rang up the embassy and found out that, for some reason, the driver had not left as scheduled. Next, the consulate put someone on the line who spoke Arabic, and after an eternity I was escorted outside to a bus. The sun was just coming up. I was the only person in the bus, and the driver just sat smiling at me. I tried every language I knew to say, "Hurry up, plane leaving! Vite! Vite!" Nothing happened. Then it struck me: "Wheels need to be oiled," so I handed him 10 pounds, and the bus turned into a Porsche!

After an hour or so we reached the airport. Being late and not wanting to miss the flight, I ran like mad. I arrived at immigrations only to be asked, "Where is your exit permit?" I almost lost it! I started screaming, "How can I have an exit permit when I went directly from the airport to jail and never even entered the country?" That was not his problem, but obviously it was mine.

Again an angel was with me. Our distributor, whom I had not been able to see, had come to the airport to visit with me on my way out of Iraq. So I gave him 10 pounds, and he returned in a few minutes with my exit visa. I boarded a rather old DC-3, which was full of Arabs and lots of hand luggage. When we stopped in Basra, the temperature was well over 110 degrees in the shade. Everyone got off the airplane except me. There was no way I was setting foot on Iraqi soil!

KUWAIT

This was my first real experience with newfound oil wealth. The hotel I stayed at was well over $100 per day (a lot for 1960). Also there was not much water. The water truck came by at about 3 a.m. and pumped water into the holding tank. I quickly learned that if you wanted water for a shower, you must be finished by 5:30 a.m.

In 1960, there was not a tree in sight in Kuwait, but there were huge roads and boulevards that went absolutely nowhere and just ended in the desert. At the end of the streets, dozens of new cars that appeared fine were simply abandoned. The brand of choice seemed to be Ford.

There were huge empty buildings lining the streets. Evidently, the government gave the Bedouin who was living on the land an exorbitant amount of money for the territory he was squatting on if, in turn, he built one of those new buildings. The Bedouin built the building, and then he found another open space to live. *Go figure!*

One evening I was invited to an Arab party. Much to my surprise after entering a lovely home, we went through a hidden door and descended to the basement where a complete American bar was in full operation. Even the bartender for the party was from the States. Needless to say I was quite shocked, as I had expected the party to be "dry."

BAHRAIN

This wonderful little island was great for a few hours' visit. I had planned to arrive midday and depart the next morning. Wrong! British Overseas Airways Corporation (BOAC), now British Airways, had other plans for me. As I was checking into the Speedy Bird Hotel, owned and operated by BOAC, the attendants asked for my ticket and informed me that my schedule had been changed. They had just switched to the fall schedule, they said, and the next flight was five days away. I asked, "What do I do?" They said not to worry; I would be the guest of BOAC at the Speedy Bird. What fun! Staying in a dry country where, after 45 minutes, I had walked the entire town!

There was an added feature during my stay: my room was a double, and as travelers came and went, the Speedy Bird periodically gave me a new roommate. So, for excitement I drank tea during the day and took a cab to the British Base at night for a beer and movie. On the third day, I decided to fly down to Qatar (Doha) and see if I could sell a few outboards. I double-checked prior to leaving to make sure no exit visa was required from Doha. It was an hour flight, and upon arrival I inquired as to the cost of a cab to town and was told 5 riyal, which was equal to $1. When I arrived at the Bank of the Middle East, the taxi driver asked for 10 riyal, which angered me. I was tired of being pushed around in the Arab world, so I gave him 5 riyal, and he promptly punched me! I wound up with a bloody nose and broken eyeglasses, but I saved $1 on the expense account!

While in Qatar, I sold five or six motors. After lunch I headed back out to the airport. My flight was supposed to leave at 5 p.m., but they announced the departure around 3 p.m., so after my second Coke, off I headed for immigration. They looked at my passport and immediately asked me for my "exit permit." This time I was ready. I responded that before leaving Bahrain in the morning I was told no exit permit was required.

Would you believe they informed me that the rules had just changed this morning because someone had tried to bomb the Bank of the Middle East the previous night? Incredible! The fact that I hadn't arrived until *after* the bombing made no difference. When I asked how long it would take for the permit, I was told 10 days. Fortunately, two people behind me had been at my sales meeting that morning and offered to obtain the visa for me. I gave one of them 20 pounds, and in about 10 minutes he was back with the "exit permit."

After clearing immigration I figured we had a long wait. But the flight was called at 3:30 p.m. It was a small plane that held five passengers and the pilot. I ended up in the co-pilot seat, and after take-off I asked the pilot, "Why did we leave more than one hour ahead of schedule?" With no change in expression, he informed me that they had oversold the flight, so they waited until the first five passengers showed up and took off. The remaining passengers scheduled, he said, would go the next week at the same time.

Welcome to life in the Middle East!

ADEN

From Bahrain I flew to Aden on a BOAC Argonaut, which was a British-made turbo prop with the seats facing backwards. I sat next to an Englishman who was a salesman for Vono beds. He had just come from Saudi Arabia, where he also had spent an extra week as the guest of the Saudis. He had negotiated a contract with the government for 5,000 beds and was on the plane to Bahrain. It had taxied to the end of the runway but then returned to the terminal and everyone was off-loaded. He said a member of the royal family had arrived with his harem and took over the plane for a shopping excursion to Beirut. So all scheduled passengers were guests of the Saudi government for one week until the next flight! Again, welcome to the Middle East!

YEMEN

While in Aden I ventured over to Yemen to visit and take a camel ride. The big deal in Yemen was that the wife of the American ambassador had just reported that her husband's good gold watch had been stolen, and she reported to the police that she thought one of the servants had stolen it. Following the Arab tradition of "an eye for an eye," the authorities proceeded to cut off the servant's right hand. About 10 days later she found the watch, so she called the police to give them the good news. Naturally, the big flap was that they wanted to remove the hand of the ambassador, who was immediately being recalled to the States, but the authorities were detaining him. Another welcome to the Middle East! A big mess! I got my camel ride, and then took off for Djibouti.

FRENCH SOMALILAND, DJIBOUTI

The country of French Somaliland easily qualifies for the worst place I have ever been. The town was not only poor but also filthy. My hotel had an abundance of every bug known to man. It looked as if it had not been cleaned in 10 years. The town was miserably hot and muggy. Dinner was so bad I don't remember it, and I was glad to leave after about 36 hours. The trip back to Aden was memorable because we were on a DC-3, and one whole side had no seats and was filled with a green weed. Upon arrival in Aden at about 3 p.m., I found out that the weed was known as "khat." It was disbursed to a waiting crowd on the ground and that was the end of the day's work, as all became very happy from its amphetamine-like effects. The balance was trucked off to make a few more Arabs happy.

ERITREA

This was a beautiful country where everyone seemed pleasant and friendly, unlike my previous experiences. I did get the worst sunburn of my life on my shoulders, however, because I forgot that we were near the equator.

KHARTOUM, SUDAN

I spent little more than a day and a half in Khartoum, and I wish I could have stayed longer. My hotel was near the Nile River, and it was as beautiful as it appears in pictures and in the movies. The atmosphere of Khartoum reflected European influence, which was pleasant when coupled with the picturesque Nile. I negotiated for two ivory hippos with a native craftsman who worked along the river. There I enjoyed watching the local boats pass by as I sipped on a cold beer. For the first time in a long while, I felt I really was returning to civilization.

CAIRO, EGYPT

Cairo was the last stop prior to returning to Bruges. Cairo is a large city, and it represented a real surprise after the last several weeks. My hotel room was a suite with a huge living room on the main level and a very romantic loft bedroom. What a waste. There I spent only one night, and I did not have time to view the famous sights. Anyhow, after my adventures in the Middle East, I was in a hurry to get home.

BELGIUM

Home at last, I had time to think about my harrowing journey to the Middle East and the lessons I had learned. I did not sell much on that erratic journey; however, my being there did establish our name and product if and when the markets improved. No one before me had ever visited the Middle East for OMC; it was considered an exploratory trip to assess the market potential. We concluded that it was pretty grim at the time.

Even though I spent a lot of time at airports as well as on other non-productive adventures, I was able to determine who would be the best firms to present to OMC once the markets opened up. All of these firms were British or French, and the local managers were extremely impressed that an American would travel to this part of the world, so my trip created good public relations for OMC.

Also important to note, at this time almost all imported products in the Middle East, Africa, and Far East were sold through major trading companies like Besse & Co (British), UAC (United Africa Company; British), CFAO (Compagnie Française de l'Afrique Occidentale; French), and Lindeteves-Jacoberg (Dutch). These huge companies controlled the sales of all imported goods to a vast majority of the then developing world. This meant that a few trading companies controlled 100 percent of all the imports and sales of every major brand that went to their empire or country under their control. Hence, there was no competition from local companies, and the major trading companies offered no economic benefit to the local economies within those developing nations.

For me, personally, traveling through foreign cultures that bore no resemblance to Europe or North America was difficult. I found their ways of life hard to adjust to and somewhat shocking. However, the frequent setbacks at airports and travel plans prepared me well for future adventures I would encounter when I traveled the jungles and interiors of South America. In the Middle East, I definitely learned patience when dealing with foreign governments. Also, starting in Beirut and throughout the trip, I learned the importance of eating the local dishes and not complaining or asking for a Big Mac. That adjustment became a major factor in establishing trust and a bonding relationship with those I met. It was obviously apparent to this American that we were not loved by Arabs. I learned later that one reason for the resentment was that when the wealthy Arabs went to college in the United States, they were thrown in with the blacks. Again, the cultures were dissimilar, and there were clashes that provoked lingering ill will.

Then, there was the impact on my marriage. The trip was a big mistake on a personal level. I left Lorna with an infant in a foreign country where the major language was Flemish. And while she spoke English and French, she did not speak Flemish, and the loneliness must have been intense. Furthermore, I am sure she did feel that the trip was not necessary. But being stoical as she was, Lorna hid her displeasure and held her disappointment within herself. During the rest of our stay in Belgium, I tried to do better by her.

Although Lorna did not accompany me on many business trips, she was able to come with me on an extensive trip to visit dealers along the coast of England. Also, she went with me when I traveled to the Far East and ended up in Japan, where OMC was negotiating a joint venture with Daihatsu [17]. Subsequently, I made several trips to Osaka, because we were slated to move to Japan. As it turned out the business deal failed and we were not sent to Japan, but we did enjoy other trips to different parts of the world.

The annual convention hosted by OMISA (Outboard Marine International Societe Anonyme) was an event we eagerly anticipated. This yearly extravaganza with a substantial budget was meant to entertain our distributors. One of the most spectacular conventions I can remember was held at the Hotel de Paris in Monte Carlo. The hotel was extremely elegant and the gala party was held at a picturesque restaurant on the water a few miles south of Monte Carlo called Le Pirate.

Pedro Wassitsch and I were tending bar, and by dinner everyone was feeling happy. It reached the point where Pedro and I greeted arriving guests by squirting them with fine French champagne. (What a waste!) Then, after everyone was seated for dinner, my dad, often the life of the party, arrived by riding a donkey to his table!

After dinner most of the guests returned to the hotel in buses, but a group of us, including Wally Britt, Alfred Wend, Tony Haag, and me, decided we should go into Cannes to continue the celebration. It was a wild night, and we arrived back at our hotel around 3 a.m. Before we turned in, Pedro and I pulled off one more foolish caper. It was a custom to put your shoes outside your room at night for polishing. We had the clever idea of going from floor to floor mixing up the shoes placed outside rooms and moving them to different rooms on different floors. Checkout the next morning was a real trip, since no one could find their own shoes, so the hotel gathered up all the shoes and placed them in one huge pile in the lobby for all to claim what belonged to them. From this episode I trust you can see that in my 20s, I still had neither outgrown my delight in practical jokes nor my indulgence in capricious "March hare" behavior.

All in all, living in Belgium was a wonderful experience that introduced Lorna and me to a different part of the world. My work with OMC traveling throughout northern Europe—and briefly in the Middle East and Far East—exposed me to varied cultures where I recognized the importance of acceptance of and adaptation to local customs, including food and beverage. Learning how not to be an "Ugly American" was an important step toward developing the successful international relationships that I, as a representative of my company and my country, needed to acquire. Now, with our little Sandy—two years old—in tow, Lorna and I looked forward to our return to the United States.

CHAPTER 21

Lake Forest, Illinois (1962–1974)

L orna, Sandy, and I moved back from Belgium in the early summer of 1962. I was 26 years old. Lorna was 23. Right from the start, our little family launched into one domestic challenge after another that characterized this busy mid-section of my life.

The first challenge involved a rug. Mom and Dad rented us a small house behind the Deerpath Inn for three months, and during that time Mom gave us a puppy for Sandy, a Saint Bernard we named Zoro. Like all pups, Zoro enjoyed chewing, and he demolished a Navajo rug owned by our landlady, who claimed the rug was an old Navajo weaving and was therefore extremely valuable. She filed suit, claiming damages of about $1,500, which was quite a bit in those days. Our attorney was Judge Dunne, a prominent judge in Cook County, and a brother of Moose Dunne [18]. He was known as "Little Moose" even though he was well over six feet tall and weighed probably 250 pounds.

"Little Moose" suggested we request a jury trial, which we did. The court was actually a tiny room above the police station (now the Market House on the Square), and the trials were held every Monday at 7 p.m. After two hours the trial was recessed until the following week.

Now, this whole scene was a comedy. The judge knew all the players and mingled freely among the audience. Several times Little

Moose, his immense size dominating the courtroom, quoted relevant valid legal points, all of which were ignored by the judge, who was not really familiar with the law. Expert witnesses testified on both sides. A witness for the landlady testified as to the value of ancient Navajo rugs. Our defense questioned that if the rug was as valuable as she claimed, then why did the landlady leave it in a rental place? Why didn't she take it up? After several weeks, the jury began deliberation, which lasted more than two hours, causing us concern that things were not going well for our side. In the end, a juror produced a rug from his home that was almost identical to the rug in question. Turns out, he had purchased his rug in New Mexico the year before for around $60! So, we won. But we also endured a lot of wasted time and aggravation.

The second challenge involved our cars. OMC had paid to move us back to the States, so it made sense to bring two cars. I sold the Opel Record and bought a Jaguar four-door sedan in England about three months before we left, since it would arrive in the United States as a used vehicle at a much lower duty rate. The Fiat 1500 was our second car. Owning foreign cars seemed like a good idea until I realized with the luxury and their driving pleasure also came some real problems. The Jag had a heater that was great in the UK, but couldn't cope with Midwest winters. The Fiat was fun when it didn't break down. When the starter failed, I called the dealer in Chicago, who referred me to the importer in New York City, who advised me that my starter would come from Italy at a cost of $125 in about 10 weeks. By comparison, a starter for a Chevy was $25 and in stock. *Hmmm.*

The third challenge involved an elegant night out. Lorna and I attended the New York Boat Show in New York City. I had read about a restaurant in Manhattan, open since 1961, in the *Chicago Tribune.* I suggested that Lorna and I go there. She was dubious about this idea because we knew nothing about the restaurant, and she did not trust my newspaper source. Nevertheless, we hailed a cab, which drove us down a street that had no restaurants, only brownstones, which further convinced her that this was not a great idea. Her opinion changed when we arrived at the restaurant, and a

French gentleman in a tuxedo greeted us at the door. This was our first clue that we had discovered an elegant place. We were ushered upstairs and seated at a lovely table, which became our second clue, and the third clue appeared when Lorna was handed a menu with no prices. Aha! Thus we were introduced to gourmet dinning.

Because I was flustered, I let the waiter make the recommendations, including wine. Everything was beautifully prepared and excellent to taste, and after the main course we enjoyed a fancy dessert and some very old Cognac.

When presented with the bill, I went into shock. It was well over $100, a major hit in those times. In 1963 there were no credit cards, and here I was, short by at least 50 percent the amount of cash I needed to pay the bill. I began a weak attempt at humor by saying, "Well, I can always wash dishes," when the maître d' appeared from nowhere and announced that my lack of cash was, "No problem!" With that, a waiter arrived with a huge checkbook on a silver platter. Lucky for us, in those days all you needed was a blank check known as a counter check. You had only to fill in your name and your bank's name plus the amount you were to pay. Very relieved, I did exactly that.

It seems that in our innocence, Lorna and I that night had discovered the ultimate French restaurant, Lutèce. The restaurant, founded by Andre Surmain, and later run by chef-owner Andre Soltner, would operate famously for more than four decades before closing in 2004. Among its specialties were an Alsatian onion tart and a sautéed foie gras with dark chocolate sauce and bitter orange marmalade. Despite my personal embarrassment over the payment solution, the experience was fabulous. Decidedly top drawer!

The fourth challenge was to purchase a home. We bought our first house, 321 Hilldale Place in Lake Forest, for $60,000. I went to Jeff Reed at the Lake Forest Bank for a loan, and surprisingly, he did not demand an enormous amount of paperwork. Instead, he looked me in the eye and asked me, "Will you pay the bank back?"

I replied, "Yes."

With that, we shook hands, and I had a 30-year mortgage at 5-1/4 percent, which was reduced about 18 months later to 4-3/4 percent. I thought, *What a great way to bank!*

When you buy a new home, it's only natural that you begin to fill it up. And that is precisely what Lorna and I began to do. Always looking for a good price, I bought appliances from Polk Brothers [19] in Chicago, which offered good deals. Here I encountered the same problem I'd had with foreign cars—distance and cost. I bought a Frigidaire refrigerator—a real bargain—because it had a left-hand door. Naturally, having the door switched proved difficult and that raised the price. Then there was the washer/dryer set—a discount deal—good until the washer broke down after about six weeks. The Polk Brothers said I was too far out of town for normal service. Could I bring it to Chicago? Then they would fix it at no charge! Lesson learned: From then on I bought all appliances locally from Highwood Appliance.

With rooms to fill, Lorna and I started going to auctions in Winnetka. I got carried away one night and acquired a large bronze Buddha and an antique Russian samovar—just the items every new homeowner needs! The Buddha didn't last long before Lorna insisted it had to go. Also we bought an antique player piano, which was an interesting addition to our living room. We found other things—a painting of a barge on a canal in either Belgium or Holland. Having just returned from Bruges, we found the painting enchanting and paid $200 for it. I have always loved that painting as it reminds me of my time in Belgium. Some 40 years later, in 1999, I had the painting cleaned by the Darvish Gallery in Naples. Our friend Charlie Szebo looked at it and asked if I knew what it was worth.

"I don't have a clue," I responded. "But the artist was Emile Gruppe."

Charlie nodded and told me that Emile had spent time in Naples, where he had painted locally. My painting was probably worth $20,000!

While we were filling up the house, Lorna sought guidance from a wonderful decorator named Jane Derrick. We had fun buying antiques. One time we were in the back room of a well-known antique dealer, Wilson's in Chicago, and we noticed a Thorne miniature room from the collection at the Chicago Art Museum that was there for cleaning. I asked if it was for sale. It was. We bought it. Jane Derrick did a great job and we continued the theme of English antiques throughout.

Even though they lived in Nassau, my parents remained non-resident members of the Onwentsia Club [20] in Lake Forest, and because of that Lorna and I were able to join as junior members. The membership was open to people less than 30 years of age with an initiation of $900 and very low dues until you turned 30 or 35, as I remember. The Onwentsia Club was a small, yet very warm club in terms of ambience, and we enjoyed it.

I took up golf. After several lessons with Hubby Habjan [21], I invested in a set of his custom clubs thinking that the purchase would improve my game. But despite hours spent at the practice range, my handicap never went below 22. In fact, my slice was so bad, my caddy often yelled, "Clear the pool!" as I teed off, because sometimes my ball did make a splash in the pool! Lorna and I played together often, as she was not only energetic but also very good in almost all sports—tennis, skiing, hiking, and golf. In some ways, she was a better athlete than I was. Once Lorna and I were playing in a tournament with Ellie and Moose Dunne. On the fourth hole, I stepped up to the tee and hit a shot that barely dribbled to the ladies' tee. How embarrassing! I had the pleasure of hitting my second shot before Ellie even teed off!

Our re-adjustment to life in Lake Forest continued, and not long after our return to the States, Mirelle Muriel, who had taken care of Sandy in Le Zoute, came to live with us for a year. In the fall, on October 3, 1963, our second daughter, "Shelley," Michelle Branch Briggs, was born, followed three years later by our son Stephen on April 3, 1966.

When children are small you don't remember days—you remember moments—like apple picking, visiting the Morton Arboretum, swimming at Onwentsia, and boating on the Chain of Lakes. These memories I hold in my mind. Looking back, it was all going so fast, that childhood ride of theirs. I felt like I wanted to catch fleeting time in the palm of my hand. Even now isolated moments rise in my mind like the bubbles in a glass of soda pop.

I remember teaching Sandy to water ski, and later the snow skiing trips we took as father–daughter adventures to Vail, Snowbird, and Steamboat Springs. Over time she became a beautiful skier, and at least once talked me down a mountain I had no business being on! I was barely an intermediate— completely terrified—but Sandy at age 12 coaxed me out of the woods and down through deep powder back to the village. What a relief!

And there was the time with Shelley, our middle child, who was known for her lack of adventurous eating habits when she was small. On one occasion we went to a Swedish restaurant for lunch. She ordered a ham and cheese sandwich, which actually was a smørrebrød—an artistic open sandwich, with cured meat that is typically sliced, served cold on buttered bread, and decorated with accompaniments to create a tasty, visually appealing creation. When served her order, Shelley took one look at the smørrebrød with the ham and cheese on top of the bread, and she refused to eat it! We were at an impasse until I got the waiter to bring us another slice of bread, which now made it into a sandwich. Voilà!

And I won't soon forget the prank with our son Stephen at around age seven when the 17-year locusts came around. "What are cicadas good for?" he asked me, again and again. Now I could be a bit of a practical joker, so I replied teasingly, "Why, they are a delicacy! Tasty when fried in butter! A must for the morning menu!" So, off Stephen went to gather cicadas for breakfast, and into my frying pan they landed. Green, big-eyed insects with clear wings and orange feet, I served them with scrambled eggs and toast. The family was grossed out, of course, but Stephen tried selling them to the neighbors. While they were not a hot sale item, "bugs for breakfast" became a memory to be laughed about for years.

In 1966–1967, when Sandy was around six or seven, we visited Wilmot Mountain [22] for night skiing. Somewhere during these years, Sandy went off on her bike to the Episcopal church fair and came home with "Buttons," a kitten that she smuggled into our house. Several days later, we discovered our new resident. Sandy claims that at one point I got so mad at Buttons, I tossed him out of a second floor window. But, being a cat, Buttons was a survivor and landed on his feet. He spent every night with Sandy on the unheated sleeping porch, which was her bedroom.

I recall the restaurants we liked as a family were The Lantern on Bank Lane where we got hamburgers; Charlie Binelicks in Highland Park on old U.S. Highway 41; the Silo east of Waukegan Road in Lake Bluff, where we enjoyed pizza and burgers; and Hackney's on Harms in Winnetka, when we wanted the ultimate burger and a loaf of onion rings. Best of all, was the arrival in our own driveway of the Good Humor man in his ice cream truck. My favorite flavor was toasted almond. I still recall just how good it tasted!

Opening of OMC European factory in Bruges, Belgium, where SFB II worked from January 1960 to summer 1962

CHAPTER 22

Moving Up, Outboard Marine Corporation (1962–1969)

During the years that Lorna and I were getting our domestic bearings in Lake Forest, I was also experiencing new opportunities with OMC. I started out as the liaison between the U.S. manufacturing division and the overseas sales operation in Nassau. As the years moved forward, I had responsibilities in both corporate market research and evaluation of potential acquisitions for the divisions in addition to staff functions at corporate headquarters in Waukegan, Illinois. This meant that I was a liaison to U.S. subsidiaries and the Belgium operation. When the company was thinking about buying a Coleman or KOA, or Irwin yachts, for example, I would evaluate whether this was a good thing and make a presentation to management. At the same time, I was realizing not only the perks of a big corporation but also learning the meaning of "golden handcuffs." I worked long hours and traveled frequently, leaving my family for extended periods.

Shortly after my return from Belgium, I was sent to South America along with Pedro Wassitsch, service manager for our international division, to evaluate the impact of competition as well as to gather data on how our outboards were being used in a commercial atmosphere. The goal was to pass on suggestions to make the outboards more durable to our OMC engineers. Since they had been designed for pleasure, they were not holding up well under commercial use. Our distributors especially wanted us to make a commercial version of the 40-horsepower model. At this time Yamaha was making major inroads into our commercial market.

Colombia was our first stop. Before the trip, however, we were required to take an intense five-day course on anti-kidnapping techniques. American businessmen were often seized, and exorbitant ransoms were demanded for their safe return. CIA agents conducted the course.

We started in Medellín, where our distributor Otto Londono lived. He covered the country for Evinrude. Medellín is in the Aburrá Valley, one of the most northerly of the Andes Mountains in South America. Londono proposed to fly us around to various high-use areas in his small single-engine plane. We were supposed to go first to his vacation home in Ayapel, which was about an hour's flight from Medellín. Unfortunately, on that day the weather was so bad we had to go by jeep, which took more than 10 hours across some unbelievable roads. Much of the way we rode over a two-track road with ruts that were filled with water. When we arrived, I was impressed with the home and its surrounding countryside of lake and swamp. Our host informed us that because the Londono family was both prominent and wealthy, it had its own shortwave telephone system throughout the country to avoid kidnapping. In addition, all members traveled heavily armed. A bit scary!

The entire area around his home appeared as one huge flood plain over which, in the rainy season, everything moved by water. Dugout canoes could be as long as 40 feet and carried up to 10 tons of rice.

In Ayapel we wanted to watch the loading process of rice that was shipped from here to all over the region. The system the locals had created was amazing. The process went on for hours. First, the rice was moved from Ayapel to the other side of the lake by dugout canoes naturally powered by Evinrude motors. Next, a work crew carried the 50-kilo sacks of rice on their shoulders up an embankment to load two sacks each on the waiting mules. The weight had to be distributed evenly on each before (you've heard the expression "stubborn as a mule") they would move. Then the mules began their journey—but strangely, no humans directed them; they had been trained to carry the rice overland by themselves on a narrow path to a point at which it was removed by humans and loaded into dugouts for further distribution to local villages. Once unloaded, the mules automatically returned along their narrow path to Ayapel for reloading. We also saw canoes packed with all kinds of things—people, bananas, Coca-Cola, and even pigs that were kept confined by wooden planks nailed over the tops of the canoes. Given their geography, the Ayapel locals had created a distribution system that worked!

From Ayapel we took off in a 16-foot aluminum skiff for another village to the east. We traveled basically cross-country through a huge area covered with lily pads that seemed to be regular roadways made by a previous boat. These paths generally closed over at night and needed to be re-made each day. In the next town we viewed more of the same traffic being transported by dugout canoes as well as two types of water taxis that served all the area villages. There were dugouts packed with 20 or 30 people, which stopped frequently at individual homes along the way. There were also aluminum boats, powered by large outboards, which represented the more expensive express method that stopped only at major villages.

When we left the Londono family retreat, we went back to Medellín to head into the interior. In El Bagre and El Banco, about a 22-hour drive northeast of Medellín, the accommodations were primitive, and the drinking water was from the highly polluted river, filtered through several large earthen jugs. This is when I learned that Coke was always available, even in the most remote jungle locations. The landing strips were small strips of grass cut out of the jungle with sometimes a wire mesh over the ground. If they had been used during World War II, they were among the newer ones and a bit upscale. We never knew when fuel would be available, as it came in 50-gallon drums mostly during the dry season, and when it was gone, that was all to be had until next year. Somehow it all worked, and I must say that flying over this vast jungle was both exciting and scary.

We went as far south as the Putumayo River, a tributary of the Amazon River. It originates as the Guamués River that flows southeastward past Puerto Asís, Colombia, after which it's known as the Putumayo. There it continues in a southeasterly course through tropical rain forest. It forms most of the border between Colombia, Ecuador, and Peru. The Putumayo is a major transportation artery, navigable for almost its total length. On its banks are numerous small river ports, and rubber is gathered from forests along its course.

We spent several days in a dugout canoe going up and down the Putumayo River, stopping at San Salvador, Barras, and Tres Esquinas. We spent one night with a local agent who was thrilled to have visiting Americans in his home. Our room was simple, with two cots, a basin in the corner, and a showerhead on the wall. The water came from an elevated 50-gallon drum outside. After dinner, which I am sure I washed down with beer or Coke, our host treated us to a couple of hours of home movies, as he had recently acquired an 8-millimeter movie camera.

Before retiring we were warned to turn over our shoes and to check them first thing in the morning, as shoes were the favorite hiding spot for scorpions. The next morning I was up before dawn, as I had visions of animals joining me in my bed. When I went down to the river as the sun was coming up, it was a beehive of activity. Everyone was loading or unloading—working before the sun became unbearable.

Before we left, our host insisted that we visit the local hospital, which had been built with USAID funds. The United

States Agency for International Development (USAID), created by President Kennedy in 1961, is the federal government agency primarily responsible for administering civilian foreign aid. Authorized by Congress, it was intended to "extend a helping hand to those people overseas struggling to make a better life, recovering from a disaster, or striving to live in a free and democratic country."

On the way to the hospital, a tall, elegant black man stopped me and spoke perfect English. This was the first black we had seen, and I was quite surprised. He insisted on tagging along for the hospital visit, wanting to know all about the Brooklyn Dodgers, as well as other sports news from the States. An interesting fellow, he had come down to work on one of the American-owned rubber plantations and he had never left.

The hospital was an old Army field unit that lacked a lot of amenities by U.S. standards, but I guess it was better than having no hospital. The most disconcerting thing was there seemed to be five river rats roaming around freely for every patient.

We spent time on the Cauca River, whose headwaters begin in southwestern Colombia, and eventually joins the Magdalena River to flow more than 800 miles from its origin to the sea mouth at the Caribbean Sea. Then we flew into Leticia, which was a fascinating town with wooden houses and raised sidewalk platforms. The town was surprisingly vibrant considering that at this time it could be reached only by water and perhaps an occasional flight. Located at the corner of Brazil, Colombia, and Peru, the area is known as Tres Fronteras, and the culture is a mixture of three countries. One can travel in deep water by boat all the way to Manaus at the mouth of the Amazon in Brazil. Leticia is the southernmost city in the Republic of Colombia, and one of the major ports on the Amazon River. It has long been Colombia's shipping point for tropical fish for the aquarium trade.

In El Bagre, as I remember, the locals were gold prospecting, and at another stop we encountered an unusual sight. A C-147 transport plane had gone off the side of the landing strip and was badly stuck in the mud. As we taxied by we noticed about 50 troops up on the wing on the high side jumping up and down while the pilot was gunning the engines to try to get out of the mud. Unfortunately, we didn't stay to see the end of this seeming disaster.

On one trip we flew into a corrupt border town between Colombia and Venezuela that was known as a hotbed of criminal activity since drug lords operated out of the mountains nearby and monitored smuggling between the two countries. The street seemed alive with local police, and we were told to go directly from the airport to our destination in our truck without stopping. The town was empty and quiet. We learned from several locals that the governor of the district had asked for the federal military to come down from Bogotá to help control unrest. A full C-147 military transport aircraft of troops had arrived. But they were greeted by rebel troops who belonged to the local bandits and drug lords. The federal military troops were stripped of all their clothes and weapons. They were sent back to Bogotá with the message that this time they were being returned alive. Shades of the Wild West.

On one of our Colombia trips we went to Esmeraldas, Ecuador, north and near the border of Colombia. This may have been the grimiest and filthiest place I have ever visited. The local fishermen are extremely poor. They harvest conch shells, fish, gather crabs, and farm. Shrimp aquaculture destroys the mangroves and pollutes the water of Colombian palm farms, where small-scale farmers struggle to survive. I found the entire area very depressing.

The entire trip opened my eyes not only to a whole different culture but also to a way of life that was strictly day-to-day with little or no concern for the rest of the world. Communication was poor, so locals dispersed most information as they traveled up and down the river, bringing greetings and stories from relatives in the different villages. Where outboards in general were used for recreation in other parts of the world, here they were almost a matter of survival because all goods and food moved on the water, which was the only means of transportation.

The result of this trip was that on my return to the States, I made every effort to convince my bosses of the extreme importance of building a high-quality product that lasted a long time and required minimum repairs. Compared to an average engine used 100–150 hours a year for recreation, these engines were operating seven days a week for 8–10 hours per day.

This eventful trip lasted about three weeks, and I made similar trips to the Orinoco in Venezuela, as well as to the shrimp fishing town of La Reforma in Mexico. Some trips were longer than others, and I returned to Colombia several more times because it was our largest market in South America for commercial engines.

Family camping trip, Saranac Lake, New York, 1973

CHAPTER 23

Times a-Changin', Home (1968–1974)

To anyone who did not live through the late 1960s and early 1970s, it is hard to convey the confusion and discord—reigning nationwide—that invaded not only our public but also our personal lives. Civil rights, a movement dominating the 1950s and 1960s, culminated in freedoms that extended to blacks, women, and anyone else who determined him- or herself worthy of being upward bound.

In Title 7 of the Civil Rights Act of 1964, the language was clear:

It shall be an unlawful employment practice for an employer— to fail or refuse to hire or to discharge any individual, or otherwise to discriminate against any individual with respect to his compensation, terms, conditions, or privileges of employment, because of such individual's race, color, religion, sex or national origin . . .

The result of such language, now the law of the land, was the freeing of people bound by custom and tradition to explore possibility in their lives, including a rejection of the status quo— religion, tradition, aspirations, homage to government, and roles between women and men.

The cold war of previous decades had turned hot, and Americans were disenchanted with the undeclared war in Vietnam that claimed millions of lives. Young people on college campuses took to the streets in protest over the military lottery and U.S. involvement in the war. Respected leaders, beginning with President John Kennedy in 1963, and including Robert Kennedy and Dr. Martin Luther King Jr. in 1968, had fallen to assassins. Clothing and hairstyles reflected defiance. Men sprouted shoulder-length hair and wore bellbottom pants; girls wore bangs, hair down their backs, and mini-skirts two inches above the knee. People experimented with substances in addition to alcohol and marijuana. Revolution was in the air and "freedom" meant anything anyone wanted to think up. In this atmosphere, when the birth control pill was in and fidelity was out, marriages were hard to maintain—even good marriages.

Meanwhile, Lorna and I adopted traditional ways: She ran the home, and I brought home the bacon. Because of my long hours and travel for OMC, I was not an involved father in the sense of changing diapers and other tasks while the children were small. Lorna was stoic; she had a strong personality. She was extremely disciplined and organized, which was evident during our marriage. More and more, where the children and household were concerned, Lorna stepped in and did it all. My lawn cutting was not up to her standards, for example, so she took that over as well. As the children became older they were expected to make their beds every morning before a sit-down breakfast and to bring down all their laundry and place it in the washing machine. One morning while I was taking my shower, my clean underwear disappeared from the bathroom and went off to the washer!

I had begun to invest in real estate. I purchased Townhouse East at the base of Little Nell in Aspen, Colorado, in 1965. In 1969, I went together with friends to buy Wonundra, later to be named Camp Cork, in Saranac Lake, New York. Both these places became delightful holiday vacation spots for us. Lorna and I continued to share outdoor adventures together and with the children, including hiking, skiing, and canoe trips.

In the winter of 1968, Lorna and I had planned to go skiing with our good friends the Kostaneckis in Aspen, but we had a couple of setbacks. Both involved accidents.

Before heading to Aspen, Lorna and I went up to Eagle River for the International Snowmobile Races. We stayed at Hazen's Long Lake Lodge in Phelps, Wisconsin, where we had vacationed with the kids for the past couple of summers. One night after dinner and a few cocktails, I challenged my friend John McGregor (his mother was Bezzie Stratton) to a jumping contest on snowmobiles. I must admit I was not using my best judgment, and my reflexes were not up to par. As a result, I hurtled down our chosen slope and crashed my Trade Winds snowmobile into a tree, severely bruising my right thigh. The accident, which fortunately was not as harmful to me as it could have been, was recorded by Stu Foundrie from Long Lake Lodge in the spring newsletter as "Tree Destroyed Accidentally by Lodge Guest." He wrote:

> Mr. S. F. Briggs, II, of Lake Forest, Illinois, received serious bruises, abrasions, contusions, possible fractures, and extreme loss of dignity in a collision between a lodge tree and a snowmobile. Mr. Briggs was operating on the Lodge grounds during the dead of night last January. Mr. Briggs . . . was extremely unnerved by his experience and even more unnerved by the apparent lack of sympathy by the immediate members of his family and Lodge management. The snowmobile Mr. Briggs was driving (a Trade Winds) was practically undamaged after the collision. The tree sustained considerable damage to bark and trunk and had to be destroyed.
>
> A volunteer committee of tree lovers has been formed to raise funds to erect a simple bronze marker suitably inscribed to commemorate the site where the lovely tree once stood. So far, no donation has been forthcoming from Mr. Briggs.

The Saturday after this incident, Lorna and I went to a dinner party at the home of Pat McKenna and his wife, along with Cherry and Bill Gillespie. The party was in Winnetka. After dinner Pat wanted us to hear his new stereo system; however, he said the sound was much better from the rafters. As I was still painfully incapacitated from my crash of the week before, I could not climb up to the rafters. Lorna, however, was game. She went up the ladder to the rafters about 12 or 15 feet above the floor. She lay down on a rafter to hear the great music. But then—catastrophe! She lost her balance and fell to the floor! She landed on her feet but then fell quickly backwards, striking her head on a marble table. (The impact from her fall broke the table, which turned out to be faux marble.) She was unconscious for a brief period, but in the ambulance on the way to the hospital she was alert and talkative. Nevertheless, the ambulance attendants were concerned.

She was taken to Evanston Hospital where the initial X-rays showed nothing, and the doctors said she had a badly strained neck and would be out of there in two or three days. The next morning, however, I called a neurosurgeon from Chicago to give us a second opinion. He authorized the hospital to do a different set of X-rays, and these showed that Lorna had a broken neck; indeed, the break was between the C2 and C3 vertebrae. The only thing that kept her from paralysis was that she was strong enough for her muscles to prevent the break from severing her spinal cord!

She was put into a Minerva cast, which covered her body from the waist to her head and left an opening for her face, ears, and hair. Wearing the cast was an ordeal that lasted eight weeks. After a while, I took the kids to visit her in the hospital, but seeing their mother in this state was disturbing. During her hospital stay, I was in charge of home discipline. What a task! The kids didn't want to do chores or eat their food. They cried about everything. They missed their mom. In self-defense,

I instituted a "cry chart" in which everyone earned stars for crying. This was my attempt at reverse psychology. It didn't cure everything, but it made a statement. Nobody wanted to win stars for crying. When Lorna came home, we had to buy her special prism glasses so that when she looked straight ahead, she was actually looking down at 45 degrees. This allowed her to eat as well as to enjoy a limited amount of reading. During this time she was a real trooper; however, at times the itch from the cast was unbearable so I used a long knitting needle to try and scratch the worse spots. As the weeks wore on, she became understandably impatient, and everyone was relieved when the cast was removed.

In time, both of us recovered from these accidents, and once again our social schedule was busy with parties on most weekends. I always mixed up a large batch of stingers—a signature creation of mine mixing brandy and white crème de menthe [23]—and served them on a silver tray after dinner to "settle the digestive tract." Often our guests could not remember them the next morning, but always when imbibed the night before, the stingers got rave reviews. We had several pig roasts on the outside grill, but after about three of those, Lorna called a halt to them. She complained the pig roasting on the fire looked too much like one of her children!

One weekend our friends Caroline and Kent Rickenbaugh decided to come for a visit from Denver. Kent was the Cadillac dealer in Denver, and he had a customer who owned Platts Meat Packing. He asked his friend to air freight some of his best steaks to us in Lake Forest. What a great idea! We picked up Caroline and Kent at the airport, and then proceed to the Continental airfreight area, but there were no steaks. It was about 4 p.m., and Lorna was getting nervous. I said, "Don't worry," but I could see panic growing in her eyes. Before too long we got a call from Continental saying the steaks were at O'Hare. Kent and I volunteered to go pick them up. We were halfway out the door when Lorna said, "You are not leaving this party to pick up some stupid steaks!"

Kent and I figured we'd call O'Hare to see if there was a limo company at or near the airport. As luck would have it, a driver was just leaving O'Hare with no passengers. So, we convinced the dispatcher to redirect the limo over to Continental airfreight. What do you know! The limo pulled into our driveway with the steaks in the nick of time just as Lorna was threatening to go out for pizza. We tipped him handsomely, and he was pleased. He informed us that those steaks were his most unusual passengers ever!

And speaking of unusual, during these years there was a fad we witnessed on a family trip to Aspen. It was called "streaking." We had stopped for lunch on the slopes, when out of nowhere came four streakers—two males and two females—skiing absolutely naked in tucked position heading down the mountain! Boy, I bet they were cold! And boy, were we ever surprised! For a while, the word was out around the resort that streakers didn't need a lift ticket; well, even if they did, there was no place to attach it!

CHAPTER 24

Times a-Changin', Work (1968-1974)

During the 1960s, public interest in novel outdoor sports offered new market potential, and OMC acquired new products accordingly. The company entered the snowmobile industry, introducing the Evinrude Skeeter and the Johnson Skee Horse in 1964. The machines sped along at more than 30 miles per hour. OMC also developed the Evinrude Aquanaut for scuba diving. This device involved a floating gasoline-powered compressor that supplied air to two masked divers at the same time. These innovations led the company into exploratory endeavors in other fields. One of these was a project with Owens Corning in 1968.

Owens Corning and OMC conceived a joint effort to produce fiberglass pre-fabricated modular rooms, complete with all plumbing and electrical. These modular rooms would be used to help renew slum areas by providing low-cost housing for the poor. The rooms would be manufactured by OMC and shipped to select major cities. There, old buildings would be reconfigured—their tops cut off, their interiors gutted, and the pre-fabricated rooms dropped into place from above with the use of cranes or helicopters. Similar rehab projects were being tried in New York City. However, the trade unions there were strongly opposed to the idea, and the rehab projects had not really gotten off the ground. Based on designs of experimental fiberglass dorms at Northwestern University in Evanston, Illinois, the OMC joint project with Corning promised to be more cost effective than those tried in New York.

As part of my research, I went with some representatives working on the project to meet with Berkeley Burrell, President of the National Business League (National Black Chamber of Commerce). His office in Washington, D.C., was located on Florida Avenue behind his dry cleaning and laundry business. As it happened, the week we traveled to Washington was the week just after the 1968 riots following the murder of Dr. Martin Luther King Jr. in Memphis, Tennessee.

During the week of April 4, representatives of SNCC (Student Nonviolent Coordinating Committee) went to local black businesses and asked them to close out of respect for the fallen leader. Things got out of hand, crowds gathered and began breaking windows. Later that evening, widespread looting began. Mayor-Commissioner Walter Washington ordered the damage cleaned up the next morning, but rioters instead got into violent confrontations with the D.C. Metropolitan Police Department. Around midday, numerous buildings were on fire, and firefighters were attacked with bottles and rocks. By lunchtime, the riot was in full effect. Police unsuccessfully attempted to control the crowds with tear gas. On Friday, April 5, the White House dispatched federal troops, including federalized D.C. National Guard troops to assist the overwhelmed district police force. Marines mounted machine guns on the steps of the Capitol, and Army troops guarded the White House. At one point rioting reached within two blocks of the White House before rioters retreated. The occupation of Washington was the largest of any American city since the Civil War.

So here we were, my colleagues and I, meeting Mr. Burrell one week later in the epicenter of violence and destruction during the 1968 Washington, D.C., riots. Probably 90 percent of the businesses had been burned out. The area looked like a war zone. When we arrived, we noticed that Mr. Burrell's establishment was intact. I observed that some of his employees were armed. We were escorted to the back to his plush office, which included amenities like a bar and a spacious sitting room.

I asked him, "Why, sir, isn't your store burned out like the others around here?"

He replied, "Writing 'Soul Brother' across the storefront is useless when an angry black crowd is rioting and burning everything in sight. My solution is to arm my employees and tell them to shoot anyone black or white that tries to burn my store."

That made sense to me. And it seemed to work! Anyway, we had a long conversation with Mr. Burrell and his assistant. They thought our idea to install pre-fabricated rooms was worthwhile, and they pledged to support it in Washington circles. However, after I researched the matter further, I realized that the unions in Washington, just like those in New York, would surely pressure contractors and city government officials to such an extent that the idea would fail. OMC abandoned the joint project, but nevertheless, while working on it, I enjoyed the challenge it presented and the idea of reducing the cost of housing with structures that could be completed quickly.

There were times when work involved a little bit of mischief. On what I refer to as the Wilmington and Rehobeth Weekend sometime in the fall of 1970, my partner in Saranac Lake, New York, was celebrating his 10th wedding anniversary. I felt obligated to come up with an original gift. Charlie, that is, C. B. McCoy [24], also known as "Kinky," had bugged me for years to get him an outboard motor, as I worked for OMC. It occurred to me that this was the perfect opportunity to gift him with a gag. So I gave him a 140-horsepower outboard with one significant alteration: I replaced the engine with a rather eager female stripper and wrapped the box with pink ribbon and bows.

The anniversary party was a special, formal affair with three generations of his family members including his wife Tory [25], a variety of friends, and other guests, as well as the Lester Lanin Band [26]. After dinner, I stood and gave my speech.

"Before now," I said, "I could not afford such an elegant gift for my friend, Kinky. But for this special occasion, I feel an outboard is appropriate."

With that, the outboard, all wrapped in pink and white within its carton, was wheeled into the center of the dance floor at just the precise moment the band struck up the tune "The Stripper." Wow! Out of the gift box jumped our female entertainer to begin a top-drawer performance before the surprised dignitaries who gasped and shrieked. Older members of the audience were taken aback. Kink's wife was embarrassed. But Kink thought it was terrific and displayed some of his best moves while the stripper commenced to disrobe. Funny thing, though, over the next 10 years, Kink never bugged me again about getting him any other OMC product. I guess the gift of one engine-less outboard was enough!

Another caper involved a cookout at my Uncle Jim Briggs's [27] house on King Muir Road in Lake Forest. Jim's best friend Ross Pulling and his wife Bitti were visiting him, and Lorna and I were invited to a dinner party for all the directors of OMC. Ross and I were in charge of cooking the steaks. We got them ready—deliciously sizzling on a platter—but as we were about to deliver them to our guests, I slipped and fell in a muddy area nearby and dropped all the steaks into the mud. What a mess! Now, let me say, the guests were all the top officials of OMC, and Ross was the account executive at J. Walter Thompson advertising firm, which had the Johnson Motors account. And to serve these important people, we had nothing at the moment but mud-covered steaks! How could we salvage this debacle?

Well . . . Ross and I put our heads together and observed that all the directors at the party had imbibed plenty of drinks and were feeling no pain. So we simply hooked up a garden hose, washed off, reheated, and served the steaks. They received rave reviews . . .

Camp Cork

CHAPTER 25

Midlife Midship (1970s)

B y the time the 1970s came blowing in, Lorna and I were in our mid-30s, full throttle into our respective spheres: she was the Type A personality, a disciplined, organized, and efficient mother and homemaker; I was the Type D personality—yes, D— the laid-back, fun-loving, prankster father who traveled all over the world making deals. As a team, we could do anything, but we couldn't do everything . . . Meanwhile, the momentum in our lives picked up speed

My parents continued living in Nassau into the 1960s, but their life together deteriorated, and they separated and divorced. My father remarried but unfortunately he did not live long afterward; he died in 1965. My mother never remarried. She returned to Grosse Pointe to live, and then in 1970 she passed away. These losses made the late 1960s and early 1970s difficult years for me. Since I was an only child, Mom and Dad were the only immediate family I had, and I thought they would always be there for me when I needed them.

Despite my sadness during this time, I was aware that life offered compensations. Lorna and I had our three children. We also had close friends who provided comfort, company, and entertainment. Naturally our lives moved forward . . .

One weekend we were invited to visit with friends on Block Island, located in the Atlantic Ocean south of the coast

of Rhode Island, separated from the state's mainland by the
Block Island Sound. I suggested that everyone go for a walk
along the shore. Lorna disagreed. I don't know what got into me,
but I overreacted and stormed off in a huff. The other couple,
accompanied by Lorna, went back to our rented house, but I
went to a bar and had a couple of stingers. Afterward, when I
went outside, fog had rolled in, and you couldn't see a thing. I
hailed a cab, but when the driver said, "Where to?" all I could tell
him was our friends' rental house. He said I was on my own. So I
started walking through the pea-soup fog looking for a haystack
to crawl into when I saw a light glimmering in the distance.
I found a lovely guest room on the second floor of a house
complete with cotton sheets. What a relief! The next morning
I wrote a nice thank you note to my unseen hosts and left the
house. Walking further, I realized I was only a few hundred
yards away from our rental house. I arrived in time for breakfast.
However, the atmosphere I found was not exactly cozy, and I had
some apologies to make.

In the Lake Forest community, Lorna became involved
in a charitable organization involving welfare for infants. She
and I met a woman who offered to donate two "very valuable"
Audubon bird prints for an upcoming benefit auction. "I hate
bird prints," she said. "But, if they're worth more than $5,000, I
want them back."

After church the next Sunday, we drove to her home to
pick up the prints. I went inside, and the maid who answered
the door called upstairs, "Visitor!" Imagine my surprise to look
up and see the woman at the top of the elegant stairway, a
peignoir tossed over her arm, descending statuesquely, wearing
not even a stitch of clothing! Trying to recover from the

shock, I glanced around the house and saw nothing but bird prints everywhere. This seemed strange as she claimed to hate bird prints! Meanwhile, with magnificent nonchalance, she completed her glamorous descent; she picked up two prints and handed them to me, reminding me that if they were truly valuable, she wanted them back. When I got back to the car and told Lorna the story, she said, "Well! I'm glad the children didn't go in the house with you!"

The upshot of this bizarre gift was that when the appraiser, Buzz Norton, priced these "priceless" prints, they came to $5 each. Just pictures from an old calendar.

During these years Camp Cork became one of our favorite places. This lovely spot was in Saranac Lake, New York. In the spring of 1969, Bill and Cherry Gillespie, our close friends from Lake Forest, invited us to spend Memorial Day weekend with them and their friends C. B. (Kinky) and Tory McCoy. At the time, the camp was called Wonundra, and William "Bill" Rockefeller [28] owned it. Apparently, Bill's mother and stepfather, who lived nearby, wanted the Gillespies to buy the place, because previously they had sent them pictures of it.

The day after we arrived, Bill showed up wearing suspenders and smoking a corncob pipe. He was driving a 15-year-old station wagon in which we toured the property, built in 1929 at a cost of $1 million—so fabulous, it's hard to describe.

Wonundra, located on Whitney Point on Upper Saranac Lake, included eight buildings on nine acres. These buildings were the main house, a guesthouse, a main garage, a boathouse, a lean-to, a maintenance garage, a pump house, a maple sugar house, and an outhouse. The driveway leading to the home was about a mile long. The main house had three bedrooms and baths, a huge living room, and a walk-in fireplace at each end with stone mantles. There was a paneled library stocked with local books. The living room paneling was knotless pine from Canada, which meant each piece was hand selected. The windows throughout the house and guesthouse were custom built. The roof was slate.

Entering the spectacular octagonal entrance, you glimpsed an impressive wood chandelier. The kitchen and pantry were pristine, furnished with stainless steel cabinets. The garage was large enough for three vehicles. The boathouse had two drive-in areas for boats, while the center section allowed room for canoes and sailboats. It offered an upstairs complete with living accommodations, a small kitchen, and a huge fireplace. The boathouse was exceptional, with a covered porch that looked out on the lake and from which hung wonderful canvas swings with full-sized mattresses, so you could sleep in the breezes.

Everything in the main house, guesthouse, garage, and all other structures was beyond perfect. Even the woods were manicured and groomed. Lorna and I, the McCoys, and the Gillespies were breathlessly overwhelmed. Even though he did not live at Wonundra, Bill Rockefeller maintained a staff or six or seven people. At the end of our tour, we all went down to the boathouse and had a few Bloody Marys while enjoying an exquisite view of Upper Saranac Lake. It was then that Kinky leaned forward and asked, "Bill, what is your best price for this place?" And Bill answered, "$180,000."

Before any of the other five of us could breathe, Kink said, "We will take it." Just like that, we three couples bought a million-dollar-plus luxury property for $60,000 each. (By 2013, this retreat had become known as The Point. Today it is considered one of the top B&Bs in the country, commanding up to $3,000 per night per room.)

Wonundra came with an Adirondack canoe, a small fishing boat, and a 1954 wooden Chris-Craft ski boat. Because of its location on Bottle Bay, Kinky renamed it Camp Cork. Every Memorial Day weekend for years, all three adult families met together to open the camp. Early on, our favorite spot became the lean-to at the point. This was a three-sided log structure for sleeping out of the weather. We often spent the night under the lean-to, reading Adirondack tales to the children before turning in. Often we gathered balsam boughs for the lean-to, an exhausting task by the time we cut them in Bottle Bay, loaded them into a canoe, and trimmed them to fill up the three-foot space in the lean-to floor. We followed these kinds of activities with a lobster bake at the cook site near the point, capped off with merriment and after-dinner drinks around the fire.

Oh, it was all so much fun! The kids played hide-and-seek, they built forts, and of course it became the spot where everyone learned to water ski. Lorna and I took all three kids on one major canoe trip a year. We'd pack two small L. L. Bean tents and take off with the kids, one dog, and two canoes loaded with supplies. What a hoot!

In wintertime we enjoyed fabulous snowmobiling and mediocre skiing at Big Tupper. One cold winter day I suggested a family picnic at the Fish Creek development located at the end of our driveway. We rode the snowmobiles out on the creek next to a small dock where I started a fire to cook hot dogs. When I gave Stephen his hot dog, he complained that the weather was so cold that when he bit off the tip it had frozen again, even though it had just come off the fire! Lorna, at this point, offered that it was a bit too cold for everyone, so we returned to camp.

Frequently, we rode down to the Loeb [29] cabin, where their caretaker filled the icehouse with blocks of ice cut from the lake. This thoughtful gesture meant the family could enjoy a cold beer on the next July 4th!

One morning at Camp Cork, I found a live bat in my shoe when I climbed out of bed. Pretty creepy. But I had to share him, right? Of course! I delivered the creature to the breakfast table exclaiming that I had a surprise—a special morning treat. Funny thing, nobody was amused except me!

Throughout my life I've felt blessed that Lorna and I had children. We felt fortunate that we had two girls and a boy; we also felt lucky that they were healthy. People say that nothing is worse for parents than to have a child who is ill. And I'd say I have to agree with them.

Although Stephen was born healthy, by about 18 months of age he was not developing normally. Lorna and I took him to the Children's Hospital in Chicago, and the doctors there diagnosed him as hydrocephalic; that is, he had hydrocephalus, a condition also known as "water on the brain." This medical condition results when there is an abnormal accumulation of cerebrospinal fluid within the cavities of the brain. This may cause increased intracranial pressure inside the skull and progressive enlargement of the head, among other symptoms. Although it does occur in older adults, it is more common in infants.

Stephen's condition appeared to be caused by a cerebrospinal flow obstruction, so doctors inserted a shunt to bypass the blockage. But as time went on, Stephen continued to have occasional seizures, which were scary, and Lorna and I became concerned about what we should do. Miraculously, an opportunity arose in February 1970 to solve our dilemma.

While we were in Naples for my grandparents Briggs' 60th wedding anniversary, one of the guests was Dr. Al Uihlein, head of neurosurgery at the Mayo Clinic in Rochester, Minnesota. The family lived near my grandparents in Naples and at the time were the owners of the Schlitz Brewery in Milwaukee. During the party I spoke with Dr. Uihlein about our dilemma with Stephen and asked him who he felt were the best children's neurosurgeons in the country. He gave me three names. One was in Seattle,

Washington, another in Texas, and a third in Cleveland, Ohio. Since Cleveland was the closest, I called Dr. Frank Nulsen, head of neurosurgery at University Hospital Case Medical System and also a professor at Case Western Reserve. When I spoke with him, he advised me that he could not see Stephen until early April since he was going on vacation. Being curious, I asked him where he was going. To my surprise, he said Naples, Florida. I told him that we also would be in Naples in March, so we arranged for him to meet Stephen, Lorna, and me then.

When I mentioned this coincidence to Tayto, my grandmother Briggs, she turned to Pops, my grandfather, and asked, "Isn't that Dr. Frank Nulsen, Cookie Nulsen's son?" Amazing! As it turned out, the Nulsens had owned a home on the beach at 10th Avenue South in Naples since the 1920s. Cookie Nulsen lived in Milwaukee during World War I, and when he was unable to find a job after the war, Pops arranged for him to work at Briggs & Stratton. What a small world! And how lucky we felt!

In April, Lorna, Stephen, and I went to Cleveland. We arrived on Sunday afternoon, and Stephen went into surgery for an air test the next morning. We returned to our hotel to wait. At exactly 10 a.m., as promised, the phone rang. Dr. Nulsen said that Stephen was fine. He did not need the shunt. Did we want him to remove it? We said yes. At noon we met the doctor in his office. He invited us to his home for a drink, and he drew us a map. As Lorna and I watched, he sketched lines that were extremely squiggly since his hands were shaking as if he had palsy. Lorna and I looked at each other and remained silent. We had the same thought: *This is the man who just performed surgery on our son?* Nevertheless, we enjoyed the evening with the doctor and his wife Ginny, who was a real delight.

After the surgery, Stephen recovered and did well. Then a year or two later, when he was about six years old, Lorna was driving to Camp Cork with all three children. About 100 miles west of Cleveland, Stephen unexpectedly had a seizure. Shelley, who was nine, acted quickly and was able to keep Stephen from swallowing his tongue by wedging Lorna's leather wallet into his mouth. Lorna stopped the car, called Dr. Nulsen, and then took off like a Porsche toward the Cleveland hospital.

Stephen was admitted to the Children's Hospital, and Dr. Nulsen met us there. After a day or so, he told us he felt the high fever had come from a virus; nevertheless, he wanted Stephen in the hospital for observation for several days. This presented a problem. Lorna and I needed to return to Lake Forest briefly, but Stephen did not like the hospital. So, with our permission, Dr. Nulsen took Stephen to his home after office hours. What a happy arrangement! Our boy would drive in with Dr. Nulsen, spend the day at the hospital, and then go home with the doctor at night. How kind of Ginny and Frank Nulsen, whom we hardly knew!

When we returned on the weekend, the Nulsens invited us to stay in their home. Altogether, Stephen was in Cleveland for about 10 days, and during his time with the Nulsens, the doctor played games and pitched pennies with him. I am confident that the home therapy with these fine people hastened our son's recovery. With Stephen at home again, we felt tremendous relief.

In 1972, I was transferred to the snowmobile division of OMC, which was located west of Milwaukee in Wauwatosa, a city in Milwaukee County, Wisconsin, and part of the Milwaukee metropolitan area. The distance from Lake Forest represented a 90-mile commute one way. Over time this became a real pain. We thought about relocating, but Lorna didn't think it would be a good idea to pack everyone up and move. Plus, there was the question as to how long OMC would stay in the snowmobile business. As it turned out, not long. The company closed the division in the spring of 1975. Meanwhile, to make the commute more tolerable, I bought a Porsche 911. That, at least, ensured the travel time would pass quickly.

In the early 1970s, we went to a formal dinner at the Onwentsia Club. I somehow had overindulged in the beverage activity, so by the time we sat down at the table, I was not in the best shape. Dinner was slow in coming and champagne was served to Lorna's and my side of the table first. Sitting across from me was Kay Phelps, a friend, and she was making noises about the fact that I had champagne and she didn't. So, I made a distinctive move to satisfy her thirst. I reached for my loafer under the table, took it off, filled it up with champagne, and passed it across the tabletop to Kay. This went over with Lorna like a lead zeppelin, even though other guests around us found it quite amusing! Within about 30 seconds, Lorna excused us both from the dinner table and escorted me home.

She's come undone

She didn't know what she was headed for

And when I found what she was headed for

It was too late

She's come undone

She found a mountain that was far too high

And when she found out she couldn't fly

It was too late

It's too late

She's gone too far

She's lost the sun

She's come undone

She wanted truth

But all she got was lies

Came the time to realize

And it was too late. . .

She's come undone

She didn't know what she was headed for

And when I found what she was headed for

Mama, it was too late

CHAPTER 26

Comin' Undun (1974)

In 1969, there was a popular song playing on the radio by a Canadian rock band called The Guess Who. A guitarist named Randy Bachman composed it, and his lyrics were haunting then and are equally haunting today. The name of the song was "Undun" [30], and a sample of the lyrics appears on the facing page. If you substitute the male pronoun "he" for the female "she" within the lyrics, you'll figure out why I find the song haunting. Lyrically phrased, the song describes what actually happened to my life in 1974: I came undone.

In that same year an investigative reporter named Gail Sheehy wrote a book called *Passages* [31]. The book created quite a stir, and according to its flyleaf, it purported to do three things: to detect personality changes common to each stage of life; to compare developmental stages among women and men; and to examine the crises that couples can anticipate at pivotal stages in their lives.

At the time, I wish I had read that book because I might have steered clear of a painful passage within my own life and my family's. Instead of reading *Passages*, however, I lived it.

In the winter of 1974, Lorna and our family were on a ski trip with friends we had known for years. We all felt easy around each other, enjoying the sporting adventure, the careless laughter in good company, and the relaxation of a winter vacation, when almost unaware, I realized things were becoming complicated. I want to say it "just happened," as everyone tells you in a situation like this, but we all know that we choose that solo late-night drink with another person; we decide to take that lonely ski run together; we confide things in one another that can be indiscreet. And what "just happens" is as old as Mother Nature herself—sexual attraction. I found myself romantically drawn to another woman.

At the time, Lorna and I were in the thick of raising children. We'd been married for 15 years, and we were dealing with the tedium and tension that come with midlife. Let's face it; life had become somewhat stale between us. Here's were *Passages* comes in. What I should have known was that these feelings were normal. They were predictable. They were indicative of my age and stage in life. I was 39 years old—almost 40— that pivotal year when men experience the proverbial "midlife crisis." Back then I wasn't familiar with the term, nor the symptoms. The key is, although I did not sense it, Lorna, at 36, was probably experiencing the same restlessness and boredom that I was feeling, because the 30s decade for women is like the 40s decade for men. So, there we were as a couple, primed for a developmental passage, which perhaps we could have worked through. Instead I fell into an affair: I acted on my rush of feelings, enjoying the intrigue, the thrill, the secret liaisons—all the while telling myself I wouldn't get caught.

As happens with many of these situations, the end came abruptly, causing damage and embarrassment to all concerned. One evening when I was visiting, her husband came home unexpectedly from a hunting trip. With that, all hell broke loose.

In the intervening tumultuous weeks, the woman and I agreed never to see one another again. And we never did.

Lorna, struggling with the painful betrayal, suggested that she and I enter counseling, but I resisted. Ultimately, when I finally agreed to counseling as an attempt to glue our marriage back together, it was too late. Lorna—hurt, strident, and unwavering—put my clothes in the front hall of our home in Lake Forest, retained an attorney, demanded that I move out, and filed for divorce.

My friend and co-worker Paul Butler accompanied me to Lake Forest to pick up my clothes and a few personal items at my home. I found that very depressing. After 15 years of marriage, what was left was a small lump of things to be hauled away. In that moment I realized a shocking truth: Midway through life, I had lost my past and also my future, for what I'd envisioned as a lifetime family with Lorna and my kids would never, ever be.

For the most part it had been a good marriage, but one that didn't make it to the finish line. Instead, I faced a divorce that proved to be complicated, expensive, vastly unpleasant, and lengthy, taking several years to become final.

In other words, my marriage took years to come completely "undun."

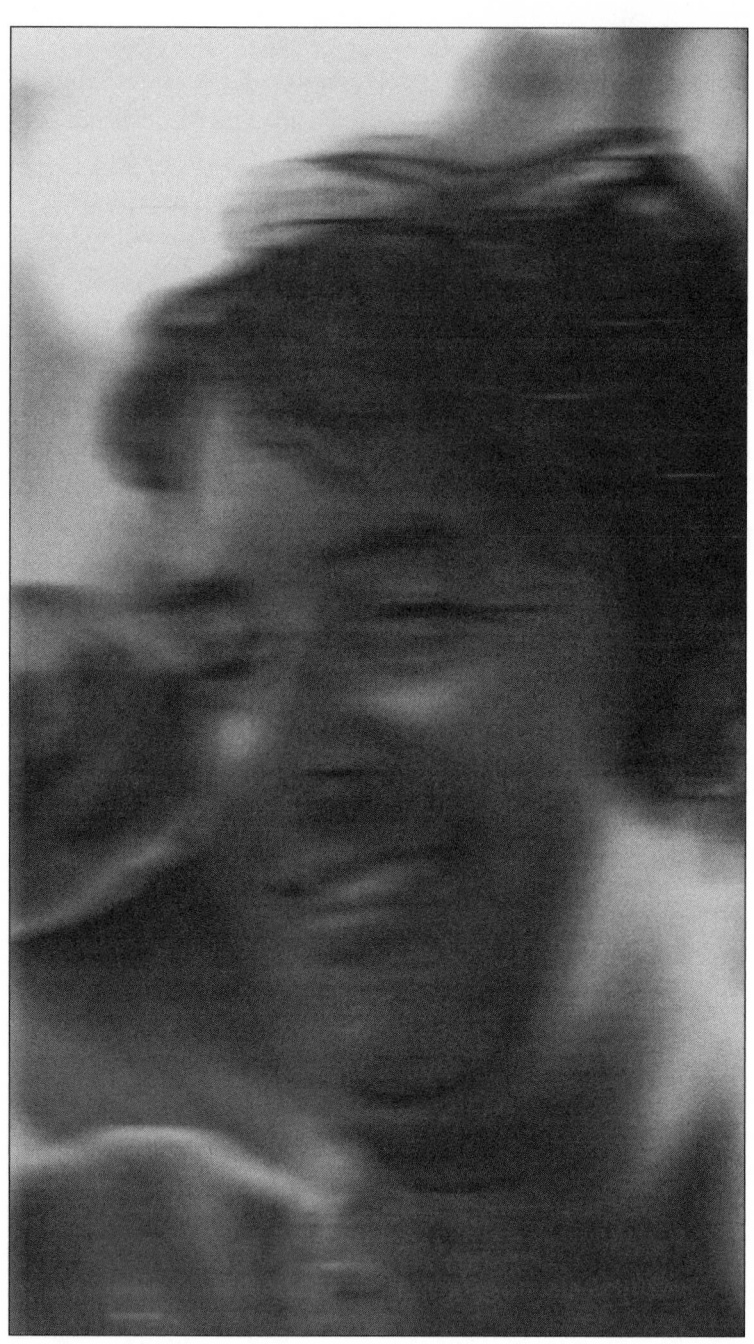

SFB II at wit's end

CHAPTER 27

Fallout (1974)

Numbed by what was happening in my personal life, I nevertheless continued my work in the snowmobile division of OMC, located in Wauwatosa, Wisconsin. Paul Butler had invited me to move into his place in Mukwonago, Wisconsin, a village just west of Milwaukee that had a geographical span of about eight miles of land and water. Gratefully, I accepted his invitation.

Originally a Native American village, Mukwonago was the tribal seat of the Bear Clan of the Potawatomi Indians. The name *Mukwonago* comes from a word that translates to "bear's den." That little piece of history struck me as ironic, since a den was what you might call our small living space—quite a comedown from the kinds of places I had grown used to. In Mukwonago, Paul had rented a two-room suite at the Heaven City Motel. We each had a bedroom with a private bath and a small living room with a working fireplace. At one end of the front room there was a kitchen, which also had a washer and dryer. Not bad for $250 per month, cash only.

The motel was a few miles from town, and the town at that time was so small, the police worked from 9 a.m. to 5 p.m. and the fire department was all volunteer. The motel was owned by Mrs. Talcott (whom we called Mrs. T.), age 92, and she lived with her sister, who was 96. They offered a small bar, very cozy, but open only on a limited basis. Strikingly, the entire room was decorated with hundreds of photographs from the 1920s, many featuring Al Capone [32] and his friends. Over several cognacs one night, Mrs. T. and her sister told us about Capone and his friends and girlfriends who would visit Heaven City on the weekends.

My work as marketing manager of the OMC snowmobile division was complicated by the division manager, a fellow named Bob West, whose management methods I would characterize as the "carrot and stick" approach. This idiom refers to a policy of offering a combination of rewards and punishment to induce behavior. Picture a cart driver dangling a carrot in front of a mule and holding a stick behind it. The mule moves toward the carrot because it wants the reward of food. It also moves away from the stick behind it, since it does not want the punishment of pain, so it draws the cart along. And while our division was not made up of mules, he treated us like dumb animals. Funny thing, you had to wonder about the intelligence of a guy who would discuss the "physical" year when he meant "fiscal" or who would describe the "allergy" on the bottom of his boat, not "algae" like most folks call it.

One day a couple of representatives from the federal government's Office of Economic Opportunity (OEO) visited our division to analyze our employment record in terms of minorities. Both of these men were black. They asked Bob what he was doing insofar as minority employment was concerned. Bob didn't seem to comprehend the concept.

"Well, I have Kneurinchild as a traffic man—he's Polish," Bob said. "Murphy, my accountant, is Irish. My marketing man, Briggs, is Catholic. Poulos, my sales manager, is Greek. My chief engineer, Edgar Rose, is a Jew. Paula, in accounting, is Puerto Rican, and oh yes! I have an 'N' in the warehouse." This bit of wisdom confounded the OEO representatives, and they left shaking their heads.

Given these examples, you can understand why, when Bob West proposed to give the employees in our division an intelligence test, we were less than responsive. When he asked us why, my co-worker, Jim Poulos, and I questioned his credentials. We told him, "If we needed brain surgery, we'd go to a neurosurgeon."

We did manage to pull off one stunt on Bob. He used to chain smoke cigars, which was particularly unpleasant in meetings. Jim and I arranged for the local sheriff to serve Bob with a fake lawsuit we concocted alleging we were suffering from black lung disease. We also insisted on an air purifier for his office.

First true love, SFB II with Merrill Stevens, 1950

CHAPTER 28

Your First True Love
May Not Be Your Last (1974–1975)

While living in Heaven City, I became bored and lonely, even though Paul was good company and we had fun together. One day at work I thought it would be interesting to try to find my first true love, Judy Kirkham Stillman, whom I had known my senior year at Canterbury in 1954. I did not know where she lived or her last name, so I called the alumni office of her private college preparatory school in Farmington, Connecticut, known as Miss Porter's School. This all-girl finishing school is highly selective and boasts famous alumnae, including Jacqueline Bouvier Kennedy Onassis, Lilly Pulitzer, Gloria Vanderbilt, and Dorothy Walker Bush, mother and grandmother, respectively, of presidents George H. W. Bush and George W. Bush.

Administrators there are not supposed to divulge information; however, I made up some story that was good enough for me to obtain her phone number in Portola Valley, California. After a few days I got my nerve up to call, and picked mid-morning as I figured her husband, if she had one, would be at work. Much to my surprise, I learned that she was divorced and living with her children just outside San Francisco. After a pleasant conversation, I flew out for a long weekend in December. We had a great time and I enjoyed her parents and San Francisco. Her dad, known as Czar Kirkham, was a well-known attorney with Pillsbury, Madison & Sutro. They were the lawyers for Standard Oil of California, and Czar had engineered the merger with Standard Oil of Indiana with the approval of the U.S. Justice Department.

Czar and his wife were in the same house at 4146 Pacific Avenue that they lived in when Judy was at Miss Porter's School. The night before I was to fly back to Milwaukee, they asked where I was spending Christmas. At the time I was depressed and had no real plans, so I accepted their invitation to spend Christmas in San Francisco.

After Christmas, Judy visited Mukwonago for a long weekend, and then we took a ski trip to Sun Valley at the end of March. Judy met me in Salt Lake and we took the small commuter plane up to Sun Valley. I noticed an extremely large man (who did not look like a skier) was sitting in the back of the plane. In a half-serious but joking voice I said to Judy, "That must be the detective that Lorna hired to follow us." I learned later that I was correct.

Sun Valley offered great skiing, although some runs were tough for me. While we were there I received a phone call from Jeff Reed, who was head of the First National Bank in Lake Forest. He gave me the unpleasant news that my bank account had been frozen by court order, and that it would take several weeks before it could be reversed. Fortunately, I had an excellent relationship with the bank, and as soon as they had the notice, they held my deposits, which were in transit. Jeff also took it upon himself to open a new account for me at their sister bank in Highland Park and mail me the new checks. I was relieved to hear that good news. Unfortunately, more bad news was on the way . . .

Shortly after I returned from Sun Valley, I discovered that I had a swollen testicle, which at first I attributed to a fall while skiing. When I went to the doctor, he told me that it was probably cancer. I called Judy in California, and she insisted that I consult with her father, who was well connected in the San Francisco medical community.

Czar, Judy's father, called me from Salt Lake where he was involved in a Mormon convention and insisted on flying to Chicago to discuss my options. He had done his research and explained to me that if it was a malignant tumor, the treatment after surgery was extremely critical. Czar advised me that the best places for treatment of testicular cancer were Sloan Kettering in New York City, Anderson in Dallas, and the University of California Hospital in San Francisco. Czar was a close friend of a leading San Francisco urologist, Frank Hinman, one of the best-known physicians in the field of testicular cancer. I chose San Francisco, and the next morning I flew to California.

After my arrival in San Francisco on April 3, 1975, I was admitted the next afternoon to Children's Hospital, where Dr. Hinman performed surgery to remove the testicle. About two days later, the pathologist, a rather tactless man, came to my room to advise me that the tumor was not only malignant but also a "choriocarcinoma." Plainly put, he would give me six months to live, and he held out little hope for a cure. Needless to say, I was devastated. However, I learned that my doctor's father, Frank Hinman Sr. had invented a procedure that entailed radiology followed by a massive lymph node dissection and then more radiology. His father had led the research for a comprehensive study on testicular cancer conducted by the U.S. Army during World War II. This was the plan Dr. Hinman Jr. recommended for me.

For radiation I went to Stanford, where my physician, Dr. Bagshaw, head of the department at Stanford, was practicing medicine. The location was convenient as I was staying with Judy in Portola Valley. One of the tests I needed was a lymph angiogram; however, they had a two-week waiting period at Stanford so they sent me off to Redwood City Hospital. What a disaster! I learned that this was the first time the procedure had been performed at this location. After a few false starts, it took about four hours to complete a procedure that normally takes 30 minutes. This test indicated the lymph nodes were negative for cancer.

Radiation treatments were tough on me, and I was constantly sick. I could not eat and went down from 160 to 115 pounds. It got to the point where I felt nauseous every time I drove to the hospital. There I learned quickly not to ask those on either side of me waiting for treatment what was wrong—they were all worse off than I was. As their treatments proceeded, many patients simply didn't show up. It didn't take long to figure out the reason.

On rare good days between treatments, Judy and I would go up to the Kirkham's house in Napa Valley. It had a little guesthouse in back where Judy and I stayed. It was near Rutherford and was surrounded by vineyards.

I tried living in Judy's home, but that proved difficult. Her children were free spirits and the house was extremely dirty even by my standards. The kids were allowed food in bed, which translated to food in the master bed, so one lived with a multitude of constant crumbs and spilt milk. Also, there was a parrot that roamed loose throughout the house, liberally shitting wherever it happened to be. That's the truth! One day I was in the shower and had just washed my hair when the parrot decided to unload on my head!

Judy did not like to cook, and most of the time I couldn't stand the smell of food. However, when I did eat I wanted something tasty, but usually it was petrified beef and overdone veggies. In general the older kids were kind to me and empathetic. I did have a problem with the five-year-old twins, who were jealous of my presence and took turns asking, "When are you going to die?" *Hmmm*. A bit trying to say the least.

The one thing you feared during treatment was being paged by Dr. Bagshaw or any other doctor. It seldom brought good news. On one trip I was paged, and the experience made my life flash in front of me. Off I went to the small cubicle of a waiting room, where I worried for over an hour. When the doctor arrived he paced the floor and hemmed and hawed for about two minutes, which made me even more nervous. Then he began by telling me what a good friend he was with Czar Kirkham and the whole family. He went on to express how difficult this news was to tell me, but he had to advise me that I could not rely 100 percent on the radiation making me sterile. Therefore, he hoped I was using some other form of contraception!! I couldn't believe it! What a relief!

My next hurdle was major surgery to remove as many of my lymph nodes as possible. I could not be operated on at Children's Hospital because the anesthesiologists were on strike. Only emergency operations were being performed at state hospitals. I was considered an emergency case, so I entered the University of California Hospital Parnassus Campus in San Francisco. My best friend Charlie Bonanno flew to San Francisco to be at my side. I remember well the night before my surgery, lying scared to death in a ward with other patients. The pre-surgery staff was supposed to prep me early in the evening and then give me something to sleep; however, at 10 p.m., no one had shown up. Finally, I called the nurse, but when the orderly came in he refused to prep me because he was a conscientious objector who had been assigned alternate civilian service as opposed to military service in the Vietnam War and would not perform a depilatory. Actually, I think his pacifist response to my situation was personal distaste for the task at hand. At any rate, he stormed out of the hospital room.

Good grief! I thought, and I rang the nurse who advised me she wasn't sure what to do, but after reading the pre-surgery directions, we got the job done. Charlie was in the hallway arguing with the doctor, who was just making his rounds and was not encouraging about my situation. My best news came from the nurse, who told me that 90 percent of testicular cancer was curable. That was in stark contrast to the doctor who told me that the operation might improve my odds by 5 or 10 percent.

The next morning they put me down in the hallway alongside 10 others waiting to be admitted to the operating theaters, which were all booked. The operation took eight hours, and the doctors removed 45 lymph nodes. After surgery I was returned to a private room with a color television. As the NBA finals were playing, I received special attention from the collection of doctors and staff visiting my room. Nothing like sports to rally camaraderie, no matter what the dire circumstances!

My radiation treatments were spaced at wide intervals, so in May 1975, Judy and I decided to go to the romantic resort called Mona Kai on Maui, Hawaii. It was lovely with a great beach and fabulous food. Most of the amenities were a waste on me, as I was only eating bananas and drinking Cokes. My big challenge was to walk to the beach and sit most of the day. I was still remarkably weak, but each day on the beach I would walk a little farther than the previous day. The meals were sumptuous; however, I couldn't eat. Nor could I enjoy all the fancy rum drinks. By the third or fourth day, Judy and I were arguing. On the beach I was reading the latest issue of *Time* and she wanted to discuss our future. But I did not feel ready either to discuss it or to make a commitment. Hence, the conversation deteriorated rapidly. I emphasized that I wanted to see if I could get well first. The next thing I knew, she headed for the room, packed up, and left to return to San Francisco. Now I was alone in a romantic, elegant hotel. What a waste.

As I was booked for the next three days, I stayed and continued my routine. Czar, Judy's father, called me at least once a day to check on me. I continued my routine of going to the beach, sitting, and walking a little more each day. On the second day alone, I walked over to the tennis courts where a foursome was playing and a very attractive woman was watching. While her husband played tennis, she told me all about her life and especially the problems she was having with her son. I asked her why they came to Mona Kai, and she told me that she really needed a rest from her work. My next question was what kind of work? She explained that she had just finished a television special that would air in the fall. That, along with her weekly series, had exhausted her. I still didn't know who she was, so as they were leaving I introduced myself, and she told me she was Mary Tyler Moore [33]. I suspect I was one of the few people who in the 1970s could spend three hours with Mary Tyler Moore and not even recognize her!

Before returning to San Francisco, I spent two days at the Royal Hawaiian in Honolulu. The first morning I continued my drill of walking the beach. On the way back I decided to spend time by the swimming pool. I noticed an attractive blond in a large straw hat who was lounging next to the pool and reading a book. I spent about 10 minutes sitting by the edge of the pool dangling my feet in the water waiting for an opportunity to start a conversation. Finally, I did and it was very pleasant. After about 20 minutes I realized that she was asking me a lot of personal questions, along with questions about my work. I knew very little about her at this point, but figured I might look her up at some future date. Suddenly she glanced up from under her large straw hat and said, "Steve Briggs, stop trying to pick up your cousin!" It turned out to be my first cousin Barbie McCulloch from Los Angeles. What a shock!

When I returned from Hawaii, Judy told me I could stay at her house but I was to move to the room off the garage. The room was dark and depressing, and there was no place for my clothes, so I got one of those hanging moving boxes. Judy's oldest son frequently smoked in the loft above my room. The ashes dropped down, landed on my clothes, and burned holes in them. Ultimately, I moved to the local Holiday Inn.

Keep in mind, I did not know how long I had to live. In desperation, I latched on to anything that was non-invasive—psychic readings, apricot pits, even the Mormon faith. During my stay with Judy, I attended the Mormon Church and studied lessons. The Mormon community at Palo Alto is above average and intelligent. I wanted to believe in anything that might cure me, so I tried my best. But I flunked my final interview. First, I tried to convince the elders that wine should be okay as it was good enough for "our Lord." Second, I asked if tithing was *before* or *after* taxes. Third, I asked why the Mormon Church had no black elders. After that, the leaders advised me I was not ready to be a Mormon. I needed more study.

Summing up that transitional chapter in my life, I'll just say that the girl of your dreams at 18 when you're innocent and star-struck may not be the woman of your dreams when you're 39 and recovering from cancer surgery. In other words, your first true love may not be your last.

CHAPTER 29

The First Day (1975–1979)

Sometimes it takes a brush with death to make you think about your life. Following my harrowing experience with cancer surgery, I spent several days in the hospital recuperating and then I was released. Facing follow-up appointments and radiation, I had time to contemplate my distressing situation: I was all by myself, and I was fighting the vestiges of cancer. Plus, my relationship with Judy was in turmoil, and I was overcome by the prospect of only six more months on this earth. Gravely troubled, I decided to take a solitary walk even though I was physically very weak. I headed toward the Presidio of San Francisco, a park on the northern tip of the San Francisco Peninsula, now part of the Golden Gate National Recreation Area. Going down the hill to the entrance to the Presidio was easy, and I welcomed the blue sky and the smell of the ocean, which reminded me of happy times with my grandparents in Naples.

Shortly after entering the park I stopped to rest on a bench under a large, old tree. I just wanted to enjoy the peace and quiet, as my life was unwinding and I was worried. There was nothing left for me in San Francisco. I had finished radiation treatment. I was alone. I longed to go to my grandparents' home in Naples, Florida. There, I thought, I could regain my strength. As I started up the hill to make my way back, I realized that I had made a big mistake going down so far, as every few feet I had to stop and rest. About halfway back, I noticed a VW van with the bumper sticker: "Remember this is the first day of the rest of your life."

It was as though someone had hit me on the head with a baseball bat. The realization was immediate. My first lives were over: the childhood life with Mom and Dad as well as the young adult life with Lorna. All I had left was life itself—the rest of it—however long or short that might be. But the point was, I had life left! Life with my children, my friends, my work, my ambition, and strangely enough, my faith. This was the first day of the rest of that life—my new life. What would I do with it? The answer seemed clear: I'd make every day count. I would work only toward those things that were worthwhile, and I would make sure that each day was not only productive, but also fun. At the same time, whatever I did, I wanted to make sure that my new philosophy did not hurt those around me. Henceforth, facing highs and lows, I would chart my daily life affirming: "This is the first day . . ."

As soon as I finished my treatments in California, I headed for Naples, Florida, where my elderly grandparents Briggs had round-the-clock nurses. The doctors had told me I should not travel until 10 days after the final radiation treatment, but I left the Holiday Inn where I was staying after 24 hours. When I arrived in Miami, I rented a car to drive to Naples, and what would have normally been a two-hour drive took me more than four. At last I arrived at my grandparents' home where, for the first time in months, I felt comfortable and secure.

I started back to work in July 1975. While I regained my strength in Naples, I found a two-bedroom apartment in Miami

at Southeast 25th Street just off Brickell Avenue on the sixth
floor overlooking Biscayne Bay and the Rickenbacker Causeway.
I had to furnish it from scratch because my divorce was not final,
and even when it did become final my allocation of furniture
was not available for another year, with certain pieces coming
to me only after 18 months. I hired a decorator and we decided
to go modern with a red, white, and blue theme to celebrate the
upcoming bicentennial of the United States. The apartment was
fun and comfortable, with a great view looking east and south
toward the causeway over to Key Biscayne and south toward
the bay. At night I could see all the lights from Miami and the
airport off in the distance to the west.

My daughter Sandy came down to help me move in, and
she worked very hard cleaning and lining all the shelves. I was
still pretty weak at the time. To regain my strength I did laps at
the apartment complex swimming pool. On weekends I went to
the beach at the sandbar on Key Biscayne.

After about six months I needed help with the service
department at work, so I convinced my friend Paul Butler from
snowmobile days to come down from Syracuse. He moved into the
apartment. Our favorite restaurant was next door, and I recall many
evenings after work when Paul and I would sit at the bar and try
to solve the problems of OMC, which was a never-ending subject.
There were many great places to hang out that were full of action
and lovely women. I also spent many hours at Monty Trainers over
their backgammon boards. It was a fun time to be single in Miami.

Shortly after I arrived I contacted Dad's old friend Bill
Simpson to see if I could find a used Mercedes convertible. He
came up with a 1972 Mercedes 350SL that had around 6,000
miles on it. The price was $12,000; however, I had a court order
from Lorna at the time that I could not write any check for more
than $500 without her permission. My solution was to write 24
$500 checks to different people and then have them endorse
them over to the Mercedes dealer!

Throughout my residency in Miami on Southeast 25th Street, I developed a great fondness for Sandy Faulkner (who was not related to novelist William Faulkner). I met Sandy in July 1975; she lived in the same apartment complex that I did overlooking Biscayne Bay. I really wanted our relationship to become a full-blown love affair, but it was destined never to happen. Whenever I was available, she was in a serious relationship, or vice versa.

Sandy was the head buyer for Jordan Marsh; she was extremely attractive and had great taste. On one occasion she invited me to New York City, where she was attending the premier fashion show of a promising new (but unknown) designer. I arrived early and was shown to my second-row seat at the Plaza ballroom. High-powered fashion buyers and the press surrounded me, wanting to know what store I was with. They were more than a little surprised when I explained that I sold outboards in Latin America. Sandy arrived and we watched the show, which was a huge success. Afterward, Sandy took me to the dressing room area to meet the designer and his mother. His name was Ralph Lifshitz, who would soon take on the name Ralph Lauren. This was his first show and the rest became multi-billion-dollar fashion designer history.

Such was the glamorous world Sandy inhabited. When I ultimately made a real attempt to put a relationship together with her, I read in the Miami paper that she had just married the president of Pan American Airways. *Hmmm.* Guess I was a little late and underqualified.

By 1977, Paul Butler and I had been roommates for more than a year in Florida and several months in Mukwonago.

One night I returned from Chile, and Paul picked me up at
the Miami airport. The airplane trip back was about 12 hours.
I was tired when I arrived around 11 p.m., and all I wanted
was to go to the apartment and crash. Paul insisted that we
go for a drink. In a strange place called the Warehouse, we
went up to the rooftop garden. After a couple of drinks, I
noticed the area contained only men. At the same time, to my
amazement, Paul told me he was gay. He went on to explain
that he was having difficulty in his relationship and needed
some advice.

My response was, "Paul, I can't even work out problems in a
heterosexual relationship. I don't think I can be much help!"

As the night wore on at the Warehouse, Paul and I tried to
solve the problems of the world and especially OMC. We ended
up going out for breakfast as the sun came up. I'm not sure if I
wasn't better off before, rather than after, I knew Paul was gay:
now I was an insider within the gay community in Miami.

Paul was one of the founders of the local gay newspaper, so
he and I made deliveries late at night to gay bars and restaurants.
I went to the gay clubs as Paul's guest, where I was treated well
once Paul announced that I was his straight friend. Among
other things, he helped organize the protest march against Anita
Bryant, who spoke out against gays and who represented the
Florida Citrus Commission. We were close to Coconut Grove,
and I learned that many establishments I thought were straight
had a huge gay following.

One night I attended my first all-gay dinner party, held in
a beautiful home on Miami Beach. There were four couples and
myself. The dinner was excellent, and as in many heterosexual
relationships, the males, as females, were responsible for the
dinner, and the males, as males, did the dishes. After dinner all
the "males" retreated to the drawing room for cigars and cognac!
So, I guess you can say, the more things change, the more they
stay the same . . .

During the years following my divorce, from 1975 to 1979, I was particularly mindful of the importance of staying in touch with my three children, and by being in touch I mean not only communicating often but also sharing experiences. As I see it, one of the most valuable things any parent can do is to create for each child a memory trail of happy events—whether it be a simple picnic in a local park or a deep-sea fishing trip to the ocean. This is particularly important if you are a single parent as I was now. I did not have custody of the children, so day-to-day memories were no longer a reality. Rather, I was faced with the challenge to create a *new* memory trail for my kids that would imbue them with a sense of continuous love and ongoing shared happiness that we had enjoyed when I was the father within their nuclear family. Also, new memories offered shared stories to laugh about for years to come.

With that goal in mind, I set about to create new experiences and new memories. In January 1976, the kids and I took a trip to the Florida Keys. In March that year, my son Stephen and I went tarpon fishing with Captain Forrest Haynes in Islamorada, also known as "Village of Islands," located in the Florida Keys. In 1977, Sandy, Shelley, Stephen, and I chartered a 42-foot sailboat from Caribbean Sailing Yachts, complete with a captain, and sailed for a week in the British Virgin Islands, leaving from Tortola. In July, Stephen, Shelley, and I went fishing again with Captain Haynes in Islamorada.

One adventure got seriously out of hand. In the summer of 1977 or 1978, Stephen and I shared an experience I never want to repeat. My son was visiting me, and I had my 24-foot Seacraft moored outside my apartment. We were planning to go to the Florida Keys for the weekend. As we left the apartment late afternoon, the weather was good with calm water in Biscayne

Bay. This all changed in about an hour as summer storm clouds started to build from the east. I thought we could easily outrun the weather and make it to Key Largo with no problem. Wrong! The storm came quickly and everything turned black in about 15 minutes. The bay became extremely rough with 10–12-foot seas.

I had no choice but to head into the wind and just try and hold the boat steady. The rain was unbelievable. I was scared but tried hard to convince Stephen that all was well. Honestly, I thought we might capsize and drown! I realized we had to head in some direction or run the risk of running aground, so I decided to head directly west. My hope was to hit land at some place where we could seek shelter without running aground. As I made the 180-degree turn, we were caught by a huge wave that drowned out one engine. With only one engine left, I asked Stephen to take the wheel and to try steering a straight course so I could go aft and attempt to get the second engine going. That did not work. The seas were so rough and coming from all directions, he just couldn't hold the helm. We had no choice but to try and make shore on one engine. With a following sea continuously crashing over our stern, it was extremely scary. The engine was out of the water at least 50 percent of the time and was cavitating a good bit. Dark had fallen when the storm started to let up, and we spotted not only shore but also an inlet. The moment we entered the inlet and were safe, I stopped the engine and went below to pour myself a stiff brandy!

As we proceeded, I realized we were on the canal where my stepmother Joan Hill [34] lived. When we reached the house we discovered no one was home; however, the lights were on at the neighbors' house. We docked the boat and knocked on their door looking like two drowned, scared rats. As luck would have it, they were celebrating their daughter's birthday and asked us to join them. This meant warm clothes, a roast beef dinner, and ice cream and cake. It became late and we were exhausted, so the neighbors let us stay in their guest room. As I lay warm and safe, my son sleeping nearby, I could only think what a mortifying experience we had endured—particularly for someone who worked in the marine industry. But also before drifting off, I realized what a relief it was to have such a pleasant ending to a terrifying event.

The children and I took one more delightful trip in 1979 when we sailed in the Lower Antilles, this time creating an extremely positive memory for everyone. Even though I was an experienced sailor, I had a newfound respect for the sea.

In the spring of 1979, we gathered to celebrate Sandy's graduation from Foxcroft School, a boarding school and day academy for girls in Middleburg, Virginia, near Washington, D.C. On Sunday following graduation exercises, a group of the graduates were invited with their fathers to a luncheon given by Pam Mars, grandmother of one of Sandy's classmates. Mrs. Mars was an impressive woman—unforgettable. Her estate was only about 10 or 15 minutes from the school and like its owner, very impressive. We toured the grounds and were told that some of the family members still believed it was a haunted house. The decor reminded me of the 1930s, and the home was lovely but very formal and somewhat dingy.

Throughout the house were numerous photographs of their racehorses, including one Kentucky Derby winner. I somehow was seated next to Mrs. Mars (perhaps in her 80s at the time) in the seat of honor at this elegant Sunday luncheon. She had been a very active businesswoman and only recently resigned as president of the American Red Cross.

Halfway through the luncheon I put my foot in my mouth by asking Mrs. Mars where her husband was and why he was unable to attend the luncheon. She responded in a very terse voice that the subject was one she did not wish to discuss as Mr. Mars was off in Las Vegas with his girlfriend—some local trollop. Ooops! Dangerous ground! I retreated quickly and tried to make it through lunch without further embarrassment.

During these post-divorce years, 1975–1979, I was learning in a variety of ways what it is like to start over in life. I've often wondered about our pioneer ancestors who abandoned the East Coast, took on the Western frontier, and carried only those possessions they could pack in a covered wagon across the Midwest prairies. I thought of my great-great-great-grandfather Joseph Briggs, a blacksmith who came from England in 1757 and settled on Block Island, part of Rhode Island, starting a new life in a new land. I thought of my grandmother Branch's family, whose lineage traced back to the 1500s. Her ancestors arrived in Massachusetts from England to plant new roots to germinate as new generations of Americans.

Now, in my own way, I was doing what they did. I was beginning again—experiencing the first days of the rest of my life. Some of them felt strange; some were lonely; some seemed thrilling; some sadly settled in despair. But as we human beings can only live life in one direction—that is, forward—I kept moving forward step by step, finding my way, mile by mile, the journey lighted, as it were, only a few feet ahead by the headlights on my boat. With such limited vision, I could not foresee the upcoming river bend I was soon to face . . .

Leaving . . .

CHAPTER 30

Leaving OMC (January 1979)

I t is important to know that OMC reigned for a time as the world's largest manufacturer and supplier of outboard motors and second largest producer of powerboats. The company had acquired fame for its brands—Johnson and Evinrude outboard motors, as well as its Chris-Craft and Grumman powerboats. OMC also produced other products including Cushman golf carts, Lawn-Boy lawn mowers, Pioneer chainsaws, Johnson and Evinrude snowmobiles, and Tradewinds campers, plus fiberglass runabouts, cruisers, performance boats, and craft for offshore fishing.

Behind my grandfather who founded OMC, my father, who was the president of international sales for several years, and my Uncle Jim Briggs who served on the board of directors after my grandfather resigned, I was the third generation of Briggs family members to be part of OMC's growth and success.

When I returned to work in July 1975, following my bout with cancer, the division that covered Central America, South America, and the Caribbean was now called OMINC, and it had returned to U.S. shores. I was told that the current division manager Jim Butler was retiring within 12 to 18 months and that I could expect to get his job. That was the good news. The bad news was there was bad blood between Jim and me. Back in 1959, when I was 23 and first started working with OMC full time,

Dad was head of the international sales operation for OMC. The company had moved to Nassau in 1958 for tax reasons, and Dad had brought Jim Butler on as his assistant. Somehow I learned that in attempting to get my father fired, Jim was critical of Dad behind his back with the big boss, Clarence Neal, in Peterborough, Ontario. When I found out what he was doing, I told Mr. Butler, "If I am ever in a position of power at OMC, and you are still with the company, make sure that the door doesn't hit you in the ass on the way out." Unfortunately, 15 years later he was my immediate boss, and I had the feeling he had not forgotten my indiscretion.

I did not have much respect for Jim, but, I reasoned, his remaining tenure was brief, and the head office had told me I would become the head of OMINC, so I bided my time. Meanwhile, my longtime friend Paul Butler became parts manager and then service manager.

OMINC was in a real battle to maintain its supremacy in the outboard field over Yamaha and Mercury. Yamaha in particular was making major inroads into our market, so I made some changes in the way we did business. First, I selected major World War II battle names, such as Guadalcanal and Bataan, to represent individual countries like Colombia and Venezuela, because we were in a real battle to regain market share and avoid a death march for our business.

Second, when our sales force expanded, I realized that most of the young trainees had no idea what it was like to travel in our territory. Most of our sales were intended for commercial use along the rivers of South America, like the Amazon, Orinoco, and Magdalena, and for commercial fishing not located near any real towns. Not prepared for the rigors of foreign remote locations, strange food, and sleeping quarters that were not your basic Holiday Inns, our early trainees didn't like the work. To remedy this problem, sales manager Tony Burgos and I designed a training program in which all new sales trainees would tour Colombia for two or three weeks with a backpack. They would accompany one of our distributors, journeying along the Magdalena River to visit rugged "garden spots" like El Bagre and El Banco. This exposure to foreign cultures and backwater regions gave the trainees a taste of what to expect if they wanted to work and travel for OMINC. In the interim, I traveled extensively through South America with several visits to Brazil, Argentina, Mexico, and Colombia.

COLOMBIA

As I have said, you learn about life when you see how it is lived in other parts of the world. In Colombia, for example, most of the outboards we sold were 25- and 40-horsepower engines for transportation throughout the interior. During the rainy season, when most of central Colombia is under water, it is a vast network of water routes both along rivers like the Magdalena and over flooded land areas. It is not unusual to see a 40-foot dugout canoe powered by a 40-horsepower outboard and loaded with up to 10 tons of rice. As a result of this trip our engineers made some major improvements to the commercial line, but most modifications were to the pleasure engines and were not up to the standards of Yamaha. Thus, Yamaha continued to increase its share of market based on durability and excellent parts availability and service.

PERU

In Peru I made several visits to the interior, primarily Iquitos, which was the center for commerce in the area. My first visit was with Bill Wershoven, the transportation and documentation manager for OMINC. He knew the local agents, so he went along. We spent a couple of days in Lima, which at the time was on rationing because of a shortage of meat. Peru at this time had inflation almost as bad as Brazil's and the local currency was worth nothing.

Iquitos is a fascinating town where the Amazon is still navigable by very large vessels. The river activity was similar to Colombia except there were far more aluminum boats being used primarily as water taxis between villages. In Lima I ate a fish called congra, whose front half looks like a fish and the back resembles an eel. Very tasty if you don't let looks bother you.

BRAZIL

On one my trips to Brazil I spent most of my time in Rio and Sao Paulo and took a side trip to Curitiba. Brazil was civilized and fun after traveling the interior of Colombia and Peru. As our business improved and the city of Manaus in northern Brazil became a free port, it became a regular stop. In Manaus the river actually rises and falls several feet. Also the current can run as much as eight or nine miles an hour, which creates a real challenge for those who are trying to paddle a small dugout canoe against the current. It's amazing to watch people work the eddies and actually go against the current.

On one occasion Bill Wershoven was with me, and we spent several days aboard our distributor's private yacht. This was the first time I saw piranhas actually devour a cow in minutes! Those freshwater fish that live in the South American rivers have powerful jaws, sharp teeth, and a tremendous appetite for meat. Some of the crew went swimming in the water right after that disturbing event; both Bill and I passed up the invitation.

On this trip we went up river toward the sea and visited several small villages that were located on tributaries of the Amazon. These settlements had sprung up when the government gave the people free land to develop the north and take some of the economic burden off the south. But a problem developed. The settlements were spread out all along the rivers for miles, and there was no practical way to get the children to a central location for education.

The river provided water for people and animals and it was the only place to bathe. It also was the number one source of food. There were huge catfish, some weighing more than 100 pounds, some of them prehistoric. With corn as bait, fishermen attached a large hook to a heavy line. When the fish was hooked they attached the line to an empty 50-gallon drum and let the fish pull the drum around for hours until it grew tired.

Mail, cargo, and passenger boats passed by the towns, usually once a week. These boats were the source of all communication with the outside world. They stopped for several hours at a village, and everyone gathered around to learn what was happening with their friends and relatives up and down river. Manaus is a thriving metropolis in the middle of the jungle.

At one point OMC considered building a manufacturing facility in Brazil, so I spent almost three weeks driving throughout the country with our local representative, Renato Azevedo. Seeking the best site, we drove through several states in that country, including Minas Gerais, Goias, Mato Grosso, and Amazonas, before returning to Rio via the coast. The trip covered several thousand kilometers . . . a real education for me.

ECUADOR

In Ecuador we had a new Evinrude distributor, and Stefano Isias owned the distribution company. At dinner the first night I was talking to Stefano about various topics, including education, and learned that he and I were at Babson together, even though we didn't know each other. We had a wonderful day of deep-sea fishing, and we caught some large marlin before we went north to Esmaraldes.

ESMERALDAS

Esmeraldas was one of the worst places I have ever been. The town was filthy and smelled rotten. But it is the largest place for the use of outboards in Ecuador. It lies on the border of Ecuador and Colombia, and distributors in both countries constantly complained that the other was stealing business by cutting prices.

In Esmeraldas we saw hundreds of canoes loaded with bananas coming out of the jungle on the way to market. Apparently, it is very critical that the bananas arrive at market a precise number of days after picking. A few days either way is a disaster.

We also witnessed another form of water-related commerce—a pig auction in which the pigs arrived by canoe and then were put in the water near shore like a corral before the auction began. That was truly bizarre.

CHILE

Although I went to Chile only once, and then only to Santiago, it was one of my favorite countries along with Argentina and Brazil. Chile has no native Indian population (like the Aztecs) and is almost totally European with a high standard of education. At the time it had more Pulitzer Prize winners than any other country in South America.

ARGENTINA

Buenos Aires is the capital and largest city of Argentina and definitely one of my favorite cities. Here outboards were sold strictly for pleasure, and no one had less than 125-horsepower engines. Key pastimes here are speed and pleasure. Around every bend there was another nifty restaurant on the water. Road signs on the waterways directed you to some resort, bar, or restaurant. In this city, brand loyalty was so strong, each marina was dedicated to an individual brand. This meant that the Johnson, Evinrude, and Mercury marinas were all separate storage facilities. These operations were advanced for the 1970s. When you wanted to go boating, you called ahead and the marina would have the boat waiting for you, fully stocked with ice and the drinks of your choice, plus a picnic lunch if requested.

VENEZUELA (1978)

Venezuela was close to Miami and our largest market in terms of dollars, so I went there frequently. Along the coast the outboards were used for pleasure on high-performance boats. The islands and the beaches are some of the best I have ever seen. At the time Venezuela was rolling in oil, so the resorts and marine facilities were first class.

In contrast, when we went to Ciudad Bolívar on the Orinoco, we found typical commercial usage of our outboards; that is, transportation of everything up and down the river.

Maracaibo was strictly oil driven and a rather dreary town. I remember that our distributor also handled the canned pre-cooked meat product, Spam. Venezuela was the product's largest market. (Oh yes, and at the time Venezuela consumed the most Scotch per capita!) While there we had a memorable lesson on the importance of reliability with the mechanic for our distributor. The mechanic insisted on showing us a video about the use of large outboards in Maracaibo. In the footage we saw a boat, about 30 feet long and powered by three large outboards—I believe they were 200 horsepower— used to smuggle booze and cigarettes from Aruba, a free port to Maracaibo. The object was to outrun the Venezuelan navy gunboats. No easy task. The video showed our mechanic friend leaning over the back of the boat changing a gear case at 40 plus miles per hour. No easy task when you could see gunfire hitting the water all around the stern of the boat. The alternative was sure death. This was his graphic way of suggesting we ask OMC engineers to make the gear cases more reliable. Point taken!

MEXICO (October 1975)

Ben Olson and I went to visit the shrimp fishing operation in la Reforma [35], also called the lagoon of Santa María la Reforma, in Mexico, on the west coast north of Mazatlán in Los Mochis. This fishing co-op is about 25 miles off the main highway on a dirt road. A huge operation, it had more than 500 boats operating out of this one harbor. We were there because Yamaha was taking control of the co-op with their 50-horsepower engine, while we were just introducing our 50-horsepower product that did not seem to have the speed or reliability of the Yamaha. Early in the morning the boats took off in pursuit of the shrimp. Each boat had a cast net with a caster, a spotter, and an engine operator. Once any of the spotters saw the shrimp boiling on the surface, the event became a giant boat race to see which boat would be the first to arrive and make several casts with nets before the competition got there, or the shrimp got smart and went to deeper water. As soon as several boats were on location, it became a real free for all with the spotter becoming a jouster trying to knock the competitor's caster into the water.

Given my firsthand knowledge of our customers from extended travel like this during my many years with OMC, the insight I had acquired, the contacts I'd made, and the deals I'd negotiated—plus the fact that I was the grandson of the company's founder and had been promised the title of division president—I was not prepared for the direction OMC was soon to take.

When Jim Butler retired, OMC reversed its promise to me. I was *not* tapped to replace him as division president. Instead, Bob West, under whom I had worked at the snowmobile division, was named division president and I was told to be patient. Be patient? I was flabbergasted! What was the board thinking?

As for qualifications, Bob West had zero export experience. He thought Chile was where Brazil is, and he had no desire to learn about either the distributors or Latin American customs. On several occasions he referred to them all as "spics." And service? When an important distributor arrived (after traveling up to 12 hours) and wanted a meeting after 4 p.m., West would just go home. I can count on *one hand* the number of times he considered going out to dinner with any of our major clients. This was my first clue that I was stuck in the job of vice president of marketing.

After a couple of years, Bob West retired in 1979, and I thought for sure I was in line for division president. When Bob Wallace, the big boss from headquarters, told me that Bob Schuler from Chrysler Outboards would be tapped, I packed it in. I knew Schuler from industry meetings, and I had little respect for him, especially since Chrysler was a miserable failure in the outboard industry. He, like West, had no international experience.

By now I figured I was going to advance no further at OMC, so I resigned. Then I immediately called my friend Moose Dunne, who advised me to quickly call back, ask for a six-month leave of absence, and reconsider the offer to stay as vice president of marketing. His reasoning was that I could get six months of pay and also negotiate a severance package if I had time to work out the details. After the six months' leave of absence, I went back and worked out six months of severance pay plus insurance for a year.

My emotions were strained raw. I had been brought up with OMC as the only thing I knew. My grandfather was the founder and served as chairman for many years, and both my dad and Uncle Jim not only worked for the company but also Jim served on the board of directors. When Dad died I thought I might be appointed to the board, but I realized I was only 29. As the years went by, I thought I was progressing well and would have settled to be president of the Latin American division, even though I felt qualified to head up all overseas operations. It was a painful parting, and my second in a four short years. I can say that after 21 years with OMC, leaving the company was every bit as difficult as my divorce from Lorna.

A bedroom at Camp Cork

CHAPTER 31

Dollars and Sense (1978–1979)

Most people who have gone through a divorce and a job
change will tell you that the experience is expensive. In
fact, I've never heard anyone say otherwise. And I certainly won't
tell you otherwise, because the high financial waves generated by
my own divorce and leaving OMC nearly swamped my boat!

After owning Camp Cork for almost 10 years, it became
necessary to sell it. By 1978, I was paying all the maintenance, as
my other owners were in financial difficulty or not interested. My
personal financial situation was dismal. I was involved in divorce,
economic times were difficult with interest rates over 20 percent,
and OMC stock was in the doldrums. The last straw came when
fuel oil rose to more than $1 per gallon, and, even with the
guesthouse closed, the resort consumed more than 40,000 gallons
of fuel in the winter of 1978–1979.

I received an offer for Camp Cork from a fellow named Ted
Carter. He was a friend of a friend, Bob Tebbutt, both of whom
were from Albany, New York. Tebbutt also represented Carter for
the sale of sea containers that were designed to take supplies and

cooling mud for drilling to offshore oil platforms in the North Sea. My daughter Sandy had concerns about Ted Carter, whom she met and pronounced to be a "little slimy." I should have listened to her, but I had no other prospects. I wanted desperately to relieve myself of the maintenance and taxes, so I pursued his offer.

We agreed on $300,000, which now seems like a song. We struck a deal with $50,000 cash paid at closing in September 1978, plus $50,000 worth of sea containers at his cost, and $50,000 cash on January 1, 1979, paid offshore. I would hold a $150,000 mortgage, which Ted Carter agreed to pay starting January 1, 1979.

There were red flags, however. The second $50,000 cash was to be paid offshore out of Ted's Swiss account, and he would record the sale at $200,000, which left out the sea containers and the second $50,000 as well. Ted promised a handsome return of more than 20 percent on my investment in sea containers, and claimed that I was getting them at his cost, 40 percent below what a regular purchaser would pay. But by closing in April 1979, the deal had changed: I had $50,000 in cash paid offshore and $100,000 worth of sea containers, plus I still held the first mortgage of $150,000.

Now, this enterprise purported to be legitimate. Carter Sea Containers was a London-based company that sold these special containers to investors and then arranged to lease them to North Sea oil operators. Sales in the UK were booming; the government, to encourage the oil business, offered a first-year total write-off. Sales in the United States did not have as good a tax advantage, but in March 1979 they were strong.

By June, I was receiving phone calls from my friend Bob Tebbutt saying he had heard rumors from London that Carter was in trouble. Furthermore, articles in the *Financial Times* suggested that the whole enterprise was a scam. I made a hasty flight to London, since Ted had assured me my containers did exist and were being used in the North Sea. I was dubious. In London I met with Carter's former controller (a British term for head of accounting), who had recently resigned. I learned that my containers did not exist. Rather, Carter Sea Containers had simply set aside serial numbers.

So, off I went to Aberdeen, Scotland, where the factory was located. Prior to leaving I told a friend that if I did not return in 24 hours to call Scotland Yard. As I drove to the factory in very thick fog, I became extremely nervous realizing that the manufacturer might be part of the scheme and I could end up in the North Sea with cement shoes. Over tea the factory owner confirmed my belief that Ted was in trouble, owing them more than £200,000, and I discovered that my containers had not yet been built. To add insult to injury, they showed me invoices indicating that while Ted's price for containers was $2,500 each, he was billing me $3,500—more than 30 percent above his cost!

Back in London, I consulted the law firm of Baker & McKenzie [36] and left copies of the documents I had acquired. Before I met Ted the next day, I called Mr. Melnor, a business reporter for the *Financial Times* in London. He had written a scathing article the day I arrived, claiming that Carter Container was a scam. I intended to use this wedge to get Ted to be reasonable.

After a heated conversation in which I narrated my discoveries and he denied my accusations, I said angrily, "Ted, the main point here is that I gave you a superior value in a residence you really wanted. In return, you gave me an empty bag!"

To make a long story short, I didn't have to involve others in the disagreement. Ted and I signed a new second mortgage [37] at his office and recorded it at the American Embassy. Ted took me there in his Rolls Royce convertible. We parted friends; I returned to the States. I waited for mortgage payments that did *not* come. Meanwhile, he had renamed Camp Cork "The Point" and had a plan to make it the most elegant bed and breakfast venture in the country. Finally, his brother and mother became involved, and we worked out an arrangement where I was paid directly from Mrs. Carter's trust fund [38]. This situation came to a screeching halt, however, when his mother died suddenly and his brother committed suicide. Once again I was obliged to renegotiate the loan.

As planned, Ted Carter made The Point a wonderful place and sold it to a group from Albany called the Black Willow Corporation. Because Carter's payments to me were irregular, we negotiated still one more contract: I became a shareholder, I received a payoff for the $150,000 mortgage, and I was entitled to one free visit a year. Later I accepted an offer to sell my stock at par to Black Willow Corporation, which was a big mistake. Sometime after I sold it, The Point was purchased by Everlands [39] for $13 million, of which my share would have been $1.3 million versus the $100,000 that I received. Oh well . . . in 2008, the whole thing fell apart, the economy tanked, and by 2013 The Point's owners were forced into bankruptcy [40].

Even now, I think about The Point, my own Camp Cork. What wonderful times I enjoyed there! And these days anyone can enjoy it! The Point is still in business and operating under the bankruptcy protection of the court. It exists as a five-star estate on the shoreline of a mountain lake in Upstate New York. The website bills it as a "Great Camp of the North Woods" with log mansions crafted of native timber and stone, which personify the "19th century romantic notion of roughing it in great comfort, style, and luxury."

Yes, that claim is true. You, too, can romantically "rough it" at an Adirondack estate. Your room will cost a measly $1,500 to $3,000 per night.

In 1979, after I had left OMC and moved to Naples, Florida, where I now lived full time, I needed to supplement my income since virtually all my assets came from OMC stock. I basically no longer had a job, and I was paying child support on top of a large sum per year to Lorna.

I joined a new, aggressive real estate agency on Fifth Avenue named Nichols Hayhoe. Some of my friends had suggested real estate sales was a good idea and suited my personality. Glena Hayhoe was a good saleswoman and a kind, thoughtful person. Lee Nichols was the business end of the operation. All in all, the agency people were great, and I felt I had found a real home in which to start my new career.

I learned, however, that real estate required more effort for sporadic paychecks than I had imagined. And it had drawbacks: I hated sitting at open houses; I was crestfallen when I had a property sale in the bag, only to see it blow up at the last minute; and I was bored stiff. Often I found myself having two-martini lunches and playing bridge with a business associate at the Piccadilly Pub on Fifth Avenue across the street from our office, wasting most of my days. During my brief career, I can recall three deals that sealed my lack of enthusiasm for real estate sales.

One was the Peppard Building, which like the Piccadilly Pub, was across the street from my office on Fifth Avenue. Glena owned the building and handed the sale to me. She told me to go to lunch and close the deal, and I would receive a nice commission. Great! At lunch the hot buyer asked me what I thought about the Peppard investment. Was it a good one? I replied bluntly that I thought the cash flow was too low for the price. By the time we had an after-lunch coffee, he had soured on the idea. When I returned to the office and told Glena what I'd done, she was surprised because the fellow had been so interested in the purchase. She asked him into her office and effectively closed the deal. The net result was no commission for me.

The next real estate deal involved a fellow named Fred Borch [41], who owned property at Indies West in Naples. One of my clients looking for condominiums in Naples was the wife of the chairman of Campbell-Mithun Advertising Agency [42] in Minneapolis. Her husband had handled the snowmobile account for OMC in past years, so I knew him.

I proceeded to show his wife every conceivable condominium on Gulfshore Boulevard in Naples. After looking around, she said she wanted to buy a condo at Indies West. No properties were available there, but I found out that Fred Borch, the retired president of General Electric, owned two waterfront units at Indies West. Would he sell one? Mr. Borch said he would, but he would not pay a commission. I asked him if he got full price, would he sell? Yes. I returned with a contract, which he refused to sign, since, as he said, "Son, my word is my bond." But, as you may have guessed, he changed his mind and wouldn't sell.

Meanwhile, I found another unit at Indies West, which the client loved and wanted to buy. I suggested sending the contract by FedEx to her husband in Minneapolis. She said she was traveling to Marco Island, located in the Gulf of Mexico off the coast of southwest Florida. She said she would gather the papers on the way home. Imagine my surprise when she called me with the news on Sunday night saying she'd bought a property in Marco! All along she had told me that she and her husband wanted to live in Naples, as Marco was too isolated! Go figure. Another lesson in the disparity between what people say and what they do.

The clincher came three months later. She and her husband visited the new condo in Marco and hated it. She called and asked me, "Will you sell it for us?" I politely replied that Marco was not my territory.

The third episode involved a former U.S. senator from Florida. By now I'd learned that real estate was a hard way to make a steady income. Commissions of $12,000 to $20,000 annually would not keep the wolf away from the door. In Fort Myers there was a large industrial development just starting at Metro Park. I felt commercial property would be easier to sell because it generally was sold on facts rather than emotion. One day I was on duty and this chap walked through the door.

He was my "up," so to speak, as he just showed up. I took one look at him and concluded he was a real "tire kicker," that is, someone who kicks the tires in a car lot, asks a million questions, takes a lot of time, and doesn't buy. He was mucho pounds overweight, he had last night's supper on his shirt, and he was just, well, grungy. I got him a cup of coffee and he sat at my desk and asked all sorts of questions about Naples, just wasting my time.

Around 11 a.m., an associate named Billy Papineau wandered in. She was a night person who enjoyed the bar scene and sang at many nightspots. While I was refilling coffee for "Mr. Grunge," she asked if she could help. Well, I could not unload this turkey fast enough, so I said, "He's your prospect if you want him."

Over the next four months I saw them out at every watering hole in town. When I inquired how things were going, Billy was evasive. Then after six months, I discovered that Mr. Grunge had bought $6 million worth of commercial real estate from Billy! He was buying property as a representative for George Smathers, a former U.S. senator from Florida. Smathers served in the House of Representatives from 1947 to 1951 and in the Senate from 1967 to 1969. He was a close friend to John F. Kennedy, since he managed JFK's campaign in the Southeast. When Smathers retired he was highly successful as a lobbyist and in business. Ultimately, he gave $24 million to the University of Florida. That did it! I realized then and there that I did not have the temperament or the judgment for this career.

I had some skirmishes with other potential sales and a successful series of purchases through my friends Moose Dunne and Bunny Dudley, which helped my cash flow and offered tax deductions. But then my firm's partners, Lee and Glena, had a falling out in 1981 so the agency dissolved. After that, although I kept my license for a few years, I gave up on real estate.

The early 1980s was a rough time financially in this country. Among other things, interest rates had soared to between 20 and 22 percent and prime reached as high as 18 to 20 percent. Since I had quit OMC in 1979, about 90 percent of my income came from dividends in OMC stock that I owned and OMC stock inherited from my grandparents. Then, too, most of the tax shelters I had invested in during the 1960s that should have succeeded didn't. In 1962, the top income tax rate was 91 percent so Citibank designed a tax shelter for top mangement of its best clients. In addition, it loaned you the money and provided management of the ventures with quarterly reports.

First, I'd gotten involved with investments in railroad boxcars for which I declined insurance against fire damage for economic reasons—plus, what could happen to a railroad car? Well, you guessed it! They burned or were destroyed in crashes.

Second, I had sunk money into vineyard production just south of Salinas, California. As a lover of good wine, this business venture had its upside: It really appealed to me. The price of red grapes was exploding from $400 a ton to as high as $1,200 per ton, and this 700- or 800-acre vineyard was planted from scratch in red grapes. Then we encountered the downside to the business venture: the high cost of improvements and maintenance. The general partner, Citibank, decided to put in a cold-water spray system to protect the crop from frost. We planted a ground crop such as sorghum between every row as a second crop. We became a huge exporter of sorghum. Those were the good seasons.

Then Mother Nature got angry, I guess, or we fell into the truism that like any farming venture, things don't always go as planned. Many of the vines died. The wine stakes kept rotting. To solve the rotting problem, we bought Philippine mahogany stakes at $4 each—expensive—but the California bugs, thankfully, did not like the wood.

Next, we tried to sell off sections of the vineyard upfront to wine producers to finance our costs. That might have succeeded, but, as luck would have it, the price of red grapes went into a permanent decline, while whites, especially Chardonnay, climbed rapidly. We kept borrowing money with the idea that we could graft the white variety onto the red stalk. Wrong. This, along with the price drop of red grapes, basically did us in. So after about 10 years, we sold out at a price that just paid off our bank loans. This was my one shot at farming.

My third and last tax shelter was an investment in government-subsidized housing in Concord, New Hampshire. It had all the problems associated with low-cost housing. People trashed the place, they left in the middle of the night, and they couldn't pay the rent. Then the project experienced a windfall. One of the government rules was that it had to remain low-cost housing for 30 years, which would mean in 1996 the owners were free to transfer to regular housing or sell the complex.

As it turned out, because hundreds of thousands of these units were built at the same time and would become available for sale at approximately the same time, massive sales would create a terrible shortage of low-cost housing. To solve the anticipated problem, the government offered us investors a new guaranteed loan. Again it would be repaid with federal subsidy funds. Most owners took the offer, as did I. In my case it meant that I received a check for $32,000 on my original $50,000 investment, plus I had all the tax benefits and I still owned my share of the complex.

Even so, things were looking bad. With the tax shelter deals that had gone wrong and my Naples real estate sales job not producing huge results, essentially I had an unsteady paycheck. Plus, I faced heavy financial obligations for alimony and child support.

Around this time I met a stock dealer by the name of Allen Edwards who approached me about putting together a group to acquire OMC. When I had left the company, I was extremely upset. I felt it was unfair that they had promised me that I would lead the South American division and then had passed me over three times. If I could find an outside investor or company to acquire OMC, I had visions of riding back into the company headquarters on my white horse.

I consulted my Uncle Jack, trustee for all the family trusts, which included 13 grandchildren. He felt it would be in the best interests of the family to diversify, a feeling shared by the Tampa Trust Bank. After some time we had about 8 percent of the stock committed to a block sale, and I felt confident we could come up with another 4 or 5 percent. We filed a 13d registration with the SEC and began the hunt for buyers. The road got rocky as soon as the directors of OMC learned of our plan. OMC made the defensive move to cut the dividend by 80 percent. At the same time, they took on debt they didn't need and offered all executives "golden parachutes." Meanwhile, the national economy was heading south along with the stock market. When we first filed our 13d registration, OMC stock was at $42. As time progressed, it sank to a low of $8.

To finance my tax shelter investments I had borrowed the funds from Continental Bank as a collateral loan. Now my collateral was disintegrating rapidly. The bank wanted to know how I was going to pay them back. I called my good friend Jack Larson, president of First National Bank of Naples. Jack reviewed my financial data and concluded that I would be like the federal government. I'd likely have a minimum deficit of $50,000 per year for several years. He promised me that his bank would loan me whatever my deficit was for the next three years. I had to promise him I would sell my OMC stock when the market improved and would use part of the proceeds to get out of debt except for my house payment, which was $494 per month. I also wrote Lorna and asked if I could defer some of the alimony payment. She and her lawyer agreed that I could defer only until the end of that calendar year. Times got really rough for a while.

Allen continued to search for a buyer for OMC to no avail. Finally, with the Reagan tax cut and tax reform, the economy turned around, and the stock market recovered. All the family trusts including mine sold all of our OMC stock at $40 to $42 per share. Also during this time Jack and I had convinced Continental Bank not to sell the OMC collateral at $8 per share.

I learned a hard lesson during those years, and from that day forward I followed the advice of Jack Larson. As soon as I had the money, I paid off all my debt and vowed never to get into major debt again. Cash was to be king. Also, I did not want to invade the principal of my investments; so, at the end of each year, if I had extra cash from dividends and earnings, I used it to pay down any mortgages on investment property. Furthermore, I built my home in Arroyo Hondo, New Mexico with cash. Once I sold my OMC stock, I never owned another share and I never looked back. By 1984, all was well again and I had recovered from a rather dismal financial period.

Now when I look back on those years, I understand why people say that when one door closes, another door opens. Amazingly, during this bleak time of financial struggle and despair following my leaving OMC in 1979, some of my old friends and former OMC employees called me with a proposal. They wanted to start a new business . . .

"Well, what kind of business?" I asked.

Well, they didn't know. Would I come to Miami to help them figure it out?

"Well, yeah," I answered. "I can do that."

AMERICAS
**TRADE & **
SUPPLY CO.

7630 N.W. 63ʳᵈ Street
Miami, Florida 33166
Phone: (305) 594-0797   Fax: (305) 592-8210

ATS business card

CHAPTER 32

ATS (1979–1993)

The day after I arrived in Miami during the fall of 1979, I found myself with Paul Butler and Ben Olsen from OMC sitting around together in Paul's home trying to come up with a business plan. Paul and Ben wanted to go into the boat rental business. There was a bid coming up to supply boats for Matheson Hammock Park on Key Biscayne. I thought that was a losing option because I felt it required too much capital and high liability insurance. Then too, people often abused rental boats and motors, which required continual maintenance.

I asked Paul and Ben how much capital they had to invest, and they said $1,000 each. Of course, that limited the choices of a new venture considerably. So, while we continued to discuss what business we could develop with $3,000, a friend of ours from Nassau walked in. Morton Turtle was a marine dealer. He was visiting Miami to buy parts and accessories for his customers. He carried a four-page list of things he needed, but he was having trouble. He had gone to Fort Lauderdale and Hialeah. Everyone there spoke Spanish, and he found it impossible to find his way around the streets in Hialeah that had Spanish names. He said he had spent two days searching for things and had accomplished only about 25 percent of what he needed to get done.

When we told Morton we were trying to start a business, he stared as us for a second. Then he said, "Well, while you're figuring out what to do, why don't you buy the items I need and charge me something for them? I've wasted enough time here! I need to get back to my shop in Nassau!"

Voila! In that instant, a new company was born—buying and selling parts. Now we needed a name. What would we call it? We settled on three criteria: one, it must have some export connotation; two, it must be at the beginning of the phone book; and three, it should be easy to remember. We came up with Americas Trade & Supply (ATS). Our company would appear first in the Yellow Pages!

Now, I can tell you this was a unique partnership. Paul was head of the gay coalition in Miami. Ben was a flower child of the 1960s and spoke fluent Spanish, having lived in Mexico for several years. I was an Ivy Leaguer from the corporate world. Our road to success proved bumpy.

We went through several offices. Our first was at Paul's home in the Grove with the telex machine located in his bedroom closet. After several months he found us an office in downtown Miami near the Miami River in the Jose Marti Building [43]. That office was a tough drug area, but the rent was cheap, and we could borrow another office when we needed it. However, the roof leaked and rainstorms produced mini floods. During the day we left boxes in the hall, because we had no room to work. By night, we stuffed them back in the offices. Ultimately, we found a new warehouse behind the county jail.

From the start, we added only 8 percent plus a $30 handling fee no matter the size of the order. We were off and running, but the first few years were difficult because we were undercapitalized. Slowly customers appeared from seemingly out of nowhere.

With no capital, we had to find a method to finance our sales until we got paid. Paul was an expert at negotiating credit from suppliers. Sometimes we got a break when our cash flow was non-existent, like the time a client asked us to sell his Chow

Lee [44] yacht for which we received $90,000 in two payments. We remitted the first half immediately, to the seller in Austria, but when time came around to send the second half, we were unable to locate the client, even though we tried diligently for several years. This incident actually saved the company.

Meanwhile, ATS experienced unique purchasing challenges, like buying trained guard dogs for our client's protection, acquiring arms for the Peruvian government, locating a complete portable landing system for Somalia for the CIA, and procuring bathroom fixtures for an apartment building in Hong Kong, where we beat out the local agent for Crane and American Standard on a landed cost.

One unusual request involved a child. In the late 1980s, our friend and now good customer Morton Turtle had a sister-in-law living in Fort Lauderdale who had problems in her life in addition to an 11-year-old son who was deaf. Morton called Paul to say that his sister-in-law had been arrested and was in jail for prostitution and possible drug charges. No one knew where the child was. Our job was to find the boy and get him on the 4 p.m. plane to Morton in Nassau.

ATS had an employee named Ivo Hodge who had been raised in New York City and was familiar with life on the streets. Ivo was tall and black. He had been born in the Commonwealth of Dominica and raised in the Bronx, New York. He possessed the ability to perform difficult tasks by not taking no for an answer. We sent Ivo to Fort Lauderdale carrying $500 for expenses. By spreading around a few dollars, he found the pimp in charge of Morton's sister-in-law. Ivo located the child and was back to Miami in plenty of time to get him on the airplane. Another successful ATS mission!

As Paul, Ben, and I had come from OMC, we naturally tried selling OMC parts and accessories. We could be of real service to OMC because we were able to get the parts to South America and the Caribbean quickly; also, we made sure all the necessary engine parts were sent at the same time. So many times a customer got pistons but no piston rings, for example. That did no good if the engine power head needed rebuilding. The ATS approach was to find all parts required. We called distributors and dealers to meet this goal. At one point we were buying more than $750,000 worth of OMC parts from Wright's in Seattle [45], which made us the largest parts dealer in the United States, even though we were the gray market (that is, not factory appointed to buy from an authorized agent and resell). Eventually OMC intimidated Wright's and all other distributors, and that source was closed down for us.

Working for ATS was never dull. At one point we sent compressor parts via taxicabs and Continental Airlines to Mullet Bay Resort [46] in Sint Maarten. We had a customer in the oil-producing region of Peru, who was also a specialist in the gray market. If he wanted to represent a company, he would simply print up a letterhead. We had a flap with Crane because they did not want to sell to us directly the valves worth several thousand dollars urgently needed to repair a major oil pipeline. Crane claimed we were not an authorized agent, even though we explained in great detail that our man in Peru would get the order because he had connections with the government. (In South America, this meant he knew whose palms to grease.) Our agent solved the problem by getting Crane valves removed from the approved list of suppliers, so we could instead buy Jenkins valves from the UK.

Another time we survived a massive IRS audit with limited expense. The audit made us very nervous. We were paying our largest customer's purchasing agent a 15 percent commission, which was then paid offshore. At the time there was a real question of whether this was allowed under U.S. law. To make this a bit dicey, we entered it in our books as "camel chow." In return the customer made sure that his hotel always maintained at least $200,000 on deposit with us. (In other words, they became our bank line of credit when we desperately needed it.)

And finally—an unusual assignment, indeed—we arranged a party including feminine companionship for a general in the Surinam Navy [47] for which we were rewarded with a deposit of $40,000 from a briefcase, counted out in twenties before our very eyes!

One incident during my ATS career afforded a moment in the presence of a world leader. In the early 1980s, Paul and I went to Jamaica with Ferdinand Mahfood, founder of Food for the Poor [48], a respected charity helping the poor in Jamaica and Haiti. We stayed in his mother's home in the mountains outside Kingston. We got there on Sunday, and Ferdinand invited us to go to church. This was a surprise, because the service seemed to be some type of witchcraft as people prayed in "tongues." The following Monday we encountered another surprise. Ferdinand mentioned that Fidel Castro was in town. Would we like to meet him?

Naturally, I said yes, having heard so much about the communist leader of Cuba. We waited more than two hours in a hotel lobby crowded with Jamaicans to greet him. When he arrived, the crowd dropped to their knees, praying and grabbing his clothes. I was astonished at how charismatic he was even to this conservative American. That was a once-in-a-lifetime event I'll never forget.

My last project for ATS in 1986 brought me real satisfaction when we helped a customer in St. Lucia to manufacture bleach [49] locally. We bought the product ingredients and a plastic extruder to manufacture bottled containers. We also provided technical support. This task was my baby, and I'm happy to say that after about nine months we had the plant up and running. It became a huge success as everyone on the islands uses bleach.

In 1993, I sold my interest in ATS and Four Star Cargo to my partners, Ben and Paul. Four Star Cargo was our freight consolidating and forwarding division. This was an important adjunct to ATS because it allowed us to control our number one market, Sint Maarten. We could purchase the product, pack it, and ship it by air or sea, making a profit all along the way. Thus, we had the whole enchilada! From the sale of these two companies, I made a nice profit, and I was pleased. I truly enjoyed my time with ATS; I just wanted out of Miami, and ATS required long hours on the phone if I was to be fair to my partners. By now, I had made other investments, specifically in a restaurant, and it was doing well.

Despite our off-the-cuff style at the beginning and our innovative scrambling approach to solving problems, I am proud to say that ATS is still thriving some 35 years later, and it is still owned by my two former partners. Founded in 1979 as a general export company, today ATS and Four Star Cargo are primarily a freight forwarding company because the Internet has changed how companies and individuals shop, no matter where they live in the world. Since its beginning, ATS has evolved into a highly successful business, having gone global from primarily serving the Caribbean and Latin America.

In retrospect, I feel that we offered our clients something special in a highly competitive business, especially in cities like Miami and New York. What set us apart and made us successful? Several things:

First, honesty and integrity. We always provided our clients with our original invoices that showed just an 8 percent mark up. Most purchasing agents charged whatever they could get away with.

Second, filling complete orders the first time whenever possible. If a client was repairing a mechanical item, only partial shipment was not acceptable; however, this is what large corporation would do. We always bought as much as possible at the best price, but we would pay retail if required to repair an automobile engine, hotel equipment, or other things.

Third, fast service. For example, a typical marine or auto parts order from overseas would have to go from the domestic factory to the export division and then may only be partially filled, sometimes taking weeks. With our ability to scavenge for parts, we could move much faster than our competition.

Fourth, personal relationships. We intimately knew most of our clients' families and always entertained them when they were in Miami.

Fifth, superior and frequent communications through telex at the time.

Sixth, our willingness to buy whatever the customer wanted—except drugs and illegal arms. This meant one-stop shopping with people you trusted.

And seventh, extension of credit. Because of our personal relationships, we could extend credit more easily than large corporations, which required payment in advance or an LC (letter of credit).

Today, ATS does business on all five continents. That makes me proud. Also, personally, I am proud of the fact that, like Pops, my esteemed grandfather Briggs, who started Briggs & Stratton, I was a founding principal in a productive and lasting business enterprise.

If you research business history in the United States, you will find that many prosperous Americans, including Steve Jobs and Steve Wozniak of Apple Computer (now Apple, Inc.), Bill Hewlett and David Packard (Hewlett-Packard), and Walt Disney of Disney Studios, among others, got their start in a household garage. While this is not to say I'm in their league, it does make for good company.

After all, ATS got its start in a humble apartment in Miami, and it became an international success.

Steve and Doris on their wedding day, October 26, 1984

CHAPTER 33

Turn That Boat Around (1982)

Brave the lonesome wind
Sail the cold deep water
Brave the lonesome wind
Sail the cold deep water
The wind will see them home
The sea will do no harm
Turn that boat around

The lyrics above are from "Turn that Boat Around" [50], a song by the Rankin Family, an award-winning Canadian family group from Mabou, Nova Scotia, made up of 12 siblings who have been singing since 1989. I particularly like the words to this song. It suggests the inevitable turning around that we all have to do in life when we get stuck—whether stranded in a cove, beached on a shoal, or adrift in the ocean. At those times we have to reverse course, tack one way or another, turn that boat around, and try another direction.

In 1982 at the age of 46, I was ready to end my seven years of midlife single status. I wanted to move on to a more worthwhile existence. I will say my encounters with the women I dated during those years were mostly pleasant, involving boating adventures in my 23-foot Seacraft, ski trips in the Rocky Mountains, and travels as far away as Brazil.

In 1979, I thought I was in love and remarried, but that ill-fated event—a rebound encounter—lasted only six months. So, as time went by, I found playing the field entertaining, yes, but lacking the substance and commitment I was looking for in what could be a lasting relationship.

Since 1974 I had changed, and so had the lives of my children. Shelley had graduated from Hotchkiss in 1981, Sandy was due to graduate from Colorado College in June 1982, and Stephen was looking to finish at South Kent by 1984. They were on their way with their individual lives, and while we continued to see each other and vacation together, I watched them begin to form solid relationships to chart their own voyages.

Also, thankfully, my health had improved and was not so precarious. My disappointment over leaving OMC had healed, and my ventures with both ATS and my investments in real estate were growing and profitable. All in all, these life factors aligned as just the right combination to usher in a new era with Doris as my companion, best friend, wife, and life partner.

Life can turn on a dime. This time, my life turned in a board meeting. Doris and I met because we were two of six partners who owned a large old mill complex called the Sawyer Mill [51] in Dover, New Hampshire. We saw each other occasionally at board meetings. By the spring of 1982, we were both free of previous commitments and entanglements. At the meeting she mentioned she had spent the previous winter miserably in frigid Massachusetts where she was currently living. I graciously convinced her to visit me in sunny Naples for a few days in March, which she did. This was the beginning . . .

She visited me once more that spring but decided she wanted to cool the relationship a bit. I took this as a creative challenge. As someone who loved fishing, I knew to make a catch I needed an irresistible hook. *Hmmm.* I began to think . . . Doris was a horse lover . . . I had a close friend who was a Kentucky Colonel, a title of honor in that state. He had a box for the Kentucky Derby. Aha! Problem solved! I invited Doris, and we shared a fabulous weekend attending the races in style and being invited to all the special parties.

Still, she was not quite on board. By that summer Doris was not convinced she wanted me in her territory. This time I became not only creative but also persistent. I sent telegrams, flowers, and made phone calls. And, amazingly, she invited me up for the summer in Wolfeboro, New Hampshire, where she had owned a cottage for many years.

During this period I was spending a great deal of time in Miami working at ATS. I needed an apartment there, especially if Doris was going to spend time in Miami. We found a nice two-bedroom unit located off 107th Avenue, S.W., in Sweetwater. On her visits sometimes she would come to ATS with me for several hours. We put her to work purchasing everything from trained guard dogs to tomatoes. She broadened her Miami experience by volunteering with Mother Teresa's Missionaries of Charity (at this time they operated only out of their small home in the center of Liberty City). Doris was amazed by the nuns' sense of order and simple life. They were faithfully disciplined to a daily routine of work, prayer, and recreation, no matter what happened in the world around them.

In October 1984, Doris and I were married at Glen Magna Farms, an 11-acre site owned by the Danvers Historical Society, founded in 1889, in Danvers, Massachusetts. Even though it rained that day, the historic gardens and mansion at Glen Magna Farms were beautiful, representing the best of America's North Shore summer living. The service was special with just our immediate family and close friends attending.

Over the years, Doris and I have been involved in real estate ventures. A few were highly profitable; others were disastrous.

On Black Monday 1987, the stock market crashed, and a major bank crisis followed. Several well-known banks folded or were ordered to merge by the Federal Deposit Insurance Corporation (FDIC). The FDIC's mission is to maintain the stability of the nation's banking system. Doris and I were caught in the calamity by our two partnership interests in major properties in Portsmouth, New Hampshire. One we resolved by convincing all partners to pony up and pay off the bank. The other one became a real mess.

In the case of the Executive Center, the venture that went south, we had never missed a payment, and the bank had agreed to renew our loan. When we were ready to sign the papers, however, we learned our banking officer was no longer there and our loan had been turned over to the FDIC. The FDIC bought the bank's portfolio and placed it with a bank in Ireland. But at the end of a couple of years, the Irish bank was allowed to "put" the loans back with the FDIC. Ours was one of those. As a result, the FDIC took over the Executive Center property and advised us they would auction it off and any shortfall would be the responsibility of the partners. Imagine our surprise when we saw a half-page ad for our property in the *Wall Street Journal!* At the last minute the partners were able to raise funds and pay off the FDIC ... but not without some arm-twisting and eloquent name bashing of the federal government!

Not one to lose her perspective during this time, Doris, a few months later, arranged two events with two couples, major real estate developers, who had been badly damaged by the bank crisis. The idea was to realize how thankful we should be for what we had—not disgruntled by what we had lost. The first event involved helping others. Doris volunteered us all to serve dinner at the local soup kitchen. Fair enough. But when we arrived at the kitchen to serve, people asked, "Where's the dinner?"

Ooops! That part had not been made clear. We thought we were only serving and a church group would provide the meal.

Immediately, we told the soup kitchen staff to "keep the natives calm," and we'd return in 30 minutes. Off we went to Kentucky Fried Chicken to explain that we needed 75 dinners PDQ! The owner of the franchise was great. He closed the store while he took care of our order. We delivered the dinners back to the soup kitchen to feed the multitudes, and I must say, just seeing those people smile made me thankful.

That same evening at home, Doris had set out tin plates and cups with plastic utensils on our outside deck for the two real estate couples and ourselves. Our menu was simply hot dogs and beans! She had set up an easel with paper on which we were to write what we were thankful for, despite our major financial reversal.

Next, she served dessert in our formal dining room on our best china, using our best crystal filled with fine French champagne. Acknowledging the contrast between supper's meager fare and dessert's sumptuous offering, our friend David Prolman stood up to make a toast. Raising his bubbling champagne flute he said, "I have been rich, and I have been poor. However, I prefer being rich!" We all shouted a hearty "Hear! Hear!" to that. After dessert, we were set to play Monopoly, the board game of chance designed during the Great Depression in the 1930s. But we were all so tired we just went to bed.

It felt soothing to crawl under the covers. Doris and I had learned that life has ups and downs. We both had experienced trauma independently; now, whatever storm came our way, we knew we would face it together—what a good feeling that was! Doris smiled at me as I reached to turn off the bedside lamp.

Old Naples Pub, opened December 1990

CHAPTER 34

The Restaurant Entrepreneur (1990)

I n the spring of 1990, I was in Naples having lunch with a
friend of mine, Don Flock, who was complaining, "There are
no casual, inexpensive places for us locals to eat! There's no place to
have fun!"

By the time we had finished lunch, Don had convinced me
that we should open a pub in Old Naples. What a great idea!
The scheme was to get 20 people with similar feelings each to
put in $5,000 to build a small pub for the enjoyment of people
in the area. After talking to dozens of prospects, we could not
find 20 investors. In fact, when it came time to sign the lease
and begin construction, there were only three of us. I put in
$30,000. We financed the equipment and the total investment
came to $75,000, with my partners Don and Tim Flock doing
the construction and design to earn their shares of stock in the
venture. Still, we were short of funds. Don took care of that
problem. Using his imagination and negotiating skills, he worked
out all sorts of deals for materials and decorating in exchange for
future meals.

We needed a manager in exchange for stock, and Don
found us one, a restaurant operator named Joe. Unfortunately,
as we got closer to the opening in November 1990, we were
getting mixed reports on Joe's ability, his operating methods, and
his philosophy. Red flags were flying. But what could we do?

We were at the point of no return. I was still basically a working partner with ATS, spending three or four days a week in Miami. My partners were full-time architects, staff was in place, and we had signed a five-year lease. My partners wanted to get started. Thus, we had no choice but to take our chances with Joe.

In early December 1990, the Old Naples Pub opened on schedule. Early on we became nervous because there were few customers and we could not afford advertising. Dinner was the worst time of the day, as many evenings you could shoot a loaded cannon through the restaurant and not hit a soul.

We wanted the pub to be small and cozy, with a horseshoe bar to lend a friendly, casual atmosphere. We had about 1,150 square feet with the kitchen occupying 250 square feet. We had 49 seats. We obtained only a beer and wine license, because our desire was to be a pub in the English tradition. By January, Joe had some basic differences with the rest of us. From the start, Don was a stickler in making sure we complied with all federal and local regulations. This applied directly to the handling of cash and the payment of wages. His feeling was, "Everything must be above board and go through the company books."

Friends of ours reported that the bartender, Joe's girlfriend, was serving drinks that were paid for but never rung up. We confronted her and she denied it. Then we experienced a couple of weeks in which dimes mysteriously jammed our receipt printer. By February, we knew we had to dismiss Joe. Not a pretty scene.

Don, Tim, and I got together to assess the situation. We agreed that we could not afford to pump money into the restaurant during the summer. The restaurant business in Florida generally suffers in the summer, and the warm season was coming up. Furthermore, we didn't think anybody would buy a new restaurant with summer coming on. In desperation, I tried to give the pub away to my local friends in the food and beverage business. No luck.

Finally, we had an idea. We called in our top three employees, the two bartenders, and the kitchen manager, who we felt were honest. We explained our problem: "We have no experience in the restaurant business. We have no time to learn it and no time to get involved. Can you guys run this restaurant?"

They nodded, "Yes."

We admonished them, "You must run it with cash in the drawer. Can you manage that?"

Again they nodded.

How do you spell relief? Eureka! This was our turning point from which we have never looked back. After the first couple of years under their management, the pub has always earned several times its investment. The Old Naples Pub opened in 1990 and the Village Pub in 1995, and both continue to be very successful. There are reasons for this. Having been in the restaurant business now for more than two decades, I can tell you that statistics show only one in ten make it.

Analyzing our successful food and beverage enterprises, I think we owed our success to several factors. First, both of these restaurants are located in a high rent area where all our competitors are much more expensive. Second, we are blessed with a fine staff, and many have been with us 15 or 20 years. Third, our staff is empowered to make decisions with a minimum of interference from us owners.

Generally speaking, theft is a significant problem in restaurants. It's extremely hard to detect, and most owners feel they have to be on location 24/7 to catch a thief. Our approach is different. We believe in developing a culture where stealing is not only unacceptable to the majority of the staff, it also becomes self-policing. We as owners have never uncovered thefts that have occurred. Rather, restaurant workers turn in all thieves, since the honest folks don't want to jeopardize their own jobs; furthermore, they feel a personal ownership in the business.

One of the amazing aspects contributing to our success is that our kitchen staff has had virtually no turnover in 15 years. Why? Well, when we replaced our American kitchen staff, we hired recent immigrants. At one of our locations the staff is comprised of Mexicans. At another location we hired all Salvadorians. We learned that you couldn't mix nationalities, because each feels better than the other. These immigrants have a strong work ethic, and they feel they are part of the American Dream. Also, there is almost no absenteeism. If they are going to a concert or if they are heading back to their country of origin for a visit, they just contact a relative, "Cousin Juan," usually in Houston. They send him a menu and a recipe book. When we go into the kitchen, we don't even realize our employee is gone: "Juan" flies over and fits right in with his relatives! One other critical factor is that in their home countries, there is no welfare! Consequently, these people know how to work!

Over the years, we have opened and closed four other restaurant locations. We've learned the importance of staying small, being in high-traffic areas, keeping to the original concept, and giving the customers what they want. So, what have we learned about failure? I'll take those stories one by one . . .

BACKSTAGE

Located in Waterside Shopping Center in Naples, Backstage was a jazz club with only 50 inside seats. The squatters killed us. They would spend no money, yet they occupied a table for the whole evening. The restaurant was small, and local musicians joining in took up to 20 percent of our restaurant. We paid three or four musicians; however, sometimes we ended up with eight or ten along with their friends and family. These constituted a major portion of the squatters. Also the jam sessions, which included sit-ins who played and their family and friends, consumed a large amount of capacity. Lastly, we had no cover charge because the locals would not pay it and there was no minimum required for food and beverages. So the ratio of true patrons to the overall attendees was too small to maintain the business and, along with a low average check, went far toward explaining this venture's lack of success.

THE LIBRARY

This restaurant, which we opened in 1991 in Cashiers, North Carolina, in Sapphire Valley, had the potential to be our best store. Unfortunately, our local partner in that venture was dishonest; he never built the culture of trust and integrity needed to be successful. We sold The Library in 1993.

NAPLES BREW PUB

We located this restaurant on the "wrong side of the tracks." It was in a shopping mall that had no movie theatre. For some reason our clientele basically did not frequent businesses that were east of the Trail (US 41). Even the banks made sure they were on the west side. Let's face it—we just couldn't give this demographic profile what they wanted at their price range.

THE ISLAND PUB

Guests loved this place; however, it was in a poor location in Naples, west of US 41 in the middle of Park Shore Resort, which was difficult to find. As a result, we were forced to discount and subsidize our guests to attract them. Although profitable in its later years, it was not worth the effort required, and our other two stores suffered from lack of attention

In business, as in most things in life, you learn from your mistakes. As I write this, our successful restaurants, Old Naples Pub and the Village Pub, have been in business 24 and 19 years, respectively, with returns well above 15 percent on sales.

This puts them among the top 10 percent of restaurants in the United States.

When I told Doris in the summer of 1990 that I was going into the restaurant business, she said, "You are crazy! What do you know about restaurants except how to eat there?" She also pointed out that most restaurants not only failed but also they can burn through a lot of cash in the process, and I represented the major financial component. Today Doris is very pleased with my monthly distribution that is more than twice my top salary at OMC. In addition, we are usually able to declare a nice bonus right around tax time.

Continuing to thrive, these establishments represent a two-in-six win in a one-in-ten game, so to speak. Overall, our entrepreneurial attempts have paid off. I attribute our restaurant victories to the loyalty and consistency of the staff, the locations, the staff empowerment, and the high morals and ethical standards of our employees. In addition, several years ago Don, Tim, and I decided we needed to make our general manager, Kent Schooley, a full partner, so we offered him stock at a major discount for which he had seven years to pay. He has now been with us more than 20 years, having started as a cook at Backstage.

As owners we also adopted some basic principles that allow small entrepreneurs to succeed in a very competitive environment. First, our motto and mission was, "Give our guests what they want." In addition, we focus on the three Ps—People, Place, and Product. Remember, the most affordable marketing tool with the greatest effect is four-walls marketing; that is, what happens within your four walls. Restaurant guests vote with their feet! In short, my life lesson learned here was, and is, if you hire ethical people, you are able to trust them. That's a reward in itself.

SECTION IV
The Stern

My best friend and hiking buddy Peter near Arrowtown, New Zealand, prior to backpacking the Routeburn and Greenstone

CHAPTER 35

Travel, Taos, and Backpacking
(1984–2001)

Following our marriage in 1984, Doris and I hit the road traveling. During the next three years, we visited some fabulous places. There was St. Lucia, with its palm-fringed Caribbean beaches, lapped by turquoise waters; Charleston, South Carolina, with its straw market craftsmen, African Americans who speak a Creole language called Gullah; and Switzerland, where we traveled all over the country and saw the Alps, still snow-capped in spring. We journeyed to England for my goddaughter, Anna Alexander's, christening in 1986. For my 50th birthday, Doris gave me a trip to Europe on the Concorde [52] and a return on the QE 2 [53]. While in the UK we had a marvelous trip to Bath and back on a replica of the Orient Express [54].

Then on a spring vacation in 1987, Doris and I drove to Taos from Santa Fe, New Mexico. Because of her interest in horses, we took a ride up to the Lobo Ranch, which is a fabulous place with outstanding views. Located about 15 miles north of Taos in Arroyo Hondo, the ranch is approached by a steep, private dirt road winding up a sharp incline to 7,500 feet. There were no houses in sight, only breathtaking views of the Sangre de Cristo Mountains with the tallest peak towering at 13,200 feet. When we toured the ranch and took in the limitless view of towering mountains, the never-ending forest known as Kit Carson, and the vast blue sky, Doris turned to me and said, "This place is the closest I will ever get to heaven."

Because we both were so taken with the area, upon returning to Naples I called the owner, Phil DeCaro, and asked if any land was for sale. It's hard to believe, but we bought 16 acres over the phone and later added another 10 acres. (Actually, I didn't tell Doris about the purchase for several days, and this was very unusual as we conferred jointly on everything—even what we were having for dinner.) Our 26 acres were one-half mile from a neighbor; the closest visible rooftop was two miles away. As an added bonus, the property bordered Kit Carson Forest, which spread across one million acres of government land.

We built an adobe style home that we finished just in time for Doris's birthday in 1989. Adobe homes are not very pretty from the outside. In fact, there is a Spanish saying, "Don't judge me by the exterior. Come into my home first." And once you've visited that area of the country, you understand perfectly what that saying means.

Taos was a few miles away, and we fell in love with the town for its diversity, its sheer beauty, the amenities offered such as hiking and skiing, its wonderful art, and its good restaurants. As an additional delight, we could ride horses from our house for miles without ever retracing our paths. Naturally, it was not long before Doris had acquired a horse and a small corral with a run-in shed. During the next several years we spent the spring and fall seasons there in our adobe home, along with Christmas, when we went snow skiing. It's hard to imagine a more perfect spot.

In the 1990s, my good friend Ben Carp from Taos convinced me to exchange hiking, which had been my interest for more than a decade, for backpacking—his sport of choice.

During my middle and late 40s, I had done a great deal of hiking, including the mountains of Switzerland. These were mostly day hikes with only a small pack for lunch. Our Australian shepherd Caramia accompanied me on most of my hiking stateside; she and I covered probably 6,500 miles during her lifetime.

Because of my experience hiking, Ben thought I'd be a natural at backpacking; so, at great expense, I purchased the gear. Now, I'll tell you I had my doubts about this sport. Was it really going to be fun? Ben assured me so. And to prove it, he took me on a trial run—an overnight into Bandelier Park near Santa Fe. What a trip! The weather was miserable, the hiking difficult, and the pouring rain leaked through our tent and nearly washed it away! With such a great start, Ben said I was ready for the Grand Canyon, which didn't make sense. Hiking the canyon is strenuous, and Ben had given me a C– on my first backpacking endeavor on much easier terrain. But, given his enthusiasm, who was I to complain?

Ben could have chosen an easy trail like Bright Angel, but, oh no! Instead, he set us up for a six-day adventure on the Escalante. Considered a wilderness hike with no maps and limited access, this trail is for experienced hikers only. There is no water available until you reach the bottom of the canyon, so you are required to carry at least six quarts, which limits room for other gear and food. In early October we were up before dawn packing and re-packing our backpacks. That morning it was snowing; and off we went on my first backpacking voyage. As it turned out we learned the temperature would be more than 90 degrees when we reached the Colorado River at the canyon bottom. That would be after an eight-hour hike down the canyon sides. With such knowledge I could hardly wait to begin . . . (I'm kidding.)

Within the first hour of this trip I must have fallen at least 12 times. I was scared, and I was tired. Ben stuck with me, offering encouragement and advice. My pack was killing me, as it kept shifting from side to side with every step. At 55 pounds it was way too heavy. I have learned since that you should carry no more than 26 pounds, not counting food. Into the second hour, the soles of my expensive, brand new boots came off. We used duct tape to bind them back on. By hour five of this "fun" adventure, I thought I was going to die. I had four hours ahead of me, and all I wanted to do was to sit down and cry. Oh how I wished I was at home in my easy chair!

By some miracle, I made it to the bottom. Like many others who take on this journey, I had developed the "Grand Canyon Shuffle," which means you are not able to walk; rather, you just shuffle along. The morning after we arrived we woke up and went on a short hike above the river along a very narrow trail with a 100-foot drop to the river. All you could do was place one foot before the other. As I stepped gingerly, I remembered Doris's parting words to Ben, "Please do not risk his life! I want him back alive!" Along the way, the challenges seemed beyond my capability. One time we lost the trail, necessitating a two-hour detour in a direction that was mostly up.

We found a lunch spot along the river to enjoy our "gorp" (good old raisins and peanuts). Our trail mix was a bit more gourmet, but you get the idea. I sat there, eating slowly, gazing at the views. In my musing state, I vaguely became aware that I could not see any cairns; that is, man-made piles or stacks of stones built to mark the summits of mountains and hiking trails. That concerned me. But another hiking buddy named Perry pointed to a cairn at the top of a cliff about 200 feet above us. Oh, dear. I swallowed the lump in my throat. That was our next challenge. I was weary already. Even without a backpack I could not get excited about this new challenge. Yet I was about to take it on with a pack weighing 50 pounds! But there was no turning back.

Gingerly we ascended most of the way. We arrived at a ledge and there we slipped off our packs. We made the last 25-foot climb by using small hand- and footholds, and then pulling up our packs on a rope. During this terrifying ordeal I could not look down to the river below until we were safely on top.

By late afternoon we arrived at a landslide area, all scree; that is, it was covered with broken rock fragments that accumulate at the base of crags, mountain cliffs, or valley shoulders. The rubble is caused by periodic rock fall from adjacent cliff faces. The landslide area was also quite steep and slippery. Ben found this difficult. I said, "It's a cake walk to me! The worst that can happen is I slide to the canyon bottom on the scree. At least I won't fall off the edge!"

During a canyon hike, in addition to learning survival tactics, you also realize you must share your supplies with the local residents—small desert mice. Rangers advise people to take about 10 percent extra food for these critters. Even though we hung our packs at night, the mice managed to find and eat their dinners. We were told not to close food packs tightly, as the mice would chew through the containers.

All these discoveries you unearth—and more. On our last night of backpacking in the canyon, we camped about halfway up on the Tonto Plateau, having come over on the Tanner and the Escalante. As a concession to weight, we left our tents at the top, since in November it seldom rained. After supper, Ben and Perry moved about 50 feet away from where we had eaten our supper to set out their sleeping bags. I thought that was foolish, because the area where we had eaten our supper was far smoother and less rocky than the one to which they'd moved. Nevertheless, we all settled down to sleep. In the middle of the night I dreamt that a mouse was chewing on my thumbnail. Wow! I woke up and discovered it was no dream! There he sat, nibbling and staring through bright brown eyes! I flicked him off, realizing some peanut butter under my fingernails had attracted him. I rolled over and went back to sleep. But, once again, I was disturbed by nightmares of mice—this time in my sleeping bag and running over my face. I woke up again to discover the persistent varmints celebrating with a lively all-night party! They wanted me to participate! *Now* I knew why Ben and Perry had kept their distance from the eating area. *Now* I knew why one does not sleep where everyone eats!

Early on the last morning we hiked to the rim of the canyon. Back to civilization at last, we went to breakfast, where I ordered a large omelet, sausage, and a cold beer. Next I was off to a hot shower before heading back to Taos. My first Grand Canyon trip was a true leaning adventure; if nothing else, next time I'd pack much lighter!

Ben, Perry, and I hiked the Grand Canyon three or four more times, including a hike down to the bottom, where we went on a 10-day rubber raft trip on the Colorado River. On this trip, everything we carried in had to be packed out—all human waste, bits of burned wood left from evening fires—everything. At the campsites two portable toilets were set up for use in the evenings; in the morning they were sealed and loaded back into a rubber supply raft.

In terms of equipment, I made one huge mistake. I took along sneakers for the raft, but always these rafts had between two and six inches of 45- to 50-degree water sloshing around in the bottom. Smarter folks had worn rubber boots like those used with wet suits. Live and learn, once again.

Along our journey we found the whitewater rapids that we had to navigate absolutely spectacular. Sometimes they were scary, especially one that dropped 35 feet! And speaking of scary, one day Perry and another river runner were packed into the small rubber ducky when they capsized near a huge boulder. The current swirled around them, pulling them under twice. I though Perry was not going to pop back up! However, they both made it out of the river safely, thank goodness. Throughout the days, the sunlight flickered along the canyon walls, changing color around every bend. It was magical. Having hiked the sides of the canyon, it was wonderful to cover so much of it that is only accessible by a rubber raft.

During the intervening years, Ben, Perry, my closest friend Peter Ordway, and I continued our journeys. We backpacked across England. We took on the Routeburn Track and the Greenstone on the South Island of New Zealand. Routeburn is a sister hike to the Milford Sound track, which is the dream of serious wilderness hikers. There were other wonderful trips with Doris, including one through the Cinque Terre in Italy with its brightly colored fishing villages perched on cliffs overlooking the Mediterranean Sea—truly some of the most breathtaking coastal scenery in all of Italy.

We went on a cross-England walk, Wainwright's Walk and the Wealdway through hundred-acre forest, where we caught up with Pooh, Tigger, and Piglet lore! I made several hut-to-hut hikes, spending nights in the towering White Mountains in New Hampshire with not only my hiking buddies but also my daughters and grandchildren. We took in part of the Appalachian Trail, which is more than 2,000 miles from Georgia to Maine.

Switzerland was by far my most favorite place to hike. I made four trips to Kandersteg in the canton of Bern, noted for its spectacular mountain scenery and sylvan alpine landscapes. Mostly agricultural, the area was relatively undiscovered by foreigners, and it offered spectacular scenery every day. An added benefit was that you are never far from a gourmet meal that included beer and wine from a Gasthaus along the trail. Plus, there was an escape route by lift, tram, or gondola. The trails ranged from easy to difficult and included a long hike up to a spectacular glacier.

With so many joyous journeys, I suppose it is inevitable
to go through a sad passage, and that's what happened in 2001
when Peter and I took one last hike together.

Peter and I had known each other since grade school. His
family and mine were the best of friends. After high school,
though, we went our separate ways, and I did not see him
again until I bought my home in Naples, Florida, in 1978. He
lived right behind me, so we spent a lot of time together. He
encouraged my interest in hiking, and in the early 1980s we
went on a 10-day excursion of day hikes in the Sils Maria area of
Switzerland overlooking Lake Sils.

After the Switzerland trip, we enjoyed more memorable
hikes, including a hut-to-hut adventure in which we stopped
along the way at shelters with prepared meals in the White
Mountains. We took trips through Switzerland, and went
backpacking in New Zealand on the Routeburn and the
Greenstone. We didn't make the quota for The Milford, but we
learned later that The Milford hikers had been helicoptered out
since they were in water up to their waists. That area of New
Zealand averages 300 inches of rain a year.

Our most rewarding trip involved almost no hiking. In
September 2001, Peter was in the final stages of losing his battle
with cancer. Not giving in, however, he insisted on one final
adventure to our favorite area, Kandersteg, Switzerland. Up until
the last minute, his wife tried to convince him just to go to the
White Mountains for a day hike. Nope. Peter would have none
of that, insisting he could make it to Switzerland. Originally,
we were scheduled to leave on that fateful day of September
11, 2001. Unable to depart because of the national emergency
created by terrorists, we got on our way two days later.

Upon landing in Zurich we missed the train to Kandersteg, because Peter insisted on carrying his 35-pound pack along with a daypack, and he could only walk a short distance before having to rest. In Kandersteg our hotel was just a block away; he insisted on walking it with all of his gear. That block took us a half hour and Peter was exhausted. Up early the next day, we started for the lift, but Peter made it only a few yards before he had to return to his room—very weak and in severe pain. He said, "Go on, Steve," but, except for brief hikes while he slept, I didn't. This pitiful scenario repeated itself for several days. It broke my heart to see his distress. He had been such a strong hiker and outdoorsman all his life.

On our last day in Kandersteg, I went out and bought two bottles of the best red wine I could find and several types of gourmet cheeses plus some wonderful French bread. With all my purchases in hand I said, "Come hell or high water, Peter, we're going hiking!" And it was so. After about an hour and a half, we sat down at a picnic bench in a park only a few hundred yards from our hotel. The next day, we endured a challenging trip back to the States.

During the previous year, I had been Peter's health care advocate, since his wife had difficulty going to Boston to confer with his doctors. Peter made me promise that—no matter what—I was in charge of seeing that he was in no pain. Since I had been through my own cancer episode in 1975, with a recurrence in 1986, I found this a difficult task. A couple of months after our Swiss trip, hospice came into his home and administered morphine for pain. Several times he called me at all hours of the night at my home in Naples. He was only partially coherent, but he insisted that I fly to New Hampshire to be with him. Of course, I did.

During his final days, he told me we had to make repairs on the sails of his boat. We had sailed together since 1988. In the Bahamas we almost got shot when we anchored off Norman's Cay in the channel used by drug smugglers on their way to Florida. In addition to these escapades, we spent 10 days sailing the coast of Maine every summer for eight or nine years. Now, bedridden and very weak, his mind was telling him to repair his sails. I suppose, in some way, he was getting ready for his final journey . . . I don't know. But even now, as I think about it, I get choked up and hardly can type these words through my tears.

To make the repairs he wanted, I had to use some ingenuity to comply with his demands, so I borrowed his wife's sewing kit and some cloth. That way we could make the repairs at his bedside. After that, he insisted that I help him up to pack his gear so we could go for a hike. With no way to talk him out of it, I began packing alongside him, and that took several hours.

Ready finally, we headed toward the door when I tried one last tactic. "Peter," I said, "we're heading into a blizzard. I suggest we postpone our adventure for a day or so." He looked me over earnestly and nodded. My words had convinced him, even though it was a lovely fall day in November 2001.

Within a few days, my very best friend was gone.

Max, Doris, Ivy, and Serena

CHAPTER 36

Other Loves: Cats, Dogs

Like many American families, ours always had animal
companions. When Doris and I married, all of our
children were grown. So we adopted a few lovable, irascible,
and entertaining four-footed family members, all of which were
individuals, to say the least. Their list of names to me is a roll call of
superior companionship . . . Max, Serena, Ivy, and Lady. Here are a
few stories about some of them.

Foster presented himself to us during the spring of 1991.
He emerged surprisingly while foraging our compost pile near
our home in Taos. Now in my experience, cats present challenges.
They whine, they don't mind, and they are not as satisfactory as a
dog. Foster whisked away my prejudices by acting like a dog: He
came when called; he followed us around; he didn't whine unless
he wanted a little tuna fish or people food. In short, he was a
fantastic addition to our family. As a result, Foster traveled with
us on more than 60 airplane rides and most of our camping RV
trips [55] through America's national parks, using up most of his
nine lives. During his last several years he spent evenings curled
up next to Doris or me, and when he left us for his tenth life in
the hereafter, we thought we'd never get over it.

Our dog Caramia helped us with Foster's leaving. In fact,
she set a new standard for me for the bond of respect that can
develop between animals and humans. From the start, though,

I was not thrilled about adopting her. We were attending a dinner party in Taos in April 1995 when Doris was persuaded to take home an Aussie shepherd named Caramia. I was less than enthusiastic over the idea. Immediately I was in for surprises. What I looked upon grudgingly as a pain in the neck, Caramia interpreted enthusiastically as companionship. She was definitely Doris's dog; however, she wormed her way into my heart and assumed responsibility for me! With Doris, she was the same, going out with my wife and her horse for a morning ride, resting awhile, and then taking off with me on an afternoon hike. As I mentioned earlier, during her lifetime, Caramia and I traveled more than 6,500 miles, enjoying hours of each other's company over and above our habitual existence at home.

Many was the time I thought she had taken one too many risks. When she was barely a one-year-old pup she chased a stick down the Rio Grande River. She got caught in the rapids and disappeared. Oh, no! I thought. But after two or three minutes, she surfaced on the riverbank, drenched and shaking. Another time she charged ahead of me to cross a rapidly flowing stream on three logs. The stream dropped 10 feet below us. Caramia slipped, and this time I just knew she was gone. But no. Using her front paws she somehow climbed back up on top of the logs. What a dog!

Taking risks seemed part of her nature. Being an Aussie, while she trotted along with Doris and me on horseback, Caramia frequently would duck out of sight—hot on the trail of a deer or rabbit, just for the chase. She'd stay gone for up to 45 minutes. These capers were always worrisome.

During summers we spent in New Hampshire, Caramia became a devoted fisherman, spending three or four hours a day in the water. We watched, amused, from our deck as Caramia quietly followed a fish with her eyes while moving ever so slowly in shallow water, then either pouncing or striking out with her paw. Once she even tried diving. Alas, she never caught a fish.

The love shared between animals and humans, I believe, is one of those bonuses in life that you often come across unaware. Once you experience their steadfastness, their unconditional affection, their constancy, and trust, there's no going back. You are irremediably changed . . . for the better. So, when they leave, their loss is immense. Caramia gave us almost 11 years of adventure and love. In the end, her cancer made her terribly uncomfortable and her eyes told us it was her time to go. Her eyes also told us more, and we decided to put down in words what we felt she would want to say. We call this Caramia's letter, 18 August 2006 . . .

Dear Doris, Steve, Allegro, Max, Tango, Diamonte, and Friends,

I will be going shortly with the angels. For 11 years I have been part of a loving family and I have always wanted to give more than 200 percent to them in return. Being an Aussie shepherd, I have strived not only to be loyal and fun loving, but also protective (as the UPS and FED EX men can attest to). My job was to assure that my family and hiking buddies like Peter and Perry always stayed together and were properly protected while stopping for lunch. Now, some of you got mad at me for herding everyone, especially children; however, it was my nature. If I offended anyone, I apologize. Yes, my barking was sometimes a bit loud, but my job was to look out for my family. I loved going with the horses; I needed to make sure Doris and Steve stayed together and that they got safely home. Steve especially needed me while hiking to keep him from getting lost, as I always knew the way home. Thank God he has a GPS now that I am leaving. I want to thank all those fish at Mirror Lake who allowed me to chase them for hours at a time without ever getting caught.

The love I gave my family was unconditional and I know now that they in turn loved me just as much. We all shared a very special relationship. Through the 11 years we gave each other countless hours of joy and happiness. Sure, everyone was grouchy now and then, but that is part of a loving relationship. Valiente, Foster, and I will be looking down on you, so be good.

Doris and Steve, special thanks to both of you for not only giving me much love, but allowing me to participate fully in all family activities. I was truly blessed to have been adopted by both of you. Lots of love and licks to you both.

Caramia

In return, Doris and I also wanted to pen the things we felt about this incredibly loving, loyal, faithful, trusting, and brave dog. We wrote . . .

Dear Caramia,

There has never been another dog or animal in our lives like you. You are the most loyal, most caring, smartest, and loving animal anyone could ask for. Your leaving will leave a huge hole in our lives. So many thousands of miles hiking and riding together. Your positive attitude through three hip and leg surgeries was truly a measure of your desire always to be there for us. After each surgery, you had the drive and desire to return to your job of taking care of us while hiking and riding, no matter what the pain might have been. We want you to know that you are truly loved and will be greatly missed. Oh yes, thank you for training Max. With all the adversities you faced, it is sad that you were unable to conquer cancer. As you proceed on your journey, you will forever be in our hearts and minds as we go about our daily chores. Don't forget to be nice to Foster and Valiente, as they also were special. We love you.

Doris and Steve
18 August 2006

CHAPTER 37

Other Loves: Horses

As my backpacking days drew to a close, I decided to replace that activity with horseback riding at the age of 66. Naturally, my family and friends thought I was crazy. But I had my reasons . . . Doris had been riding since she was 30. We shipped her horse to our home in New Mexico every spring and back to Naples in the fall. Me trying to ride seemed a good idea. That way we could spend more quality time together. Backpacking had not been of interest to her.

In those days she had a semi-retired horse living in central Florida, which she intended to sell. Over the years I had become fond of him, so one day I asked Doris, "Do you think I could learn to ride him?"

She said, "Yes." And just like that I fell into her trap. I later learned that she had no intention of selling the horse; she was only trying to trick me into learning to ride. Now this is the point at which I could begin a tirade on how spouses learn effectively to outmaneuver their mates, but I will refrain. Instead I'll relay that Doris followed up her trick by admonishing me that she had zero interest in teaching me to ride. I needed to take lessons.

Oh, great! As I proceeded with the project, I realized three things: One, I was scared to death. Two, I didn't know the front from the back of a horse. Three, I needed a good teacher. I signed on with an instructor at our stable in Naples. She was terrific. After six lessons on a very calm quarter horse, she told Doris that I was ready to go out on the trail. I was grateful. This became my last lesson, as I hated riding around a ring, which bored me and was a lot of work. We brought Doris's horse Valiente down to Naples and my new sport began. It was more challenging than I expected; nevertheless, I was lucky as Valiente was a Paso Fino, so I did not have to learn to post. These horses are naturally gaited, which makes them extremely smooth. Our barn was located at the edge of the Picayune Forest, so trail riding always promised adventure.

There were times we took trails into the Everglades, where we saw deer, wild pigs, wild turkeys, snakes, alligators, and an occasional panther. In times of danger, horses have only one defense; that is, to run. Consequently, I had several "unscheduled dismounts." From those I learned you had to be in the moment—no daydreaming or solving the problems of the world while in the saddle. In central Florida I learned a useful tool for riding in dangerous settings. The one-rein stop will force a scared horse to go in a circle, which he doesn't like, as opposed to galloping off, when pulling on the reins to slow him has little effect. Early on I learned to follow the basic rule taught by nationally recognized equine trainer Clint Anderson: Never do anything that will endanger your horse or yourself.

After a couple of years, we had to put Valiente down. I then acquired Diamonte, a four-year-old Paso Fino who had flunked out of the show circuit on his first show. As they say in the Paso world, "He did not have the fire in the belly." Just what I wanted: I had to rely heavily on the horse taking care of me since I was still a novice. Diamonte was a gentle soul who somehow knew from the beginning that I did not know what I was doing. He seemed to sense he needed to take care of me. Over the years he and I have bonded, and he, indeed, looks after me with one exception: When he hears air brakes—an 18-wheeler or a dump truck—he turns into a racehorse at Churchill Downs!

As Doris was no longer shipping her horse to New Mexico, we decided to buy a two-horse trailer and haul the horses north to New Hampshire for the summer where Doris had a cabin in Wolfeboro on Mirror Lake. After taking several short trips with the dogs and horses to ride in central Florida, we thought it would be fun to make an adventure out of going north and stopping to trail ride at interesting places along the way. We would take about 10 days to two weeks going up as well as returning. This turned out to be much more challenging than we expected, as we wanted to be on a trail system with direct access, including a place for us and the dogs and horses on site. We quickly learned that many of our hosts shaded the truth a bit.

In 2003 and for several years following, we rented a farm outside of Woodstock, Vermont, for six weeks every fall. The farm covered 400 acres and had an old cow barn with direct access to the GMHA (Green Mountain Horse Association) trail system, which went off for miles in all directions. This was still early in my riding career, so I experienced some surprises. At the time I was riding a leased quarter horse named KC that I did not know well. While I was riding him through a field at a quiet walk, KC suddenly took off like a rocket! I tugged him in a tight circle, and then I went flying in an "unscheduled dismount." While on the ground with a few aches and pains, I realized the horse had stepped on an underground beehive. Doris explained later that I should have let him run so he could get away. Oh well. Live and learn.

Another time KC and I were riding around a local reservoir near an airport landing strip when 200 feet above us an extremely loud jet took off. This made for another wild accelerated ride for several hundred feet. Terrifying! I had not yet learned to read the mind of a horse. In fact, just to show how naïve I was, one day Doris was practicing in a nearby ring, and I was seated on KC watching. After 15 minutes he started to go down on all fours. Immediately I interpreted this as he was just like a camel—going down so I could easily dismount. Wrong! Doris yelled at me to immediately get off, as he really was about to roll with me on board. Live and learn again.

One time in north Georgia we rented a cabin in the mountains. The road leading up to our destination was definitely grim, more like a goat path with ruts, rocks, potholes, gravel, and dirt. Derelict cabins surrounded the local dump. There was an old rundown school bus with weird sayings and graffiti reflecting the hippie days of the 1960s and protesting the Vietnam War. We arrived at the cabin, which turned out to be fine; however, the horse pasture was surrounded by barbed wire, a big NO NO for horses. We spent a couple of hours placing reflective tape every few feet and then walking the horse around the perimeter several times.

I decided to take our dog Caramia to walk the trail. We could not find it; and anyway, the woods felt very unfriendly and a bit scary. We learned later that we were actually in the area where *Deliverance* was filmed. During our ride I had an opportunity to test Diamonte's concern for my safety as we came to a small stream. I dismounted, and walking right ahead of him, I was leading him across only to have him take a giant leap across to land at my side. Doris yelled that you never lead a horse across without being at his side!! So, coming back, I stayed mounted on Diamonte and prayed he would walk through the water. Nope. He took another giant leap and cleared the stream with plenty of feet to spare, while I was trying to hold on and stay in the middle of the saddle.

After several years of trying new places to ride, we settled on two: Shalimar Farm in Cass, West Virginia, and Acadia National Park in Bar Harbor, Maine. Despite the fact that Cass is in the middle of nowhere, it became a favorite as we had 1,000 acres to ride on the farm, and the town was surrounded by a national forest. Acadia in Maine has more than 45 miles of carriage trails with spectacular views at every turn, ranging from mountains to ponds to the Atlantic Ocean. When Rockefeller built the carriage trails he made sure they were the focus of beauty and required that all the roads pass under the trails, thereby providing the best views for the trail riders. Now, at age 78, I am not riding as much; however, I still especially enjoy riding in the Hitchcock Woods with our three dogs and Doris. Although we no longer are going to Bar Harbor it is still our favorite.

Our most moving and exhilarating experience was riding the battlefield in Gettysburg, Virginia, with our own horses. The wife of the head forest ranger was in charge of taking us around. We stayed at the local campground and the horses were in a small corral nearby. Once we were on the actual battlefield, we felt as if we had stepped back in time. It is impossible to describe the feeling of looking out over ground where American history has been made. We could visualize Pickett's charge as if we were part of it—truly an awesome experience.

When all is said and done, many friends and family members think I'm a bit touched to still ride, so why do I do it? First, as Winston Churchill once said, "The outside of a horse is good for the inside of a man." Since I have experienced this, I can say it's true. When riding, one must be in the present, one with your horse. No cell phone or daydreaming. A horse can sense when you are truly upset or in bad mood, so don't ride until you calm down. Now, more than 12 years since I started riding, I can say it has been a great experience. In fact, I'm not sure why I missed out for so many years since Doris is such an avid rider. Horses are loving companions who give back a hundred fold once you have bonded with them. I never realized how sensitive a 1,000-pound animal could be with a human. I truly believe that if I am kind and tuned in to Diamonte, he will do his best to take care of me while we are out on the trail.

Life on the farm, Aiken, South Carolina, 2009, sans one dog and one horse

CHAPTER 38

Moving to Aiken (2008)

Sometime in 2006, Doris and I, with our two horses and two dogs, were traveling from Naples to Wolfeboro, New Hampshire, and we stopped in Pennsylvania at a bed and breakfast that would take all of us on site. As I have mentioned, it was not always easy to find places that would accommodate a traveling bunch such as ours. During the cocktail hour at the B&B, we chanced to meet a woman who lived in Aiken, South Carolina. I had never heard of the place. We fell into conversation about desirable places to live, particularly if you were horse lovers, which of course we were, and she suggested that we stop by on one of our trips south. She described an area in the center of Aiken called Hitchcock Woods, with 2,200 acres and more than 65 miles of trails for horses, dogs off lead, and walkers.

"Sounds like our kind of place," I said, "although we've lived in Naples, Florida, for 30 years."

On our trip south, Doris and I did stop to ride the Hitchcock trails and immediately we fell in love with Aiken. "This is Nirvana at a reasonable cost," I said to Doris. She agreed. In addition to Hitchcock, there was a section of town known as the Horse District, less than five minutes to town with no paved roads and easy access to Hitchcock Woods. Doris and I could not believe that Aiken offered every discipline from racing training tracks to driving. There are more than 55 polo fields along with five hunts!

In the late 19th century, Aiken, South Carolina, became known as a wintering spot for wealthy people from the northeast. The Aiken Winter Colony was established by Thomas Hitchcock Sr. and William C. Whitney. Over the years, Aiken became a winter home for notable people with last names such as Eustis, Astor, Vanderbilt, Harriman, Grace, and Knox. History records that the roots of the Winter Colony reach back to Celestine E. Eustis. Celestine was the guardian of her niece Louise and brought her to Aiken for visits. Louise, who married New York financier Thomas Hitchcock Sr. joined with him to establish the foundations of the Winter Colony. The climate and the loamy clay soil, it seems, were perfect for their stables of horses. Today, the Aiken Winter Colony Historic District, listed on the U.S. National Register of Historic Places since 1984, features more than 30 properties, most built between 1882 and 1948, and many of which are impressive mansions with stables.

In addition to attracting the super rich, Aiken in the 1950s at the height of the Cold War saw the construction of the Savannah River Site (SRS) to refine nuclear materials for deployment in nuclear weapons. It required some 30,000 workers to build the site, which at its peak employed 25,000 workers. Covering 310 square miles, it is owned by the U.S. Department of Energy. This project brought top-ranked scientists, nuclear engineers, and support teams to the town, which at the time had a population of around 10,000. Meanwhile, the winter horse people were going to Ocala and Wellington in Florida. But in the 1990s, they re-discovered the horse amenities of Aiken, its mild winters, great footing for horses, costs lower than Florida, and the absence of hurricanes.

Doris and I are among these "new" horse people. In November 2008, we moved into our home on 18 acres with three pastures and a four-stall barn. Doris and I are animal lovers, obviously, and we wanted our dogs and horses to enjoy all the attributes of a place where they could be free—not housed in a stall with a tiny turnout or a small lot in Naples, Florida, bordering two busy streets.

In one sense, the move to Aiken was difficult for me as I had deep roots in Naples. However, we found our only regret now is that we did not do it sooner! We found the Aiken community extremely welcoming and friendly. In fact, it reminds me of Naples as it was 50 years ago. Within six years we had made more good friends in Aiken than we did in 22 years as residents of Naples.

Aiken is 20 miles northeast of Augusta, Georgia, along US routes 1 and 78. Interstate 20 passes six miles north of the city. The city itself encompasses little more than 20 square miles. We have hot, humid summers and cool, dry winters. Rain occurs mostly in the more temperate months and sometimes it snows in winter. In addition to its canopied streets, its wandering trails, its history, and its attention to beautiful environs, I suppose what I love most about Aiken is the freedom we have to enjoy it all—a variety of outdoor pleasures with our animals. And recently, to my delight, the interaction of the Aiken community and my animals brought me to a surprising avocation that offers a new and individualized definition of the phrase *giving back.*

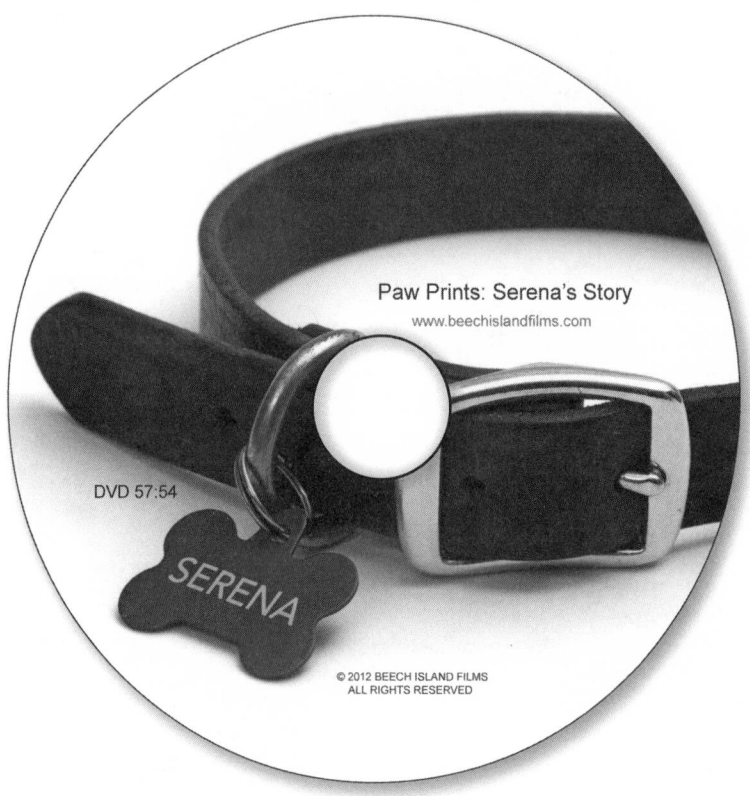

Paw Prints: Serena's Story
www.beechislandfilms.com

DVD 57:54

SERENA

DVD titled *Paw Prints: Serena's Story* shares Serena's improbable journey from stray to highly ranked therapy dog, 2012

CHAPTER 39

Serena's Story

I n the spring of 2007, prior to our move to Aiken, Doris and I
headed north with our two Paso Fino horses and our Tibetan
terrier Max. We stopped in Aiken to visit for a week and ride in
the lovely tree-lined trails of Hitchcock Woods. While we were
there, Doris casually looked in the local paper and found an ad
for an Aussie shepherd being fostered in nearby Augusta by a
group called Molly's Militia. Curious, she checked the website
and called me over to have a look. There was Serena. She was
certainly not an Australian shepherd; nevertheless, she was very
appealing. Doris was intrigued by her name. "Serenity," she said
out loud, and proceeded to look into the dog's past. It seems that
Serenity had been picked up as a stray when she was about three
years old. She had been living on the street for several months,
and she had a litter of puppies. Beleaguered and hungry, she was
in pretty dismal shape. The rescue group Molly's Militia had
rescued Serenity from the local county animal shelter, where she
had only a few hours left to live.

Doris and I drove to Augusta to see Serenity in her foster
home. She was timid and shy, but her eyes and demeanor were
both beguiling. We had our Tibetan terrier Max with us; she got
along well with him, so we took her back to our motel in Aiken
to see what might develop. Two days later we left Aiken and
headed to Cass, West Virginia, to ride in the mountains for a

week. We experimented with Serena—our version of her name—leaving her off lead. We were afraid she might run off. Nope. She was happy to stay with us, even as we traveled on horseback for two or three hours at a stretch. Serenity, now Serena, was not only well named, she was also well suited to us. We knew she was meant to be family.

We continued north to New Hampshire and stayed for the summer. I took Serena to clicker training and the instructor there felt that she was so laid back, she might make a good therapy dog. In January 2008, I found myself training her to be a therapy dog, and she and I passed the Delta Society test with flying colors. Delta gave us a "complex" rating, which is the highest level and qualifies us to work in adverse and fast-changing situations.

Voila! Both of us had new jobs!

In the past several years, Serena and I have made trips to nursing homes for the elderly, hospitals for the sick, and schools for challenged children. Serena has a sixth sense about people in difficult circumstances. She has been featured in a book, titled *To the Rescue* by Elise Lufkin, about dogs with a special mission. In October 2012, she was the focus of a full-length documentary, *Paw Prints* (now on DVD), which tells her story. Serena is truly remarkable; she can detect people with cancer, and she brings healing to impossible situations.

On a visit to a children's hospital in Augusta, Georgia, we were in the intensive care ward visiting a three-year-old girl. That day several other therapy dogs had visited ahead of us in the hospital, and we were the last to go in. In her hospital room, the nurses told us the little girl had been immobile for hours. She was huddled in a fetal position in the corner of a narrow bed in her room. Serena and I walked in quietly. I told Serena to jump up on a chair next to the child's bed. Serena sat. The child stared. Then, amazingly, the little girl unwrapped her stiff limbs, moved over toward the dog, placed her arms around Serena's neck, and hugged her for at least three minutes! After we left, the head nurse intercepted us in the hallway. She exclaimed, "This is the first time the girl has moved at all in more than two days!"

On another visit, we saw a stage IV cancer patient under hospice care in his home. The man was surrounded by his family. When we entered Serena asked permission of me to get up on the couch where he sat to lie next to him. He was fidgeting strangely and looking vaguely straight ahead. Serena jumped up on the couch, lay down, and put her head on his lap. Unaccountably, the man began to pet her head and continued for about 15 minutes. Then, amazingly, he began to talk to his family in a coherent manner.

"That is so incredible," his wife told us as we were leaving. "He hasn't spoken a word in weeks!"

They lost him two days later. All I could think was: *What a blessing that family had received from Serena!*

While working on the rehabilitation floor at Huggins Hospital in Wolfeboro, New Hampshire, I asked permission of the administration to visit a lady there. It was granted, but when we knocked to get permission to enter, the lady groused, "I don't like dogs!" I told her that Serena was special; furthermore, we would not stay long. She nodded and we entered. Surprisingly, Serena in her own way asked to get up on the bed. I could only think, *Why?*

But Serena prevailed. She lay next to the lady for about 20 minutes. She didn't want to leave, and both dog and patient seemed very relaxed. The visit ended and we left.

On our next trip to Huggins Hospital, a nurse on that same floor rushed over to Serena and me. "That lady was released two days after your visit," she said. "And we never did find out what was wrong with her. She was severely agitated, you remember, and unable to sleep. But 20 minutes after you left, she fell sound asleep!"

One day on a visit to Naples Community Hospital, Serena and I called upon a man who was bedridden. When it came time to leave, Serena grew stubborn. She would not leave his side.

I had to drag her out of the room—highly unusual—as Serena always followed my instructions without hesitation. I came to find out that the patient died a few hours after we left. I could only marvel. Serena must have known.

Serena is marvelous with challenged children, particularly those with autism. It is heartbreaking to see those children struggling in their own worlds. Many have not spoken for weeks. But when they do, if only to a limited extent, it is heartwarming to watch. After a few visits from Serena, some of these children simply open their arms while they smile to reach for a dog that accepts them and loves them immediately.

All in all, because of Serena I have encountered many people in trouble we have been able to help, however briefly. For these experiences, I am grateful.

Serena at work, inspiring challenged children

SECTION V

The View From Here

SFB II, 2005

CHAPTER 40

Perspective

I suppose when you reach your seventh decade and you're looking at the horizon of your 80s, you are inclined to view your life in terms of meaning. In this life I've had opportunities: I was born into a family in which I was loved. I've met some fantastic people. I was educated. I've traveled much of the globe. I've run several businesses. So now I sit back and ask, how did these opportunities shape me? Did I make the most of them?

Opportunities lead to choices. What were my critical choices, and where did they lead?

As a youth I chose Babson College by default and discovered my aptitude for business. After that I married Lorna. We had three wonderful children. They had children, and that led to the joys of grandchildren. In my 40s, I decided to quit OMC. That choice brought on some rough years. But ultimately those years led to rewarding business endeavors with friends and on my own. I was divorced midlife. That was a critical time—painful—a period of self-assessment and regret. But, then I found Doris, with whom I've shared the second half of my life very happily. After more than 30 years in Naples, Florida, I moved to Aiken, South Carolina, a place I'd never heard of, but one that guided me toward new friends, appealing activities, and an appreciation of animals. I discovered with Serena a late-life pastime of giving back and helping others.

Then there are the mistakes I made. I went into mechanical engineering, for which I was not suited, because my grandfather Briggs was a mechanical engineer. At the age of 29, I insulted my boss. I had a misguided affair when married the first time. I stayed too long in one place of business. I overextended myself financially—living beyond my means. Why did I make such mistakes? Were they inevitable? Perhaps even necessary?

What about the lessons I've learned? Ah, now there is the meat in the hamburger! We are supposed to learn, are we not? After all, learning is the substance of guidance, of maturity and wisdom . . . wisdom that we might pass along to others . . . to young people, for instance, who will follow us.

In a nutshell, I suppose I've learned a dozen or so lessons while puttering around in my lifeboat of experience. And for what it's worth (it's free!) I'll share a few . . .

I have learned that the universe is so constructed that you can find meaning in everything—hardship and success, mistakes and opportunities, long-familiar landscapes and new places, illness and health, times of doubt and confirmations of faith. We learn from those people close to us how to live and how *not* to live. Frankly, lessons conveying meaning abound at every turn.

But more to the point, personally I've learned to be less impetuous. I've discovered I'm happier when I am financially conservative. I've found I can trust and believe in myself. I think I should have spent more time with my family when I was young; I wish I had expressed love and affection openly and sincerely at all times. I've realized the positive impact animals can have in my life. I've grown to know that faith is important to explore while you are young and retain when you are old.

If I had it to do all over again . . . well, I don't. But I can say it's important to be honest with yourself and with others . . . that dreams are worth pursuing and taking risks is the cost of reward. I'd steer away from hurting other people when I could, and I wouldn't let work interfere with adventure. I've found that

physical activities are renewing. That recreation is exactly that—
re-creation. In times of joy and sorrow, you can always get in a
boat . . . or ride a horse . . . or pet a dog.

After almost eight decades of highs and lows, I find myself
reflecting on what truly brings me happiness now on my farm in
Aiken with my wife Doris and our four horses and three dogs . . .
I enjoy keeping in touch with my family and friends. I like taking
mini trips with Doris every few weeks for an overnight without
animals. I find it peaceful in the mornings to have Doris beside
me, along with three dogs stacked up in bed, while we watch
television or gaze across green pastures outside the window. I
find it wonderful to walk with my dogs in beautiful Hitchcock
Woods. It's exhilarating to ride horses there—or anywhere—
with Doris. In the evenings I enjoy quietly sharing cocktails
with my wife on our deck while the horses graze before us and
a scattering of songbirds sing for supper at their feeder. It's at
these times that I realize that I've reached calm waters, and I feel
intensely the blessings I've known.

All in all, life is valuable. Your life and my life. That any of
us is born is a miracle. (Some analysts estimate it as a 1 in 400
quadrillion chance.) Given the odds, I'm glad I didn't miss out.
I'm thankful for the journey.

For those of you mid-travels, I wish you the best as you
chart your distinctive path. Truly I can say, navigating a life is a
unique experience. And always it's a meaningful ride.

Grandfather Briggs

Grandmother "Tayto" Briggs

Grandfather Nichols

Grandmother "Duckie" Nichols

Mom and Dad

Three generations, 1950

Sandy, Shelley, and Stephen, 1971

Foster, Doris, and SFB II

SFB II and grandchildren

Family reunion, Naples, 2004

Caramia

SFB II, Diamonte, Tango. and Doris

Sandy, SFB II, Shelley, and Stephen

SECTION VI
Afterword

Throughout my life I have experienced fortuitous events. First, I have known some remarkable people as friends and family. I've had a long-standing interest in what they accomplished and how their roots spurred them toward the heights they reached. Several years back, I began to research my own genealogy to understand how my ancestors fit into the landscape of a developing America as well as how they influenced me. You will find them in the following section.

Second, during my life adventures I have encountered individuals who demonstrated enough interesting quirks to be considered "characters"—for better or for worse. You will meet them here, too.

Third, I have traveled to some of the most fascinating far-flung areas of the world. You will visit many of them alongside me through my recollections.

To help you follow my journey, in this memoir I have included numbered endnotes to provide you with further information that may be of interest. I gathered this information from research through public records, museums, libraries, online sources (notably Wikipedia), and family archives. The people I discuss were influential and involved in private and public events. Some made enduring contributions to history; others were passing acquaintances with only momentary significance. In all instances—including how and where they lived—they made my life interesting. And for that reason, among others, they are part of the story.

SFB II

Reference Notes

CHAPTER 1

[1] Briggs

My father was Stephen Albro Briggs (1911–1965).

It is believed that the Briggs roots go back to Norfolk, England, and that Briggs was Brigg, which meant the person(s) lived near a bridge. The first member of the Briggs family to come to America was Joseph Briggs, born around 1734. He was a blacksmith on Block Island in 1758, where he had two shops. It is written that he had a monopoly and high prices.

There is little known about his son Samuel Fiske Briggs (1772–1822), born on Block Island in 1772. He was a sailor and spent most of his life on the island, and members of his family were active in the marine trade. Three were masters of large schooners, while others owned and operated several firms in the shipping trade in New York City from 1823–1872. The best known firms were Briggs & Company, J&N Briggs, and the Swiftshure Line.

Jeddidiah Briggs (1800–1869) might be called the "black sheep" of the family. When he married his second wife, Francis Albro, her father drew up documents that forbade Jeddidiah from receiving anything that belonged to the Albro family. His third wife was equally cautious, as she had him sign a pre-nuptial agreement giving up all dower rights. He spent his final days at Seaman's Retreat Hospital on Staten Island, which indicates that he must have been a seaman and was single at the time.

My great-grandfather Stephen Albro (S. A.) Briggs (1838–1907) was born in Rhode Island, and after passing through Ohio, ended up in Shakopee, Minnesota, with his brother George (Welcome) Briggs, where they were in the mercantile business. S. A.'s first wife died shortly after childbirth in 1879, leaving him with three young daughters. A year later he married my great-grandmother Flora (Muzzy) Foster from Millbridge, Maine. Immediately after their marriage they took the train to Watertown, South Dakota, where he was an insurance agent and part-time farmer with his brother George. My grandmother told me that he also was the manager of the opera house. As I was duly impressed, when I visited Watertown, I asked the lady in charge of the local historical society where it was located. With a smile she asked me, "Which one? We had three." I was speechless, and then she added. "Well, young man, I guess you didn't know that 'opera house' was the name given to the local bar and brothel!"

[2] Nichols

My mother was Joan Taylor Nichols (1912–1970). She married Stephen Albro Briggs in 1935.

The first Nichols from our family that I can identify is Asa (1765–1813), who was killed in the War of 1812. He was born in Vermont before moving to Crown Point, New York. His son Eliakim (1794–1838) was born in Onondaga, New York, in 1790. The family had come from England sometime earlier. By 1848, they were in Battle Creek with John Nichols (1814–1891), who had been a farmer in Clinton, Michigan, prior to moving to Battle Creek. He and his son Edwin (1838–1924) were extremely successful and influential in Battle Creek. John founded Nichols-Shepard in 1849. In 1850, he took off for California in pursuit of gold with 5 men, 3 wagons, and 12 horses. This adventure was short lived, and he returned to build Nichols-Shepard into a major company. In 1854, Nichols-Shepard built the first steam engine tractor that was highly successful. In 1859, the company built 10 vibrator threshers, and by 1911 John Nichols had introduced the gas-powered tractor. In 1873, he became director of the Chicago and Huron Railroad. In 1875, he founded the Old National Bank, where he remained as director for 50 years.

In 1876, William Butts Mershon featured the Nichols Deer Hunting Camp in the book *Fifty Years of Fishing & Hunting*. The camp was so remote that when a group arrived, its members would spend six weeks hunting and fishing. When they returned they would parade through town showing off their trophies.

In 1880, John founded the Nichols Hospital. He became mayor of Battle Creek and the first president of Union School Furniture. In 1929, John sold his company, Nichols-Shepard to Oliver Farm Equipment Company. By 1951, Oliver built an outboard motor in competition with Outboard Marine Corporation (OMC). In the early days he bought fuel for his men and was the first to build homes and sell them on easy terms to his workers. During the difficult years, 1873, 1893, and 1907, he kept full employment. His financial standing in New York and Chicago allowed him to survive.

CHAPTER 2

[3] DeMorat

Oliver Boudrais DeMorat (1835–1902) came to the United States from Canada in 1868 and settled in Philadelphia, where he became an accomplished portrait photographer. His most famous photo was of the notorious Doc Holiday (1859–1887) taken in 1872 at the occasion of his graduation from the Philadelphia College of Dental Surgery. Doc was a gambler, a gunfighter, and a dentist. He was a good friend of Wyatt Earp and is best known for his involvement at the gunfight at the OK Corral. My grandmother Helene DeMorat was born in Philadelphia in 1879.

[4] Branch

The Branch family arrived in the United States in 1638, represented by John Branch (1628–1711). His father died on the trip over from the UK to America, and John was 11 years old, having come from Kent. For many years the family lived in Duxbury, Massachusetts, before moving to Preston, Connecticut, near Norwich, where Peter Branch (1682–1713) was one of the founders. Next, they traveled north on the Connecticut River and settled in Norwich, Vermont, prior to going to Tunbridge, where they raised sheep. The family moved to Meigs County, Ohio, and then Jeffersonville, Illinois, where Jasper Branch (1798–1875) was a founder, and the city was laid out on his farm of 1,600 acres, which he had received as bounty from the War of 1812. The Baltimore & Ohio Railroad (B&O) was the first common carrier railroad, and it offered scheduled freight and passenger service to the public. The railroad came through town in 1854 when there were only three small clapboard houses constructed. Truly a "one-horse" town!

Prior to the Civil War there was an active saloon in town, but it did not last long, as Jasper along with other locals formed the "Sons of Temperance" and quickly ran the owners out of town. Jasper's cousin was S. S. Branch, a first-class preacher who had his own church in Jeffersonville. However, after he died in 1862 the church folded. From the Lamard (also LaMard) Township history in Wayne County, Illinois, I found this item:

> The church flourished for a time under the efficient labors of its pastor, who was a earnest, practical preacher of Gospel truths.
>
> After his death the church struggled on, but removals, death, and

dissensions ere long reduced the number and disheartened all. The "Lions by the Wayside" caused many to retrace their steps to the enticing shades of sinful pleasure.

In 1870, John Elrie Branch, my great-grandfather, was 12, and his mother, Maria Cornell Branch, was "keeper of the hotel" in Jeffersonville. They both eventually moved to Yankton, South Dakota. My grandmother (Tayto) had told me he was an Indian agent. Needless to say this had always impressed me. In doing research on him, I learned that he really was a sales agent for Swift Meat Company selling to the Indians!

[5] Briggs & Stratton

In 1908, Briggs Electric supplied Ole Evinrude vibrator spark coils for his outboard. By 1909, Briggs & Stratton (B&S) was making ignition equipment and locking switches for the auto industry. During World War I in 1915, B&S manufactured V-B rifle grenades. In 1918, the company invented the "Motor Wheel," which was a gas engine attached to the rear of an ordinary bike. This led to the development of the first two-wheel scooter, on exhibit at the Museum of Science and Industry in Chicago. My grandfather S. F. Briggs actually rode one of these into the lobby of the Ritz Carlton Hotel in New York and persuaded the bell captain to leave it on display in the lobby. In 1920, the first Zenith radio was built at B&S. The company also introduced the "buckboard," which was an engine attached to a rubber drive that could be raised and lowered on the pavement. It had a top speed of 25 miles per hour with two leather seats. By 1922, B&S teetered on bankruptcy. However, in 1924, the company became a major supplier of auto locks and reached $4.8 million in sales by 1927. In 1928, B&S had doubled its sales. In 1930, B&S built a large number of engines for water wells and washing machines in rural America. Note: B&S actually supplied the Zenith Company with gas engines for their washing machines.

S. F. Briggs and Harry Stratton, buckboard, 1920

[6] Outboard Marine Corporation (OMC)

In 1935, my grandfather S. F. Briggs, along with Ralph Evinrude, purchased the Johnson Wheel Co., which manufactured the Johnson Outboard. They merged Evinrude, Johnson, and Elto to become OMC. By now B&S had acquired Elto (Evinrude Light Twin Outboard) and my grandfather had turned his interest to pursuing the outboard industry. From 1939 to 1945, OMC was dedicated to the World War II effort, producing firefighting pumps, generators, navigational equipment, and so on. In 1949, OMC's largest selling outboard was 10 horsepower. In 1952, OMC bought Lawn-Boy, the largest manufacturer of rotary lawn mowers. Around 1956, my uncle R. P. McCulloch decided to go into the outboard business and acquired Scott-Atwater. This upset my grandfather, so OMC purchased IEL (manufacturers of Pioneer chainsaws). As the McCulloch chainsaw was number one in the country, they became truly friendly competitors. During 1957, OMC acquired Cushman, which at one time was the largest motorcycle builder. The company concentrated on building golf carts and other three-wheel vehicles. In 1963, my grandfather resigned as chairman of the board. My uncle Jim Briggs took his seat on the board and Ralph Evinrude became chairman.

The 1960s saw the introduction of the OMC boat, which was a disaster, losing $42 million in a few years. Also in the same period, OMC entered the snowmobile industry and lost its shirt, as the product was never able to compete with manufacturers like Ski-Doo, Artic Cat, and Polaris.

By 2000, the company was in real turmoil, having gone through several presidents as well as making some major blunders. In my estimation these included allowing the Japanese to steal the market with a much more reliable product than OMC could produce and by not switching from a two-stroke engine to four-stroke soon enough. As the country was very environmentally concerned, a four-stroke engine was a much cleaner burning engine, even though it was much heavier.

I believe OMC also erred in buying a large number of boat companies, a step that demoralized their dealer network. Also I fault OMC for not having engines in the same horsepower range as Mercury. The same horsepower engine from Mercury outperformed OMC. Probably the single largest error, however, was adopting a revolutionary fuel system from Germany known as FICHT. This fuel injector was to provide less pollution and greater fuel economy while maintaining performance. Wrong! Two problems emerged: First, the engines kept blowing up at rapid rate, with pistons and rods exploding out of the crankcase. Second, the engines stalled when transitioning from slow or trolling into performance required for water skiers. Ultimately, in 2000, OMC declared bankruptcy. In 2001, Bombardier of Canada bought the company remains on the courthouse steps.

Note: Among other products, the Gale Products Division produced the first room coolers (that is, air conditioners). Gale Products was the plant in Galesburg, Illinois, that produced parts for OMC. Gale was the major producer for OMC's World War II war effort and then for Lawn-Boy as well as several contract brands for Sears, Montgomery Ward, Goodyear, and others. It also produced the Gale Buccaneer outboard.

CHAPTER 4

[7] The Dream Backfield

Also known as "The Million Dollar Backfield" by the NFL Football Hall of Fame, the group consisted of these players: fullback Pat Harder, halfbacks Elmer Angsman and Charlie Trippi, and quarterback Paul Christman.

CHAPTER 5

[8] "Tayto"

My cousin Richie McCulloch was the creator of this nickname for my grandmother. He used to call her "Dado Larado Mashed Potato."

CHAPTER 6

[9] Tony White

Having fully recovered from polio as a child, Tony went on to become an admiral in the United States Navy. As he spoke two dialects of Chinese and Russian fluently, he was in charge of intelligence in the Bering Sea. Later he organized a naval bird watching society that would take naval enthusiasts all over the world to identify rare birds.

CHAPTER 7

[10] The Quarters

This was the black neighborhood in the 1950s that is now an upscale residential area called "Aqualane Shores" in Naples.

[11] The Quonset Building

This structure was located off Third Street in Old Naples south of Broad behind The Beach Store.

CHAPTER 9

[12] Micky Briggs

He was not related to us; his family was from Detroit and owned Briggs manufacturing that produced automobile bodies for Chrysler. Ironically, his mother was a Fisher and "Body by Fisher" was the motto for General Motors' autos.

[13] Robert McCulloch (1911–1977)

Robert McCulloch married my dad's sister Barbara Briggs, whom I called Aunt Basie. Uncle Robert was a successful industrialist; yet at the same time he was highly eccentric. (See also Endnote [15].) He graduated from Princeton with an engineering degree at age 17. During World War II he built drone engines for military target practice. By 1946, he was the second largest stockholder in Pan American Airways after Juan Tripp. That same year he went to California and bought a large tract of land next to an old military airport to start McCulloch Motors. Today that land is adjacent to the Los Angeles International Airport. By 1947, McCulloch started to manufacture lawn mower engines in direct competition with Briggs & Stratton. His first order was for 5,000 from Modern Tool and Die, which made lawnmowers in Ohio. When they arrived, the engines would not start. McCulloch immediately dispatched another 5,000 engines, knowing they had the same problem. But the difference was, with this order, he sent his chief engineer and close friend in a car with several thousand dollars to be given to switchmen, etc., to make sure they never reached Ohio. When he solved the problem, he called my grandfather, who shut down OMC for three days while he made ignition coils for his son-in-law McCulloch to save his company.

In 1945, Uncle Robert began manufacturing McCulloch chainsaws. In 1950, he started McCulloch Oil and Gas. In 1953, he built the Paxton automobile, which was a rear-engine coupe powered by a two-cycle supercharged engine or a steam engine. By 1956, he bought Scott Atwater Outboards, which put him in direct competition with my grandfather's company, OMC. My grandfather retaliated by buying the IEL chainsaw company in Vancouver to compete directly with McCulloch chainsaws. In 1957, my uncle developed and sold the number one racing engine for Go Karts, which dominated its class.

During 1963, he bought 26 square miles in the barren Arizona desert, known as Site 6 of a World War II military installation, for $75 per acre. He already owned 3,500 acres, so he developed the property as Lake Havasu City, known today as "Arizona's Playground," a popular vacation site on the Lake Havasu reservoir. In 1964, he moved his chain production manufacturing division from Los Angeles to Lake Havasu to provide an industrial base for the area. In 1968, he bought the London Bridge for $2.46 million and moved it to Lake Havasu, but he constructed only the exterior of the bridge on the site. Next, he re-routed the Colorado River to go under the bridge *without* governmental permission. By selling small bridge pieces, which he periodically shipped from the UK, he was able to recover the cost of the bridge. His last venture, in 1971, was to build the McCulloch J-2 Gyrocopter with the dream of seeing one beside every house, as it could be landed in a driveway. Only 100 were built.

CHAPTER 17

[14] Dr. Jack Briggs

A well-known thoracic surgeon in Los Angeles, Dr. Jack Briggs was also the heart doctor for the first chimpanzee (named Ham the Chimp) to go into space. One time when he was in surgery, Dr. Jack received an emergency summons from the hospital to report immediately to his office. It seems the chimp had gotten loose and crossed the boulevard and was having a ball, swinging from the chandeliers in a high-end decorator's store. Dr. Jack was the only one who could catch him. This little caper ended up costing the U.S. government several thousand dollars.

[15] Uncle Robert McCulloch (again)

My uncle Robert McCulloch was one of the founders of Thunderbird Country Club in Palm Springs, and also a friend of President Dwight Eisenhower (president from 1953–1961). As President Eisenhower was an avid golfer, McCulloch would frequently allow Ike to use his home for vacations. When John F. Kennedy (1961–1963) became president, he had his staff call McCulloch to secure the use of his home at Thunderbird. Uncle Robert replied emphatically no! He was a staunch Republican and didn't even know Kennedy. Shortly after this he received a call from Robert Kennedy, attorney general for the United States, advising him that if his brother could not use the home the federal government would immediately start investigating and possibly bring suit claiming that McCulloch Chainsaws was a monopoly and therefore controlled pricing. Uncle Robert never gave in. (See also Endnote [9].)

CHAPTER 20

[16] Aramco (American Arabian Oil Company)

At the time this was a consortium of U.S. oil companies, which, in partnership with Saudi government, produced all the oil in Saudi Arabia.

[17] Daihatsu
This was the oldest Japanese car manufacturer.

CHAPTER 21

[18] Moose Dunne and Family

Ellie Dunne was a classmate of mine from the Bell School. Over the years we became good friends, and I invested in several ventures with Moose, ranging from oil and gas production in Michigan, to real estate in Naples, and in an ice skating arena with Michael Kirby, a well-known figure skater. Moose's brother, Judge Dunne, called "Little Moose" despite his enormous size, was our attorney in the case of the (fake) antique Navajo rug.

[19] Polk Brothers

This was a large appliance store that was the original discounter of appliances. Up until then, the business was dominated by the major department stores that charged full retail. At its peak in the 1980s, Polk Brothers had 17 stores in the Chicago area and controlled appliance sales.

[20] The Onwentsia Club

Located in Lake Forest, Illinois, the Onwentsia Club is a wonderful old golf and country club dating back to 1895. In the early days it offered a stable, a polo field, and a number of cottages for the members who came out from Chicago for weekends. In the 1960s and 1970s, you could only use a golf cart with a doctor's order and there were no tee times.

[21] Hubby Habjan

Hubby Habjan was the golf pro at Onwentsia for more than 30 years starting in 1965. He was a member of the Illinois Golf Hall of Fame, past president of the Illinois PGA, and past vice president of the National PGA.

[22] Wilmot Mountain

This mountain, located in Wisconsin just over the border from Illinois, has a vertical drop of 200 feet. When we went there, we would see several thousand skiers on weekends using the three rope tows. This location may have been among the first to offer night skiing under the lights.

CHAPTER 23

[23] "Stingers"

This drink was a mix of brandy and white crème de menthe. Very smooth!

CHAPTER 24

[24] C. B. McCoy

Also known as "Kinky," he was the son of the first president of the DuPont Company, who was not a DuPont. He tried forcing Kinky into the business, which Kinky hated. C. B. had a fabulous talent and ear for music and could play any tune on the piano by memory. His forte was Broadway tunes. He should have been a musician.

[25] Tory McCoy

As Kink's wife, Tory was a member of the DuPont family and they lived on the family compound in Montchanin, Delaware. The party was in a huge ballroom on the property and many members of the family were in attendance.

[26] Lester Lanin Band

Considered the top socialite band at this time, it performed at every presidential ball from Eisenhower to Carter.

[27] Uncle Jim Briggs

Uncle Jim was my father's youngest brother and started out raising top field trial dogs. Later he went on to be partner in Erwin, Wasey, Ruthrauff & Ryan, an advertising agency in New York City. When my grandfather retired from the OMC board, Uncle Jim replaced him. He was vice president in charge of all non-marine products. I worked for him for several years on various projects and research initiatives.

CHAPTER 25

[28] William "Bill" Rockefeller

William was a descendant of John D. Rockefeller, co-founder of Standard Oil. He preferred Bay Pond, which had been a family retreat and large game preserve located near Paul Smith, New York. At one point it included two-thirds of a section of land along with a private park. Several buildings were located on the property, among them a lumber mill, a stock barn, a store, a station post office, and large garage. At its peak 150 people were employed. William bought most of it back from a third party, which had acquired it from the Rockefellers.

[29] Loeb

This name descends from the Loeb who became infamous in the Leopold and Loeb kidnapping case in 1924.

CHAPTER 26

[30] "She's Come Undun" song lyrics

Available online at http://www.azlyrics.com/lyrics/guesswho/undun.html

[31] *Passages: Predictable Crises of Adult Life.*

Sheehy, Gail. 1974. New York: E. P. Dutton & Co., Inc.

Chapter 27

[32] Al Capone

Capone was one of the most notorious gangsters of the Prohibition Era in the United States.

Chapter 28

[33] Mary Tyler Moore

Born in 1936, Mary Tyler Moore is an American actress and an Emmy Award and Tony Award winner for television shows including the "Dick Van Dyke Show" and "The Mary Tyler Moore Show."

Chapter 29

[34] Joan Hill

Late in life my father and mother divorced. A few years before his death in 1965, my father married his longtime secretary, Joan Mandrey, in Mexico.

Chapter 30

[35] la Reforma

Every day around noon in the village, the fishermen returned to shore, and a large church bell would ring. The schools would close and all the women and children reported to the factory to process the shrimp, which would then be frozen. Several waiting 18-wheelers would be loaded to head for the States when the dispatcher received a telex that the price was high enough. These local fishermen were extremely poor, and many lived in shelters that were made from the shipping cartons that the engines came in.

Chapter 31

[36] Baker & McKenzie

Baker & McKenzie was the number one international law firm that set up and managed the structure used by many of the Fortune 500 companies who wanted to take advantage of the tax laws allowing profits to not be taxed in the United States if kept overseas for expansion of the company. This law is still in effect; however, there is a great deal of pressure to repeal it.

[37] Second Mortgage

Although I really needed the cash, I was advised by Baker & McKenzie that if it was proven that any of the funds had come from investors, then if and when Carter Containers went under, I would have to give the money back. Being concerned that other liens might be ahead of me, I discovered that if you recorded a document at an embassy overseas it was effective immediately, and you had 30 days to record the document in your home jurisdiction.

[38] Mrs. Carter's Trust

As luck would have it, both Mrs. Carter and I lived in Naples, so the arrangement was convenient. Ted's mother was delightful and very saddened over the situation, since his brother was manager for the local Paine Webber brokerage firm and treasurer for the George H. Bush campaign in Collier County. These facts gave me a feeling of security about the arrangement.

[39] Everlands

According to spokesperson Helen Patrikis, Everlands is "structured similar to an equity country club on a global basis where the members are owners, and because of its conservation ethos, the model of stewardship through ownership is fundamental. This differs dramatically from traditional models of fractional real estate and destination clubs. Everlands it is all about conservation ... A portion of each membership fee helps to fund the Everlands Conservation Foundation."

Bob Burch, Everlands' co-founder and chairman explains, "Our vision in creating Everlands was to bring together a global community of likeminded individuals who share a love of people and family and a passion for nature and the great outdoors, defined by a desire to preserve and protect it ... for future generations."

[40] The Point Bankruptcy

Shares were $1 million each, and membership was limited to 100. Until this was reached, the resorts would remain open to the public. The shares sold never came close to the goal before the financial crisis in 2008. The Point loan was with Lehman Brothers, which went bankrupt!

[41] Borch

With his credentials as president of GE from 1963–1967, chairman 1967–1972, and Businessman of the Year 1970 by a two-to-one margin in *Saturday Review*, you would think his word would be his bond!

[42] Campbell-Mithun Advertising Agency

The president of the Campbell-Mithun agency, Stan Blunt, was the husband of the woman I showed property to in Naples and secured an agreement on her behalf with Mr. Fred Borch. Ultimately, without telling me, she bought a place on Marco Island. This surprised me, as I had known her husband fairly well. In the 1970s, the agency handled the advertising for the OMC snowmobile division, for which I was the advertising manager.

Chapter 32

[43] Jose Marti Building

Jose Marti (1853–1895) died in 1895 fighting for independence from Spain. He was exiled in 1871 and spent several years in jail. He is known as "The Apostle of the Cuban Revolution."

[44] Chow Lee Yachts

This line was founded in China in 1870. They moved to Hong Kong in 1936. By the 1960s and 1970s, they were best known for their trawler-type yachts. Descendants of the original family still run the business.

[45] Wright's in Seattle

Wright's was the largest independent Johnson parts distributor in Seattle. At the time, OMC owned all its parts distribution outlets except in the West. These included distributors in Seattle, Alaska, Denver, Phoenix, and Bose, Idaho. The three-hour difference in time meant that if we ordered by 5 p.m., the parts could make the overnight flight to Miami. In the morning we would immediately canvass the local dealers to make every attempt to ship the order complete.

[46] Mullet Bay Resort

The Mullet Bay Resort and Casino was our largest account, averaging between $750,000 and $1 million per year. We bought all their linens, toilet paper, casino equipment, and even change for the casino, which was a weekly order for $8,000 in coins. From 1980–1995, it was one of the finest resorts in Sint Maarten and the Caribbean. In 1995, Hurricane Luis completely destroyed the property. The resort never was rebuilt and was in a legal battle until 2011 and remains a war zone.

[47] The Surinam Navy General

It was ATS's policy that all customers, whether large or small, should be treated equally. In the fall of 1983, the United States invaded the island of Grenada using all branches of the military. Shortly after that, a Mr. Cheng from Surinam (formerly British Guiana, which was a colony on the northern coast of South America, now known as the independent nation of Guyana) arrived at our warehouse.

His opening line was, "I am a friend and neighbor of Mr. Rousheval, who says you are not only the best but also the most honest purchasing agents in Miami." Now Mr. Rousheval was a client of ours who had purchased two large container loads of ketchup. I sent him Heinz ketchup, which he liked and wanted more. It's difficult to find anything in ketchup that is not either Heinz or Hunt's, and Mr. Rousheval wanted a supply of ketchup rather quickly, because the authorities in his country were closing the borders to make their own ketchup, which he felt would not be very good. He wanted Heinz, but he wanted it cheaper.

I called a growers' association near Naples, the largest producer of winter tomatoes at the time, but those tomatoes were not used to make ketchup. Only

California tomatoes were used in ketchup! So I located a brand called Brooks Ketchup, talked to Mr. Brooks, who just happened to have a carload of Brooks Ketchup because someone had cancelled an order. So he sold it to me at a price 15 to 20 percent cheaper than Heinz. And Rousheval loved it!

Next, Mr. Rousheval came to ATS and said Surinam didn't have satellite TV, as you could only get it through an account in the States. He and his friends liked to watch weekly productions like "Bonanza" or soccer at Surinam social clubs, so he made a deal with us to record the show, take them to the airport, and send them on their way. The task represented no profit and lots of work, but we did it because it showed Rousheval the extent to which we would go to "give a customer what he wants."

It was with this confidence in our ability to produce anything that we met Mr. Cheng. Cheng was requested by the Surinam government to come to Miami to buy spare parts for its four naval vessels that did not run. Also they were scared of a U.S. invasion! He went on to say that his superior (whom I'll call General X) was coming on Friday, and he wanted to be entertained. Doris, who was working at ATS at the time, offered to host a dinner party for him. Wrong! That kind of party was not what the general had in mind.

After Mr. Cheng counted out his deposit of $40,000 in cash, we opened a few beers to decide how to handle his request. Ben and I quickly appointed Paul, our gay partner, to make all the arrangements, since he would not be biased. The arrangements were made. But the morning after the general's rendezvous, we heard that the general had not had a good time. *Now what?* we thought. *File a warranty claim?* As luck would have it, the general's next stop was London, where we arranged for our contact Simon to take over. Five days later, Simon called us, and as was his custom, began by saying, "This is the mother country calling, and we have done it again when you Yanks have failed." The general had not been heard from in five days.

[48] Food for the Poor

Food for the Poor is one of the largest non-profit charities just behind the Red Cross. Founded in 1982 by Ferdinand Mahfood, it serves the Caribbean and Latin America, having given away more than $4.8 billion in 17 countries. Its emphasis is on food, medical supplies, and education. Unfortunately, the organization has been plagued with a series of scandals starting in 2000. Ferdinand was replaced by his brother Robin for having diverted $275,000 to two female employees. Robin was no better, as he feathered his own nest, as well as those of a large number of family members. It seems they just could not "keep their hands out of the till."

[49] Bleach

What made this project unique was that our customer, Tom Rosarie, was managing a small bleach factory for a local who spent most of his time in Ohio. Tom also was a wholesaler of the bleach and realized the price was way out of line, so he wanted to start his own plant to "eliminate the middleman." While his boss was based in Ohio, he started making his own bleach in his employer's factory. The turning point came when the owner showed up unexpectedly. When I first visited Tom, his entire house was filled with all the supplies he had quickly liberated from the factory, especial hundreds of unfilled plastic jugs. Welcome to the islands.

CHAPTER 33

[50] "Turn That Boat Around" song lyrics

Rankin Family, "Turn That Boat Around" lyrics, MetroLyrics website therankinfamily.com

[51] Sawyer Mill

The Sawyer Mill was located in Dover, New Hampshire, and contained 240,000 square feet. Built in 1849, it manufactured cashmere, flannel cloth, and yarn. Doris and I were two of six owners. We rented a large portion of the space as cold storage to Davidson Rubber Co., which stored molds that were used for Chrysler parts. A problem developed when the sprinkler system did not work, and the fire marshal kept coming to inspect it. Our realtor told him that it was under repair; however, this was a ruse as repairing it would have cost us more than we paid for the building. The fire marshal tired of our excuses, so we sold the property for a nice profit in 1983 to a developer. Today it is lovely apartments.

CHAPTER 35

[52] Concorde

The online encyclopedia, Wikipedia, has this to say about the Concorde: "The Concorde is a retired turbojet-powered supersonic jointly developed and produced by Aérospatiale and the British Aircraft Corporation (BAC) under an Anglo-French treaty. First flown in 1969, Concorde entered service in 1976 and continued commercial flights for 27 years. Among other destinations, Concorde flew regular transatlantic flights from London Heathrow and from the Paris

Charles de Gaulle Airport to New York JFK, Washington Dulles and Barbados; it flew these routes in less than half the time of other airliners. With only 20 aircraft built, the development of Concorde was a substantial economic loss. It was retired in 2003."

[53] QE2

Queen Elizabeth 2 is often referred to simply as QE2. Wikipedia records that she is an ocean liner built for the Cunard Line, which was operated by Cunard as both a transatlantic liner and a cruise ship from 1969 to 2008. She was designed for the transatlantic service from her homeport of Southampton, UK, to New York, and was named after the earlier Cunard liner RMS *Queen Elizabeth*. She served as the flagship of the line from 1969 until succeeded by RMS *Queen Mary 2* in 2004.

[54] Orient Express

The Orient Express was originally a long-distance passenger train service that ran from 1883 to 2009. There are variants, which exist today. The name has become synonymous with intrigue and luxury travel.

CHAPTER 36

[55] RV Trips 1991–1998

In the spring of 1991, Doris and I purchased a 26-foot Winnebago, better known as "Minnie Winnie." Doris complained that when I was tracing my roots, we usually ended up in some remote locality, and she would have nothing to do except to listen to me talk genealogy with other family researchers who were quite elderly and often deaf. Her suggestion was that we acquire an RV so she could have a place to go and read, plus we could use it to explore the national parks.

For seven years, we spent 7 to 10 days traveling in Minnie Winnie in the spring and fall, mostly in the West. Then we would leave the RV and fly home. After we got our dog Caramia, she and Foster the cat made all the excursions with us. Our favorite parks were Custer State Park, the Tetons, especially Jenny Lake, and Bryce Canyon. Our most favorite was Glacier National Park. On the one hand, traveling that way was a wonderful time for us to become closer as there were no outside distractions. On the other hand, more than two weeks living in a 26-foot box could have been a disaster!